M000104945

Sin, Sex, and Democracy

SUNY series in Queer Politics and Cultures

Cynthia Burack and Jyl J. Josephson, editors

Sin, Sex, and Democracy

*Antigay Rhetoric
and the Christian Right*

Cynthia Burack

State University of New York Press

Cover photo: Istockphoto/Amanad Rohde.

Published by
State University of New York Press, Albany

© 2008 State University of New York

All rights reserved

Printed in the United States of America

No part of this book may be used or reproduced in any manner whatsoever
without written permission. No part of this book may be stored in a retrieval system
or transmitted in any form or by any means including electronic, electrostatic,
magnetic tape, mechanical, photocopying, recording, or otherwise
without the prior permission in writing of the publisher.

For information, contact State University of New York Press, Albany, NY
www.sunypress.edu

Production by Ryan Morris
Marketing by Fran Keneston

Library of Congress Cataloging-in-Publication Data

Burack, Cynthia, 1958–
    Sin, sex, and democracy : antigay rhetoric and the Christian right / Cynthia Burack.
        p. cm. — (SUNY series in queer politics and cultures)
    Includes bibliographical references and index.
    ISBN: 978-0-7914-7405-1 (hardcover : alk. paper)
    ISBN: 978-0-7914-7406-8 (pbk. : alk. paper)
1. Gays—United States.   2. Democracy—United States.   3. Homophobia—United States.
4. Christianity and politics—United States.   5. Homosexuality—Religious aspect —Christianity.
6. Homosexuality—Moral and ethical aspects.   I. Title.

HQ76.8.U5B85   2008
306.76'60882773082—dc22   2007025413

10 9 8 7 6 5 4 3 2 1

To my best old pals,
without whom living the gay lifestyle all these years
would have been no fun at all.
Patricia Davis
Joyce Enoff
Suzanne Franks
Jyl Josephson
Jeff Mann
Laree Martin
Michelle Powell
Stacy VanDeveer
Alayna Waldrum
Diana Zoelle

Contents

Acknowledgments

The prophet Ecclesiastes wrote, "Of making many books there is no end, and much study is a weariness of the flesh." True, but I can't imagine anything I'd rather do. And the process of making books is especially fulfilling when it brings one together with good interlocutors. The following people read parts of the manuscript as I wrote, offered suggestions, or contributed materials: Sean Cahill, Jason Cianciotto, Jyl Josephson, Valerie Lehr, Laree Martin, John Parrish, Claire Snyder, Joan Tronto, Rebecca Wanzo, Angelia Wilson, and Ara Wilson. Thanks to Lu Zhang, Lacey Dalby, Min Sook Heo, and Kathryn Linder for research assistance on the project and to my partner, Laree, for editing and for assistance with formatting the final manuscript. Much love to Suzanne Franks, Jeff Mann, and Diana Zoelle for sharing all the emotions and allowing me to read parts of this manuscript to them aloud. For all this and more, I appreciate their good-humored forbearance.

My greatest thanks and appreciation go to my friend and colleague, Jyl Josephson. My collaborations with Jyl have been a great source of pleasure in trying times. Together, we attended Focus on the Family's Love Won Out conference in Minneapolis, Minnesota, in September 2004. We wrote a part of what appears here as chapter 3 and presented a paper at the 2004 annual meeting of the American Political Science Association entitled "Origin Stories: Same-Sex Sexuality and Christian Right Politics." Sean Cahill, then director of the Policy Institute of the National Gay and Lesbian Task Force, invited us to contribute a report of our attendance at Love Won Out to the NGLTF website, and writing that report helped me to clarify my ideas. Thanks also to NGLTF's Jason Cianciotto and Roberta Sklar for shepherding the report to publication.

Thanks to the following for providing access to materials or otherwise helping me out: the Chick archive at Michigan State University for providing copies of materials in their non-circulating collection; Political Research

Associates (especially Chip Berlet) for use of their archive and materials; the Ohio State University Cartoon Research Library; the Augustana, South Dakota, University Library (and collections staff); Dan Moshenberg and the Women's Studies Program at The George Washington University for designating me as a Research Associate; and the Centennial Center of the American Political Science Association for its Visiting Scholar program, which provided office space during final revision of this manuscript. Alayna Waldrum provided the perfect title for this project, and it is no reflection on her ingenuity that I did not use it.

Thanks to Clarissa Hayward at Ohio State for providing opportunities to talk, first about "Getting What 'We' Deserve" at an Interdisciplinary Research Seminar on Democracy, Citizenship, and Identity, and then about the Christian Right and separation of church and state (under the title "Getting the Christian Right Wrong") at a lecture series on Political Theory and Political Science in Dialogue. A portion of chapter 2 appeared as "From Doom Town to Sin City: Chick Tracts and Antigay Politics," *New Political Science* 28, 2 (2006): 163–179. A portion of chapter 3, co-written with Jyl J. Josephson, appeared as "Origin Stories: Same-Sex Sexuality and Christian Right Politics," *Culture and Religion* 6, 3 (2005): 369–392. And an early version of chapter 5 was published as "Getting What 'We' Deserve: Terrorism, Tolerance, Sexuality, and the Christian Right," *New Political Science* 25, 3 (2003): 329–349. I'm grateful to Joseph Peschek of the journal *New Political Science* for his interest in this project.

In what follows, all quotes from the Bible are from the King James Version (KJV). There are debates among Christian conservatives about the relative merits of different translations. I use the KJV because it's the translation I learned in as an adolescent and because I still find its language lovely and poetic.

Abbreviations

ACLU	American Civil Liberties Union
AFA	American Family Association
APA	American Psychiatric Association
AUSCS	Americans United for Separation of Church and State
CBA	Christian Bookseller's Association
CFV	Colorado for Family Values
CWA	Concerned Women for America
DSM	Diagnostic and Statistical Manual of Mental Disorders
ELCA	Evangelical Lutheran Church in America
FOF	Focus on the Family
FRC	Family Research Council
FRI	Family Research Institute
GID	Gender Identity Disorder
GLSEN	Gay, Lesbian, Straight Education Network
EI	Exodus International
HRC	Human Rights Campaign
HRW	Human Rights Watch
LGBT	Lesbian, Gay, Bisexual, and Transgender
LWO	Love Won Out
NAE	National Association of Evangelicals
NARTH	National Association for Research and Therapy of Homosexuality
NGLTF	National Gay and Lesbian Task Force

PFLAG	Parents, Family, and Friends of Lesbians and Gays
PFOX	Parents and Friends of Ex-Gays
PPT	Presidential Prayer Team
PRA	Political Research Associates
SBC	Southern Baptist Convention
TFP	American Society for the Defense of Tradition, Family and Property

Introduction
We Are Family

The LORD shall cause thine enemies that rise up against thee to be smitten before thy face: they shall come out against thee one way, and flee before thee seven ways.

—Deuteronomy 28:7

Though I speak with the tongues of men and of angels, and have not charity, I am become as sounding brass, or a tinkling cymbal.

—1 Corinthians 13:1

Born-Agains and Other Strangers

The fruits of Reverend Bernard Coffindaffer's spiritual vision are familiar to travelers on American highways. In the early 1980s, the Holy Spirit directed Coffindaffer, a West Virginia minister and ex-Marine, to spend his personal fortune to plant 1,800 cross clusters across the United States. The familiar wooden poles—"Jerusalem" gold for the larger center cross of Jesus and light blue for the smaller flanking crosses of the thieves—stand alongside highways, on church lots, and in the yards of believers. They stretch from Delaware to New Mexico, from Florida to Kansas, from the church grounds of Washington, DC, to the mountain escarpments overlooking West Virginia's New River. Even if Coffindaffer was not more ardent than most Appalachian conservative Christians, the scale and grandeur of his witness distinguishes him from his peers.

No doubt many who travel the nation's roads do not know of Coffindaffer, just as many were taken by surprise by the runaway success of Mel Gibson's

The Passion of the Christ. The day of the film's general release, Ash Wednesday, 2004, religion critic Kenneth Woodward wrote in the *New York Times* that evangelical Christians would not be likely to "recognize" the Jesus of the film because of their "inherently non-visual" "sensibility."[1] Perhaps Woodward has never attended a conservative Protestant church service in the weeks leading up to Easter Sunday and heard a graphic and lingering description of the wounds inflicted on Jesus during the Passion. Even so, Woodward's analysis of the as yet unrealized reception of Gibson's film struck me as curiously disjoined from my own experience of conservative Christian theology and worship.[2]

Even as Gibson's *Passion* was bringing conservative Christians to movie theaters in record numbers, many Americans were missing, misreading, and misunderstanding their conservative Christian fellow citizens. Garry Wills is funny and accurate on this point when he writes that "it seems careless for scholars to keep misplacing such a large body of people."[3] To obtain a workable understanding of American conservative Christianity after the turn of the millennium we need history, theology, sociology, politics, rhetoric, psychology, and patience. Fortunately, it does not take a childhood drenched in Southern Baptist, Pentecostal, or Holiness Christianity to understand the theo-politics of contemporary Christianity. Scholars and the culturally curious acquire this knowledge by setting aside their own expectations and listening carefully to the thought and aspirations of conservative Christian leaders and followers. In this book, I hope to carefully record and comment on the political rhetoric and aspirations of the Christian right with regard to queers and same-sex sexuality. But first, I'd like to explain my claim to interest in the Christian right, if not any particular authority on or to it.

For a time, I was a youthful member of the First Baptist Church of Copperas Cove, Texas. Texas is "God's Country."[4] As recent students of the Texas Christian right confirm, "one constant in Texas is support for religion."

> Texans consistently profess some form of religious commitment and identify religion as "important" in their lives. . . . A majority express a traditionalist view of religion, with an additional 19 percent characterizing their faith as fundamentalist, evangelical, or charismatic. . . . Most (54 percent) are God-fearing Christians who "say that they have been born again or have had a born-again experience."[5]

If anything, traditional religion is more ubiquitous in Texas now than it was in the early 1970s. But conservative Christian faith was big even then. First Baptist, where I first became acquainted with it, sprawls along West Avenue B on the wrong side of the tracks from a decrepit downtown. Its rambling buildings represent decades of growth and additions, including three separate sanctuaries that testify to the ways in which God has blessed this one of seven Baptist churches in the Cove.

You don't know Copperas Cove, but chances are you've heard of its nearest neighbors: Fort Hood and Killeen. At 339 square miles, Fort Hood is the largest military training post in the world, occupying barren land in sparsely populated central Texas. Killeen is the contiguous city that became famous in 1991 for the "Luby's massacre," with twenty-three fatalities, the worst mass shooting in American history until the murders at Virginia Tech University in 2007. Copperas Cove is an army town, patriotic and religious. I arrived there as a sixth grader and escaped one year shy of high school graduation.

Although I went to central Texas as a nominal Catholic, it was at First Baptist that I learned about fundamentalist faith and the basic precepts of conservative Christianity. I didn't go to First Baptist by choice. My mother—reared a Methodist and a Catholic by marriage—had undergone a religious conversion a few years before our arrival in central Texas. In the wake of her conversion, she joined a small charismatic congregation in Colorado Springs, just outside Fort Carson. In time, she determined that she could not be both born-again and Catholic. And that is how I joined the world of Baptist youth, Sunday School, Wednesday services, church choir, tent revivals, Baptist summer camp, prophesy, and mandatory scripture reading. At twelve, I entered a world of apocalyptic hope and solidarity. At seventeen, I left that world with enthusiasm. In contravention of the proverb, although I'd been trained up in the way I should go, I departed from it as quickly as possible. For some time, the only obvious legacy of fundamentalist training was my ability to quote from the King James Version of the Bible. Given my distance from it today, my sojourn in the world of the Southern Baptists might never have happened at all except for a few lingering details. When I left the world of fundamentalist faith I was on the verge of coming out as a lesbian; my mother remains a conservative charismatic Christian, and the marginal fundamentalists of my Baptist adolescence have become more powerful social and political actors than any of us ever could have imagined.

As it turns out, I learned a great deal in my few years as a Southern Baptist. First, although I am no scriptural exegete, I have a functional grasp of the Protestant Bible. I have come to think of this as cultural knowledge, a useful tool, and a good defense. The first year I taught at Ohio State, a rattled teaching assistant came to me to report that two students had responded to a mention of lesbians in an assigned reading by bringing their Bibles to a small group discussion. The two had witnessed to the class, telling their group that Jesus taught that homosexuality is a sin. It could not be the point of our academic lesson, but as Appalachians in my birth state of West Virginia might say, "he said no such a thing."

A second lesson I brought away from my Baptist youth was an appreciation for the protean forms of emotional and intellectual enrichment that strict forms of religious belief deliver. Among well-educated agnostics and religious liberals, it is common to understand the payoff of exacting religion as comfort, a specific psychological deliverable that gives the individual what she needs without threatening the broader (secular) social order. Minnesota Governor Jesse Ventura probably relied on this trope when he made a controversial statement, which he later retracted, about religion being a "crutch" for "weak-minded" people. I don't deny that many people take great comfort in the promises of their faith and the proximity of a god whose eye is on the sparrow. However, this is not nearly all that traditional forms of religion offer.

Students of religion suggest an array of rewards and motivations for religious commitment that are as diverse as human motivation itself. These include moral certainty or clarity, confidence, fear, greed, a sense of chosenness, freedom from choice, the desire to reverse humiliation or wounded masculinity, a desire for intellectual mastery, and a sense of community. Jessica Stern discusses all these motives in her study of religious extremists who are willing to kill to achieve their goals.[6] By invoking categories Stern's analysis shares with others, I am not suggesting that Christian conservatives are religious terrorists. On the contrary, I want to suggest that these motivations are human ones, in some sense profoundly prosaic and widely shared among religious terrorists, Southern Baptists, and academics in research universities. In other words, whatever factors can be used to explain distinctions between believers and unbelievers, they must be less trivial than these categories. In order to grasp them, we—that is, we critics of the Christian right—must examine our vulnerability to the kinds of stabilizing identities and discourses on which we routinely rely for our own sense of exceptionalism.

Finally, I grew up appreciating the humanity of people who believe—as I do not—that some day God will remove his followers from the earth as they drive cars, endure business meetings, or visit with their neighbors. The popular bumper sticker from the 1970s, "Warning: In Case of Rapture This Car Will Be Unmanned," is still with us; but more important, the belief system that lies behind this sentiment remains influential.[7] These are the beliefs I was taught as a Southern Baptist, and although I do not share them, to me they are not the system of some alien tribe. I have been close to many people who love Jesus, pray daily (including for me), and look forward to the end-times when evil (including the evil I represent) will be vanquished from the earth. I do not have to wonder if the intelligence of people who hold these views is impaired; I know it isn't. I don't have to wonder, as many of my students and companions have, whether they *really* believe what they profess; I believe they do. We just disagree. What's changed between then and now is that this disagreement is no longer a matter of private lives and personal beliefs. It has gone public, political, national, and global.

The Vision Thing

Analyses of the conservative Christian right acknowledge the importance of regional differences in the United States. Today we have the overgeneralized differences between "red" and "blue" states. We also have the complex historical legacy of the cultural, economic, and political conflicts between the North and the South. These two cleavages form the umbilical cord between the American past and the American present. I confronted Southern Baptist faith in one of its natural habitats in rural Texas in the 1970s, but "Southern Baptists [are] no longer geographically Southern Baptists."[8] Indeed, "all America, not one region, is a 'Bible Belt'."[9] As Angelia Wilson puts it, "One cannot fully grasp American politics without understanding the extent to which normative Christianity dictates the political, social, and sexual agenda. The comfortable well-established home of that conservative Christianity is the American South."[10] The themes, values, and appeals of Southern conservatism at the mid-point of the twentieth century are in many important respects now those of the "center" of American political culture. Politicians have lead, ignored, resisted, and accommodated themselves to this shift.

Conservative Christians never trusted George H. W. Bush, but they love his son. G. H. W. Bush hailed from the Episcopal High Church tradition, did not talk about his personal relationship, if any, with Jesus, and did not champion the social and political agenda of the Christian right. George W. Bush, on the other hand, has turned out as president to function effectively as the de facto leader of the Christian right even if he has not delivered on much of the movement's agenda.[11] Indeed, the benediction of the Christian right has been bestowed upon our president with little dissent and discomfort from other quarters. In this respect, if not in others, Bush can be compared with Ronald Reagan, the president who sparked the conservative revolution.

During the early 1980s, many Americans—cultural elites though they may have been—were shocked when Reagan speculated about the prophetic inevitability of the nuclear battle of Armageddon that would take place in the Middle East within a generation. Reagan's biographer, Lou Cannon, suggests that "the story [of Armageddon] appealed to Reagan's adventurous imagination and met his requirement of a happy ending." After all, in the Armageddon story of that time, the Soviet Union is defeated as Christ returns to earth in glory.[12] When questioned about his belief, and its nuclear implications, Reagan demurred, offering instead that nobody could know *when* this fateful battle would occur. Many Americans remained suspicious of what the president might do under color of his roles as head of state and commander in chief of the military services. Others were no doubt reassured by Reagan's chronological agnosticism.

We know that as a candidate and as president, George W. Bush has been packaged and scripted against the risk of embarrassing slips and disclosures, including disclosures of ignorance on important issues. In spite of a pronounced interest in addressing matters of the spirit in public forums, George W. Bush has not spoken publicly of nuclear Armageddon, the Rapture, the Antichrist, the tribulation, and other aspects of conservative Christian eschatology. We cannot know whether these ideas and categories are important to him. However, we do know that both his advisors and the institutional Christian right prefer not to discuss these ideas too openly in public media. There is no point running the risk of frightening and alienating Americans who do not already share these beliefs. In this, Bush is not alone. One example of such strategic discretion is the email Pastor Ted Haggard, then president of the National Association of Evangelicals (NAE) and Colorado Spring's New Life Church, sent to "New Lifers and friends of New Life Church" in May 2005. The message, widely dubbed the "don't be weird" email, alerted parishioners to behave themselves when members of the national media visited the church to film services and conduct interviews. Haggard encouraged parishioners to "use words that make sense to [journalists]. Speak their language. Don't talk about the devil, demons, voices speaking to you." Oh, and "don't be spooky or weird."[13]

During the course of Bush's first term in office, a handful of scholars and pundits stepped up to translate some of the language in Bush's speeches and extemporaneous public addresses for the theologically disinclined. These interpretations largely appeared in recondite settings that were unlikely to attract wide attention. For educational purposes, what we need is a brief reference guide that sets up the translation in the form of a *Cosmo* quiz: When politician X (who is courting the Christian right) says ____ s/he means ____. It would be useful to include chapter and verse for each reference, many of which are likely to pass over the heads of those who have not read the Bible closely, sung traditional hymns, or listened to the tropes and cadences of Bible-believing preachers.

It is also imperative to concede that with regard to religion Bush has given the American people what they want. In the July 2003 poll on "Religion and Politics," the Pew Forum on Religion and Public Life concluded that the majority of Americans are either comfortable with the way that Bush relies on his religious faith to make policy decisions or would like him to rely on his faith even more than he does. Interestingly, even the majority of citizens classified by Pew as "seculars" indicated that religious faith exerts an appropriate influence on policy.[14]

Yes, the President and his corps of speechwriters have routinely spoken to the American people in a language of conservative Christianity, even when it appears on the surface that they were doing something else entirely. And yes, both greater transparency and greater comprehension about the messages political leaders send would constitute a democratic achievement. I return to this concern about transparency later in the book, but I expend most concern on the question of comprehension. Political discourse is a form of pedagogy, and those of us who do not appreciate the complexities of conservative Christian pedagogy will have a more impoverished understanding of American politics than those who do.

The Pew data tell us that Americans want as much or more religion in President Bush's policy formation and public discourse as he has given them. Such a finding might suggest that American citizens know to what extent religion constructs our policy and public discourse, but this is probably too robust an assumption. I suspect that there is some level of ignorance about the meanings that lie behind many of Bush's sub rosa religious references. After all, I'm sure my undergraduate students are not the only people in America who don't understand completely what Bush is saying when he speaks his Bible-believing tongue. Putting these two claims together, we might read the Pew data in this way: perhaps if Bush's speechwriters did not bother to encode his messages to conservative Christian followers Americans would draw a different conclusion about how much theology the president has offered them in his role as head of government. Indeed, such understanding might tip many respondents over into the group of Americans who believe that Bush actually overemphasized his role as head of the Christian right and underemphasized his other, constitutional, roles. It's a theory.

In any case, there is no mistaking both that Bush has presented himself and has been presented by a significant subset of his supporters as chosen of God to lead the nation in traumatic times. However, this appeal would be nothing without the Protestant theological backdrop with which such a representation resonates. For example, in the first week of the 2004 election year, Pat Robertson, founder of the Christian Broadcasting Network and the *700 Club* television program, announced that God had informed him that Bush would be elected in a "walk" against a Democratic challenger. "It doesn't make any difference what he does, good or bad, God picks him up because he's a man of prayer and God's blessing him." Many liberals and conservatives denounced Robertson's arrogance, some noting in web logs and other informal venues that not all of Robertson's predictions—such as a 1998 threat concerning the destruction of Tampa, Florida, over its putative sponsorship of homosexuality—have come to pass. Robertson, who cannot leave any challenge unanswered, defended his prophesy record in a CNN broadcast a month later. He noted that he has "had a pretty remarkable track record" interpreting God's communications to him.[15]

Later in the campaign, the late Reverend Jerry Falwell publicly made the conservative Christian case for Bush's inevitable second term. Leaders in the Christian right sometimes seem to adopt temporary divisions of labor in communicating with the faithful. If one speaks in a prophetic register, telling followers and the American people what will be, another speaks in a more recognizable political register. He exhorts and motivates conservative Christians to go to the polls to fulfill the prophesy that God has already delivered. It is no accident that Falwell performed his task with regard to Bush's reelection soon after political pundits and representatives of the parties clarified the importance of turnout to the hopes of both presidential candidates.

Before the 2006 midterm elections, other Christian right leaders spoke of Bush and the Republican Party in biblical and prophetic terms and reminded followers that it would be a sin for Christians to abstain from voting. In late September 2006, the Family Research Council (FRC) and other organizations sponsored a Values Voter Summit in Washington, DC, a political, rather than religious, event for Christian conservative activists. The impressive roster of speakers included governors, members of Congress, and leaders of Christian right organizations, and all who spoke in an explicitly political vein praised President Bush and the Republican Party as advocates for Christian conservative causes and values. Besides predictable rhetoric against abortion rights and gay rights, these leaders roused the crowd in the Omni Shoreham Hotel ballroom with appeals to God's blessing on Bush's leadership and the importance of supporting Bush on such issues as the treatment of detainees in the "war on terror."[16] Indeed, even implicit criticisms of Bush on the issue of immigration policy—conferees supported the most punitive policy among the options then being debated—failed to staunch enthusiasm for the Bible-believing president.

On the other hand, critics of the Bush administration have made much of George W. Bush's personal and political capacities and motivations. Many have played the president's linguistic calamities and his putative intellectual deficiencies for laughs.[17] Others have cast a cold eye on his language of the heart. These judgments are not unrelated: while for some Bush's "incessant references to blood-pumping organs" signal an inability to exercise political judgment, others recognize political intelligence in such references.[18]

Bush used talk of the heart—his and others'—to position himself and his socially conservative policies for a constituency of born-again Christian conservatives. Analyzing Bush's autobiography, *A Charge to Keep,* as well as many of his public utterances, David Gutterman concludes that Bush's conversion narrative situates him as a "modern-day Moses," his "quest for the White House" a "divine mission."[19] Another scholar concludes that Bush is Esther to his followers rather than Moses, but these Biblical parallels are not mutually exclusive. Rather, their proliferation may simply confirm Bush's stature as a man of God for believers. Bush's political adversaries also suspect him of using Christian conservatives to advance his own prospects. However, Bush did not come to his relationship with the Christian right during his first campaign for president beginning in 1999. He was one of his father's emissaries to this restive constituency during the G. H. W. Bush years, and he forged many relationships with Christian right leaders that served him well as his political ambitions expanded. In *A Charge to Keep,* George W. credits Billy Graham with leading him to Christ. He is close to Graham's son, Franklin, and Focus on the Family (FOF) founder, James Dobson. Dobson reciprocated the president's trust by departing from his usual neutrality in a presidential election season to endorse W. in his winning bid for (re)election.

W. has even built a relationship with Pat Robertson, a man who ran against his father in the 1988 Republican primary and later, during the first Gulf War, spoke out against the president's putative dream of a New World Order. In his own book, *The New World Order,* Robertson rehearsed many of the details of Christian right eschatology for the faithful. In a move that might have doomed Robertson with the notoriously loyalty-obsessed George W., the Christian right leader suggested that George H. W. was ignorant of his role in bringing end-times prophesy to fruition. But this pointed critique did not exile Robertson from political influence in the George W. administration. Although he has been supplanted in many respects by other, more savvy and flexible, leaders, Robertson instructs and represents a broad swath of Christian conservatives and has been an important political strategist. Aside from small disagreements over the Texas execution of Karla Fay Tucker and the implementation of the White House Office of Faith-Based and Community Initiatives, George W. has come to terms with Robertson. In his turn, Robertson has been a reliable voice for Bush's policy agenda and for his larger legitimacy as the anointed president. I mean here, of course, anointed by God and not by the Supreme Court.

As it is currently constituted, the Republican Party cannot do without the Christian right in terms of electoral politics. The Christian right constituency was necessary to elect the Republican freshman class of 1994 and, thus, to launch the "Republican Revolution" that stymied Bill Clinton for much of his presidency. And the Christian right positioned George W. Bush for his dubious ascension to the presidency. Far from distancing himself from the theology and politics of the Christian right, President Bush courted this constituency with his personal witness and with a range of concrete policy positions on welfare, reproductive rights, lesbian and gay rights, and church-state relations.[20] It is not all the Christian right had hoped for, and in this respect Bush compares with Reagan. The Christian right's extravagant pro-Reagan and Bush rhetoric to the contrary, the Bush administration has been a disappointment in many concrete respects. It is important, however, to remember that this sense of disappointment is in direct proportion to the high—and rising—hopes of the Christian conservative movement. For Christian conservatives, Bush was neither all talk and no action nor the man of their dreams. In fact, his administration has deftly negotiated the differences that make up the Republican coalition.

Within the conservative coalition that has governed the United States for much of the period since the early 1980s, cultural and economic conservatives exercise different kinds and degrees of influence, largely in different arenas of decision-making. For example, neoconservative foreign policy and neoliberal business considerations drive most Bush administration foreign policies. Meanwhile, the administration actively courts the Christian right in areas of domestic policies related to education, reproductive rights and other health issues, lesbian, gay, bisexual, and transgender (LGBT) issues, and faith-based provision of public services.[21] This is not to say that the Christian right does not also extend its influence into the international arenas. As many observers detail, Christian right initiatives are well institutionalized in the broad area of family policy, on issues relating to women and sexuality, on Israel, and on religious freedom and discrimination abroad.[22] It is merely to suggest that there is a tacit division of authority over particular spheres and kinds of decision-making that enables New right constituencies to cooperate rather than conflict. This is only one of many reasons why the distinctions of interest between economic or market conservatives and social conservatives has not always been as troubling to the New right and its Christian right wing in the ways that left political wisdom might suggest.

Startling as it is to citizens of other liberal democratic nations, the common coin of political discourse in early twenty-first-century America includes debates about the divine standing of the president and the godly nature of his policies. Observing this political discourse as a scholar and citizen, and having a particular kind of stake in its consequences, I begin with a number of assumptions, which are closely related to one another. First, with most students of the Christian right, I know the movement is not merely a curious and anachronistic ideological phenomenon on the American social landscape. Rather, it is a significant contemporary social and political movement with long historical roots. Second, I assume that the Christian right aspires to control the levers of government in order to enact a broad agenda of social and political changes that are consistent with conservative Christian beliefs and aspirations. This is not to say that there are no differences between the "centrist" Christian right and some of the more extreme manifestations of right-wing Christianity. However, these differences shouldn't efface an important similarity. Christian conservatives of many stripes want to "reconstruct" the fallen American social and political landscape and to institute biblical law as they understand it.

Finally, I believe that the Christian right poses a threat to secular democratic government and to the political rights of minorities, perhaps especially sexual minorities. Their—our—social and political presence represents a threat, a challenge, and in some respects, a confirmation, both of Satan's activity in the world and of God's final justice. Those of us who disagree with the theological foundations and political aspirations of the Christian right can only hope to oppose the movement's sexuality politics by understanding its theological politics. Without this understanding, we are uninformed about matters that lie at the heart of American politics.

Moving from these assumptions about the Christian right, I will make two main arguments. First, I want to show that an often-remarked-upon feature of Christian right politics—its willingness and ability to direct different political messages to different audiences—is central to its current, and future, successes. Some scholars of the Christian right argue that the need to direct different public discourses to insiders and outsiders is a weakness of the movement, one that has the potential to undermine its outward effectiveness as well as its internal mobilization.[23] In contrast, I argue that the Christian right has become more and more effective at designing and deploying multiple modes of address, different rhetorical tones, emphases, or arguments directed at ingroup and outgroup audiences.[24] Perhaps more than secular opponents would like to acknowledge, these modes often overcome the liability that is posed by the simultaneous existence of publics with diverse beliefs.

Second, I will show that even though the Christian right has become adept at developing and implementing a variety of more or less successful political strategies in the course of its various projects, the conservative Christian movement is not strategic without remainder. To describe a broad, grassroots political movement that from its most to its least activist tail encompasses nearly one third of the American electorate, this is far too singular an explanation. This is to say that sometimes the critics and political adversaries of the Christian right misunderstand the movement, at least in the context of particular social and political projects. Because I take the antigay political convictions and projects of the Christian right as my text here, I'm particularly concerned that lesbian, gay, bisexual, and transgender people and their political allies not overlook the many motivations behind Christian conservative belief and activism. Like all human beings, Christian conservatives and their leaders are moved by emotions and psychological defenses as well as by intellectual and social status aspirations. Critics should take account of these as much as we take account of the strategies and calculations that are an unavoidable dimension of mass and institutional politics.

The Privileged Position of the Christian Right

A sense of grievance and narcissistic injury frequently marks the memory of group members, particularly of those groups whose history records a high-profile defeat. In the United States, we have the "Lost Cause" whose contemporary proponents practice a set of quixotic rituals meant to summon the martial spirit of their ancestors.[25] A similar narrative accompanies contemporary fundamentalists, whose cultural—if not legal—defeat in the Scopes trial is recalled with every discussion of the phenomenon of literal Biblical Christianity. The problem with this narrative is that while fundamentalists and their theological kin in the Christian right today cling to the lost cause mantle they exercise enviable political influence. True, the inability of contemporary Christian conservatives to choose between the narrative of downtrodden minority and the narrative of universal truth creates a knotty problem of consistency. But what is a knotty problem from one perspective is just invisible reality from another.

Howard Winant points out that the breakdown of white racial supremacy as a result of the Civil Rights movement shattered the ideological consistency of both white and African American identity. Thenceforth, these identities were constituted of "racial dualisms." The hybrid "white" identity was reinterpreted as "on the one hand egalitarian, on the other hand privileged; on the one hand individualistic and 'color-blind,' on the other hand 'normalized' and white."[26] Sound familiar? There is no reason that Christian conservatives should have to be more consistent in the representation of their collective identity than white people as a whole in the United States. But more important: there is a considerable overlap in "white" and "Christian conservative" identities, particularly when we consider the whole ideological package that defines Christian conservatism. As Winant and many others suspect, there is more than a little sense in which the real but limited successes of the Civil Rights movement propelled the real, and thankfully still limited, successes of the white conservatives who fill the Christian right movement.

However, such an abstract take on the intersections of race, ideology, and party doesn't do justice to our fractious history. Throughout much of the nineteenth century and through the mid-point of the twentieth, Christian conservatism was virtually defined by its support for slavery and then for the unequal social and legal statuses of the races in America. The largest Protestant denomination in the United States, the Southern Baptist Convention, apologized for its support for racism, slavery, and segregation in 1995, and some older Christian right leaders have closeted identities as youthful supporters of racial separation and inequality. By contrast, today's Christian right strives to be a racial big tent, actively recruiting socially conservative African Americans with the same appeals to moral issues—notably abortion and gay rights—that it uses to solidify its authority with similarly situated whites. A brilliant political move is to accuse liberals, and even sometimes gays in particular, of racism while denying the movement's own history of solidarity with the "Southern strategy" that propelled the Republican Party to virtually complete dominance in the states that once comprised the Confederacy.

So what is the relation of the movement known as the Christian right to political influence and power in the United States? I will not be able to answer this important question in one essay, but here are some preliminary thoughts.

In 2003, *New York Times* editor Bill Keller penned a defense of sorts against charges that as president, Bush caters to a specific Christian right political agenda. For Keller, Bush's religion entails neither a particular pope-like coach nor a "very specific playbook." Rather, Bush's faith is ecumenical, moving him to respond positively to believers, whether Vladimir Putin or Tony Blair. Unfortunately, the observation that Bush feels comfortable with believers of many stripes and that he neither reports to nor receives guidance from some institutionalized religious authority do not prove Keller's main argument: that the "White House is not powered by fundamentalist Christianity." Neither—just to cover all the bases—does the claim that the Christian right is "dying . . . as an independent political structure." Indeed, it is one of the great successes of the Christian right to have become absorbed into the Republican Party as well as into the politically influential professions.[27]

As far as anyone can tell from his public statements and limited published writings, George W. Bush has a quite specific set of religious beliefs, and these are all beliefs he shares with the Christian right. This is not to say that he does not feel affection, and a sense of common purpose, with those who are Christian, and perhaps more generally religious, believers of some sort. But this general bonhomie, for which Bush is famous, is not what has discomfited politically attentive Americans who are not conservative Christians. Perhaps what Keller means to suggest is that Bush's commitments are not exhausted by his religious beliefs. I will concede that President Bush is no theologian and that his administration has pursued *other* agendas besides a conservative Christian one. Indeed, to all appearances, he is neither a particularly perceptive nor a vigorous student of conservative Christian theology. He does not appear to be able to discuss his choice of Jesus as his favorite philosopher as Thomas Jefferson could when he stated the same preference. Comic pundit Al Franken investigated the president's well-rehearsed autobiographical narrative about his "Acts of the Apostles" study group in Midland, Texas, and irreverently submits that reading the book of Acts over a period of a year is not a strenuous course of scriptural study.[28] However, even with all the caveats we might concede about Bush's biblical comprehension and stamina, it will not do to instruct us that Bush's faith "has no political agenda." As the political orientations and vague religious convictions of millions of Americans demonstrate, deep thoughtfulness about matters of faith is not essential to the formation of strong political views and preferences.

However, Keller is on to something. He notes that the best way to gauge the relationship of the Christian right to the Bush administration is to consider it as just one more interest group that the administration must feed and mollify, like business or other groups in a conservative coalition. This loose hypothesis does encourage us to use both theory and empirical evidence to investigate the Bush administration's—and Republican Party's—orientation toward a Christian conservative political agenda.

One robust family of theories about the influence of groups and the relation of groups to the state has been pluralist theories. In its simplest formulation, pluralism understands civil society to be made up of competing interest groups, none of which has a timeless monopoly on political power. These groups vie with one another for resources and outcomes; the role of the state is to mediate between groups and make sure that they observe the rules of the game of political competition. Pluralism is usually contrasted to theories that postulate a "power elite."[29] Either groups compete in a public arena or power is wielded by particular groups—say, those who own the means of production or Anglo-Saxon men with Ivy League educations—that control resources and institutions for their own good. But there is more to the argument than this debate. Political theorists worry that pluralism expresses relative or complete indifference to a number of important political issues. These include: asymmetries of power between groups, the origins of preferences (including moral preferences), and the roles of democratic deliberation and participation in a liberal democratic public sphere.[30]

Another kind of empirical and normative take on pluralism is offered by political scientist Charles E. Lindblom. Considering the competition for influence over political decision-making, Lindblom formulated the idea that the business community, far from being merely one of many interest groups in American liberal democracy, occupied a "privileged position" in comparison to other groups.[31] Is the "privileged position of business" a helpful concept for understanding the relationship of the Bush administration to the Christian right? The market-oriented private enterprise economy of the United States leads business leaders to decide matters that have "momentous consequences for the welfare of . . . society."[32] Because business leaders perform so many "public functions," public officials are concerned with inducing business leaders to perform their functions. Business leaders are induced by receiving "whatever [they] need as a condition for performing the tasks that fall to them." And business leaders themselves define what is necessary for them to perform the tasks that fall to them. As a result, they occupy a "privileged position" vis-à-vis other interest groups in the polyarchy.

The relationship between the Bush administration and the Christian right is unprecedented in modern American history. Even the market-fundamentalist Reagan administration did not cater to the central culturally conservative issue positions of the adolescent Christian right in the 1980s. On the one hand, Christian right leaders and organizations engage in traditional kinds of practices to influence policy outcomes, including making political donations, placing advocates in influential positions in the Republican Party and the federal government, lobbying, executing "grassroots" campaigns to pressure law- and policy-makers to favorable decisions, and developing new government programs or changing the terms or implementation of existing programs. These are all routine ways for groups in liberal democracies to participate in government on behalf of their ideological positions and constituencies. They are not unique to the Christian right. It is not even unusual for groups such as the Christian right to exercise well-placed blackmail threats, such as the threat to instruct followers to sit out an election to demonstrate their value to the party. Focus on the Family's James Dobson tendered one such threat in 1998 when he told GOP lawmakers he would not turn out followers to continue to vote for a party that ignored their socially conservative agenda on such issues as abortion and sexuality.[33] Such maneuvers are an attempt to avoid electoral capture. They get the attention of decision-makers and make it less likely that important blocs of voters will be taken for granted in electoral and policy-making processes.

On the other hand, political decisions that favor the perspectives of the Christian right are not only a result of these forms of proactive politics. In many ways, large and small, the Republican Party and the Bush administration preemptively seek out Christian right leaders to deliver political goods and secure their support. Christian right organizations and congregations occupy a central structural position in organizing electoral support for Republican national candidates. National Christian right organizations such as the Christian Coalition and, more recently, the Family Research Council (FRC) produce voter "guides" that favor Republican politicians, but these guides are produced by and for Christian conservatives.

A more aggressive and troubling relation between the state and churches began to coalesce during the Bush years. In 2004, the Bush-Cheney campaign teamed up with pastors and congregations. The effort began with an email message to Christian conservatives in Pennsylvania to identify 1,600 "friendly congregations" where Bush supporters could "gather on a regular basis." From there, the program escalated to an action plan listing twenty-two "duties" for Bush supporters that included turning church membership directories over to the Bush-Cheney campaign, encouraging pastors to hold voter drives, recruiting church members to volunteer for the Republican campaign, and holding campaign-related potluck dinners.[34] In the uproar that ensued, perhaps the most interesting critique of the Republican campaign effort was offered not by the Democratic Party or by Americans United for Separation of Church and State (AUSCS), but by a group of religious ethicists and theologians. Ten spokespersons who hailed from a variety of theological positions signed a letter that called on Bush to "repudiate the actions of [his] re-election campaign." The letter characterizes cooperative church members, if not the Bush-Cheney campaign itself, as engaging in a "scandalous secularizing of the sacred."[35] The campaign, having formulated the action plan with its attorneys, was unrepentant. Focus on the Family, and other Christian right organizations, defended Bush and alleged that the signatories to the critical letter were liberals in conservative Christian garb.

And this process of outreach is not new. A past president of the NAE, Robert Dugan, describes the relationship between the Republican Party and Christian conservatives in this way:

> I am often asked: why do evangelicals align themselves so much with the Republican party? The reverse may be even more the case. The Republican party aligns itself with evangelicals because, as Paul Weyrich and many others have observed, evangelicals are more conservative, generally, than are most other segments of the population. Republicans have been actively cultivating evangelicals, and the Republican party was a natural place for them to end up.

Dugan goes on to explain the difference between the Democratic and Republican parties with regard to interest in NAE political perspectives and organizing. To contrast the parties, Dugan notes that the Democratic Party has had a gay and lesbian caucus since the early 1980s but has devoted little space and interest to evangelicals and their concerns. He concludes, "given this state of affairs, it is not surprising that evangelicals identify more with Republicans. This may not be ideal, but it is the way things are because the Republicans have been cultivating us for over a decade."[36]

A final piece of the privileged position puzzle is the likelihood that government officials will voluntarily turn over decision-making to interest group advocates. As we know from the legal fracas over Vice President Dick Cheney's refusal to turn over to the General Accounting Office and other petitioners records from meetings of his National Energy Policy Development Group, the traditional privileged position of business is alive and well. The same kind of process operates with Christian right representatives and interests in the Bush administration. Indeed, many—though certainly not all—of these representatives have been absorbed into government service as political appointees in the executive branch and on a variety of government commissions. Other Christian right leaders remain off the government payroll but exercise considerable influence over government policy through lobbying, "consulting," producing faux journalistic "reports" on administration policies, and participating in informal networks with law- and policy-makers. As Lindblom points out, governments do not have to be "bribed, duped, or pressured" to turn over decision-making authority to privileged interest groups. Rather, "collaboration and deference" between government officials and interest group representatives become standard operating procedure.[37]

Incorporating the courtship of Christian conservatives by the Republican Party allows students of Christian right politics to bypass the common question of whether any particular political figure is as personally committed to conservative Christian law and social policy as his admirers believe him to be. Examining the relationship through the lens of Lindblom's "privileged position" can displace the question of politicians' personal commitments. Instead, it refocuses attention on the electoral considerations that underlie party politics and the more specific electoral concerns of conservative Republicans who seek the endorsement of Christian conservative leaders and organizations.[38] Of course, to observe that the Christian right occupies a privileged interest group position within the Republican coalition does not invalidate another proposition: that Bush and other Christian conservative politicians assume the moral rectitude of their own conservative impulses and principles and see them as the most appropriate inspiration for political action. Both can be true at the same time. And both probably are true at the same time.[39] A pithy summation—one that is consistent with the evidence—is Richard D. Land's commentary on Bush's faith in the PBS film *The Jesus Factor*. Land, president of the Southern Baptist Convention's Ethics and Religious Liberty Commission and a friend and supporter of Bush says, "There's no question that the President's faith is calculated, and there's no question that the President's faith is real, that it's authentic, that it's genuine. I would say that I don't know and George Bush doesn't know when he's operating out of a genuine sense of his own faith or when it's calculated."[40]

Although the "privileged position" is a workable thesis, we cannot rule out the possibility that what the Christian right is expected to deliver to the nation is not limited to electoral assistance for Republican candidates and policies. Based on what we can surmise about President Bush's beliefs and those of his close doctrinal kin, it is certainly possible that Bush subscribes to conservative Christian eschatology. Such an eschatology pins the fate of the nation to the social and political success of a conservative Christian agenda. President Reagan subscribed to this eschatology and articulated its terms in a variety of public venues.[41] If Bush and other prominent conservative Christian Republican political leaders also subscribe, then we can understand the present relationship between the Republican Party and the Christian right as overdetermined. The relationship has its electoral and policy dimensions, which may be considered to comprise the crux of the arrangement. And it may well have other, theological—and following from the theological, political—dimensions that constitute a less-publicly acknowledged agenda.

If Bill Keller is right—and here, at last, I think he is—it is fruitful to think of today's Christian right in America as occupying a privileged position like that of business. Indeed, it is accurate to say that the Christian right occupies another privileged position alongside business, since the precepts of conservative Christianity have hardly displaced those of business. Far from it—the Christian right distinguishes itself from other recent religious social movements in being aligned with business interests and with the market fundamentalism of the new right coalition. The identification with business interests and market fundamentalism is so key to the Christian right that one sticking point between Protestant and Catholic conservatives remains the remnants of the Catholic social justice tradition. John Dilulio Jr., political scientist and former director of the White House Office of Faith-Based and Community Initiatives, cites this tradition when he refers to himself as a "pro-poor Catholic." Dilulio found himself in conflict with the Bush administration which, during the period of Dilulio's tenure, was loathe to "suffer the term, 'social justice'."[42]

The Catholic social justice tradition continues to create a low wall between many conservative Catholics and conservative Protestants. As Catholics well know, there is also the abiding—even if unvoiced—Protestant Christian conservative conviction that Catholics who do not undergo a particular sort of (Protestant) salvation experience are going to hell. The doctrine of "cobelligerency" articulates Catholics and Protestants as having common interests toward which they can work in spite of theological differences.[43] Whatever the theological issues, I can only be grateful for political reasons that on economics Catholic and Protestant conservatives do not always see eye to eye.

Indeed, identities and the bedfellows and contradictions they create are central to any story about social movements. Whenever I see Coffindaffer's crosses I know the strangeness of belonging to a club that does not want you as a member, multiple clubs, in fact: Appalachians and "real" Americans, to be sure. That strangeness is compounded by my own sense of connection to the red state America—wherever it is found—that so vigorously renounces me and my loved ones. Back in 1987, at the second Washington, DC, lesbian and gay civil rights march, my friend Jeff threw his arms wide in a theatrical gesture, pointed to the many stripes and hues of our queer compatriots, and said in a voice wry and bemused, "these [pause] are my people." I recall that sentiment because it captures for me the messiness and fretfulness of identity. My partner, Laree, tells me that when I take her to Christian bookstores she feels like an anxious porn consumer. She avoids eye contact because she believes, magically, that those who belong in such a place will look into her eyes and find her out. I don't experience that sense of displacement or dread of discovery. I am comfortable even as clerks smile and call me "sister," even as I browse through the most virulent antigay materials. I am critical of much of what these decent Americans hold dear. At the same time, I strive to have a more accurate understanding of them than they have of me and my kind.

I will attend little in what follows to the kinds of political institutions most political scientists study. This introduction suggests a political backdrop against which the ordinary beliefs, theology, and psychology of American conservative Christianity play out. However, even if electoral and institutional politics constitute an unarticulated background to these chapters, it is important to bear these matters in mind. Against the organization and persuasiveness of conservative beliefs about immorality, lesbians and gay men have a number of weapons and defenses: varying personal assets, networks, contracts, protective legislation, court decisions and, sometimes, the kindness of strangers. What we do not have is full inclusion in the model of citizenship that prevails for heterosexual Americans. Particularly for those of us who are poor, working class, and even middle class—and we are many—we must often rely upon our wits, our friends, the irregular practices of our employers, and footholds of protection in our legal and political system to negotiate our existence.

Am I exaggerating? I finished a draft of this book in South Dakota. I was there because my partner, an employee of the federal government, had been posted to a temporary position in Sioux Falls. Because of the 1996 federal Defense of Marriage Act (the original DOMA) I have no legal standing in her life that her employer—our government—is bound to respect. In Sioux Falls in 2005 there was no visible gay community and virtually no visible lesbians and gay men. Although they were invisible, we knew they were there, however. We eventually found the one gay club in Sioux Falls that served people in a wide radius of four states. It is located in an ally behind a restaurant, and its unmarked door reminded me of my 1970s youth. In the autumn of 2004 my partner and I joined the city's small AIDS march with thirty or so others; we rallied at the edge of town and marched directly into the woods where we could not be seen by passersby. Yet even in such a closeted environment, the city and state were alive with Republican Party denunciations of queer trespass. During the 2004 campaign, John Thune, who would unseat minority leader Tom Daschle to become the junior Republican Senator from South Dakota, guaranteed the citizens of that state his support for a constitutional amendment to ban same-sex marriage. There, in that outpost—what Sioux Falls was in its nineteenth-century white Manifest Destiny incarnation—I was reminded of the hegemony of a particular notion of the good that defines itself as universal. Many Americans will recognize this notion of the good as the way the privileged position of conservative Christianity is instantiated in everyday American life as traditional morality and family values. I strained to hear whatever disagreement there might be to the agenda of those who would deny my citizenship, but it was very quiet.

My Gay Agenda

Like other social movements, the Christian right contains great diversity under its umbrella. The movement does not consist of a monolithic and disciplined force of intellectual and ideological automatons. As Charles Strozier discovered when he talked to fundamentalist Christians in New York City about the expected Apocalypse, even beliefs about a particular element of Christian eschatology reveal important differences among believers.[44] There are other cleavages that must be of interest to those who investigate the ideology and practices of the Christian conservative movement. These include cleavages between leaders and followers and between activists and those who are not so inclined. Other systematic differences may appear, depending on the subject and the circumstances: differences of age, race, gender, region, denomination.

Acknowledging these differences, I will still step back and try to give a particular kind of account of the antigay theology and political rhetoric of the Christian right—one that captures the salient dimensions of conservative Christian acts and activism. This perspective does not deny the existence of doctrinal trees. It remains attentive to the political forest nonetheless. In this book, I take a broad approach. Rather than focusing on one arena of antigay conservative Christian activism, I look at several sites or venues of antigay thought and action.

In chapter 1, "Speaking Right," I give more attention to a well-documented aspect of the Christian right movement's political rhetoric—the strategy of directing different kinds of theological and political ideas and emphases to different audiences for political effect. The Christian right often has not received appropriate credit for its sophisticated ability to wield multiple modes of address. This may be because tracking such multiple rhetorics requires attending closely to aspects of doctrine and theology that may—particularly in our present hard-knuckled political environment—attract charges of religious bias to those who criticize Christian right theological politics.

To introduce a general theoretical model of multiple modes of address, I look at the recent explosion of thinking and writing about tolerance among conservative Christians and the way this thinking about tolerance is closely related to Christian right political efforts against LGBT rights. Next, I link Christian right ideology about tolerance to conservative Christian beliefs about eschatology, outlining distinctions between the ideas and arguments that Christian right opinion leaders routinely share with followers and those that are routinely occluded in public political speech.

Especially when we set out to analyze the ideology or rhetoric of a social movement, scholars try to be as careful as possible to sample the movement's discourse widely. In chapter 2, "The Nightmare of Homosexuality," I go to an unusual venue to examine conservative Christian political rhetoric: Chick tracts, the most popular and recognized of all Christian religious tracts. The comic-book format tracts, distributed since the 1960s and translated into over ninety languages, are produced by Jack T. Chick, a conservative Christian artist, self-professed propagandist, and entrepreneur. Strategic Christian right leaders regard the tracts with ambivalence, and the buzz on Chick is that his tracts are no longer welcome in Christian bookstores. However, Chick tracts continue to reflect internal Christian right positions on abortion rights and same-sex sexuality, even as they complicate conservative Christian outreach activities to members of the Jewish, Mormon, and Catholic faiths. In this chapter I interpret the politics of Chick publications and trace Christian right ambivalence toward Chick tracts as a function of efforts to "center" Christian right politics for mainstream audiences.

Chapter 3, "Origin Stories," co-written with Jyl J. Josephson, turns to a venue that is more familiar to those who follow the antigay politics of the Christian right: the ex-gay movement. The ex-gay movement consists of many sites and projects, but we concentrate here on the particular segment of the movement that is connected to ex-gay literature and to the institutional Christian right in manifestations such as Focus on the Family's Love Won Out conferences. The Christian right's antigay politics usually focus on one narrative of homosexual origins, that of individual choice to engage in homosexual acts. The claim that same-sex sexuality is a "choice" often has been successful in neutralizing both claims of discrimination and public support for potential legal remedies. On the other hand, a second and overlapping narrative of development is often ignored. This psychological narrative circulates tacitly through a different set of public debates than those usually associated with the narrative of choice, particularly debates regarding children and adolescents. This chapter surveys Christian right literature and the teachings of the ex-gay movement to explain how two quite different narratives of the origins of same-sex sexuality forge the foundations of different kinds of organized antigay political activities.

There are times when a single set of utterances contains within it a world of meaning. In chapter 4, "Getting What 'We' Deserve," I focus on the brief conversation Pat Robertson shared with fellow minister and televangelist Jerry Falwell on Robertson's *700 Club* television show two days after the September 11 attacks. Together, the two ministers forcefully expressed a "politics of desert" that links American tolerance of lesbians and gay men, feminists, atheists, and others with God's punishment on the polity. Falwell and Robertson were widely denounced for their comments. However, mainstream media provided little analysis of the theological and political content of the Christian right's premillennial politics of desert or the importance of the movement's multiple modes of address. In this chapter I argue that their comments communicate much about the mainstream Christian right's interconnected positions on tolerance, the nation, eschatology, same-sex sexuality, and separation of church and state, as well as the meaning of "terrorism."

Finally, the afterword, "Another Gay Agenda," reflects on the importance of democratic citizens attending to the political exertions of interest and identity groups. As many pessimistic observers of national politics have noted, the demands of democratic citizenship can be rigorous. Because most of us are not blessed with the leisure to pursue politics as a full-time avocation, we rely on filters, shorthands, impulses, and the recommendations of trusted leaders. I don't have any solutions to the demands of democracy except to deepen the pessimism by suggesting that for those whose religious and political views place them outside the Christian right, it is more crucial than they might think to listen carefully to the political arguments and aspirations of Christian conservatives. In the final analysis, this book is not a call to be seen and heard by voting against the right. Instead, it is a call to see and hear Christian conservatives as fellow citizens who want to lead the nation, crafting particular kinds of laws and policies and engaging in particular forms of reward, punishment, and exclusion.

As a social and political movement of great breadth, complexity, and internal diversity, the Christian right cannot be contained within any particular set of disciplinary analytics and epistemological perspectives. It takes the combined interests, skills, and methods of many scholars and other interested parties to assemble and interpret pieces of a vast empirical and theoretical puzzle. This book is not exhaustive, even of the intersection between the Christian right and LGBT people or identity. Its contribution is to closely examine a particular issue across a range of antigay topics and contexts. This issue—the careful management of political rhetoric and argument to advance political interests and the beliefs and convictions that lie beneath political rhetoric—is one that many students of the Christian right observe and comment upon. I hope that the light shed on it here advances the conversation about an important domain of American social and political life.

CHAPTER 1

Speaking Right

If my people, which are called by my name, shall humble themselves, and pray, and seek my face, and turn from their wicked ways; then will I hear from heaven, and will forgive their sin, and will heal their land.

—2 Chronicles 7:14

But the natural man receiveth not the things of the Spirit of God: for they are foolishness unto him: neither can he know them, because they are spiritually discerned.

—1 Corinthians 2:14

Queer Is as Queer Does

In the Southern Baptist church of my youth I never heard any of the graphic descriptions of same-sex sexual practices that have been commonplace in the years since. I knew that although there are many sins that grieve Jesus, homosexuality is particularly loathsome, perhaps not only to his people but also to the creator himself. This I learned in the indirect way that constitutes much socialization and folk knowledge transmission. In the rare moments when Southern Baptist elders spoke of homosexuality, even if they denied that it was any worse than, say, bearing false witness or lusting (heterosexually) in one's heart, they managed to convey the opposite. As we listened, we knew that God saved his most severe disapprobation for homosexuals. And perhaps we even doubted that homosexuals could *really* be saved, not because sexuality is inextricable from the impressive constellation of traits and feelings that constitute the self but because homosexuality is so, well, icky. As a teenaged "prehomosexual," I was alert to every pronouncement—indeed, to every unspoken nuance—on the subject. What was clear to me then was what my mother, upon learning of my sexual orientation, made explicit: being

sexual with a person of the same sex was the worst violation of the laws of God
and nature that any person can accomplish. Like her co-religionists, when she
learned of my orientation she wanted me to repent and change.

Fittingly, I encountered my first "ex-gay" in a lesbian bar. Before the
mainstream popularization of ex-gay and reparative therapies, if not before the
medical and psychological treatment of homosexuals, an ex-gay witnessing to
practicing gays would need to go where the gays were. And in those days the
gays were in bars, clubs, baths, and other settings where queers could congre-
gate away from the attention of straights. I don't want to suggest that ex-gays
only haunted queer gathering places back in the "old" days of the 1970s and
early '80s, when I met "my" ex-gay. Queers today wryly note that ex-gays still
have an affinity for gay spaces. In 2000, activist Wayne Besen sprinted several
blocks through the Dupont Circle neighborhood of Washington, DC, to con-
front and photograph the ex-gay John Paulk in a now-defunct club called Mr.
P's. Paulk's late-night comfort stop only exemplified the many cases of back-
sliding of putative ex-gays who seem to be more "gay" than "ex."

The ex-lesbian I met in Washington, DC, in 1981 was in her mid- to late
forties, about as old as I am now. She sat at the bar of a popular club called The
Other Side and tried to share her Christian witness. Over the pounding beat of
dance music, the woman tried to chat with us—two lesbians half her age—
about her journey out of homosexuality. This was not a journey I had any interest in making. But my girlfriend was intrigued by the oddness of someone
lying in wait in a noisy lesbian club to try to turn women away from the pursuit
of love, and she wanted to hear more. Alas, that longer conversation would not
take place that evening. When my girlfriend and I shared a light kiss, the ex-
lesbian intoned a paraphrase of Hebrews 13:4: "thou shalt not defile the marriage bed."[1] Looking back, I wish I'd taken the time to talk with her. Instead, I
banished her from our company and waited many years before I began to think
seriously about what motivates such a reformation of identity.

The ex-lesbian did not succeed in persuading either of us to turn away
from homosexuality—not even close. She seemed to me a forlorn representative of a world that was disappearing. But I was wrong. Instead, she was in the
vanguard of a dynamic movement that has branched out into academic research, public relations, and political influence. There was a time when I could
just walk away from the message of the Christian right's antigay movement, but
that time is no longer. To paraphrase Hannah Arendt, if one is attacked as a homosexual, one must defend oneself as a homosexual. Not as an American, not
as a world citizen, not as an upholder of the Rights of Man, or whatever.[2]

Defiling Beds, Hearts, and Minds

For a quarter of a century, conservative Christian groups have been advertising
the perversions of lesbians and gay men in sermons, literature, and fundraising

envelopes marked for adult eyes only. Many mass mailings have featured photos of costumed (and sometimes semi-nude) lesbians and gay men, usually snapped at Gay Pride events in major cities. Photos such as these—young women and men semi-clad or in leather paraphernalia, same-sex couples embracing and kissing—found their way into mass-market public relations vehicles like videos and political advertisements.

Christian conservatives pointed to representations like these to demonstrate the hidden gay agenda, ignoring, as many queers have enjoyed pointing out, the *other* gay agenda of working, shopping, paying taxes, visiting with friends, and all the pedestrian activities of daily life. While humorous, such rejoinders to accusations about the gay agenda fail to acknowledge that while lesbians and gay men perceive the pace of change in our social and legal status to be glacially slow, those who disapprove of same-sex sexuality and relations perceive it to be swift and terrible. For them, a world that would reverse the stigma of same-sex sexuality, even slowly and unevenly, is a world that has lost its soul. And they have had no choice but to gird themselves for battle on as many fronts as necessary. This they did, beginning in the 1970s with such efforts as Anita Bryant's Save Our Children campaign and the Briggs Initiative. And they do so today with ever more media and intellectual sophistication.

In the early days of new Christian right formation, opprobrious depictions of lesbians and gay men were directed to both in-group and public audiences. Today the conservative Christian leaders are more careful about how they manage images of the movement and its adversaries. As we shall see, some Christian right leaders and arenas still direct censorious representations of queers to Christian right insiders and to those perceived as likely allies. Depending upon the speaker and context, gay men may continue to be portrayed as raunchy, sexually promiscuous, diseased, atheist, and threatening. In addition, and Justice Antonin Scalia is on record on this point, they are rich. This claim is important because it reverses the legally and politically marginal status of gays.[3] Representations of homosexuals as "sexually depraved, superrich, and intent on domination" are still useful to dissolve or hold at bay identification with those marginalized by their sexuality.[4]

But this generalization is too simple to capture the intersections of narratives and venues in which conservative Christian talk about LGBT people appears. One apparent counterexample occurs in counseling and ex-gay literature where sympathetic portrayals, especially of those "struggling" with homosexual attraction, are routine. Another distinction appears when we factor sex into consideration of political rhetoric, disarticulating the L-word from the G. When conservative Christian opinion leaders differentiate lesbians and gay men, we can see that they treat these groups differently.

First, lesbians are often ignored in lubricious discussions of rampant sexuality. It is as though the sexuality of women who have sex and partner romantically with women must remain a black box. This is odd in its own way because if gay male sexuality has been until quite recently largely absent from popular culture, "the lesbian" is a staple of pop culture's lower depths. Perhaps this repression of lesbian sexuality helps conservative Christians defend themselves against the potentially arousing flood of sexually explicit popular media images in which "lesbians" appear. Second, when lesbian sexuality comes to the fore it is of the stereotyped masculine variety: aggressive, preying on the innocence of girls and women, mostly indescribable except for its dimensions of hypermasculine (gay, rather than straight) violence and control. One useful conduit for such conceptions of lesbian sexuality has been the recent emphasis in feminist scholarship on violence in lesbian relationships. Paul Cameron's Family Research Institute (FRI) and other antigay sources use such scholarship as a resource to publicize the risks of lesbianism.[5]

Finally, lesbians may not be considered a threat at all, but rather "sad" and "weak."[6] However, when we are designated a threat, lesbians are often an ideological threat, the thinking person's homosexual menace. From Jesse Helms's dismissal of Clinton nominee Roberta Achtenberg as a "damn [damned?] lesbian" to the widely circulated intimations of Hillary Rodham Clinton's same-sex sexuality, the charge of lesbianism clings to women who have the effrontery to transgress gender rules. In the conservative Christian narrative, even those girls and women who cannot be induced to yield to sexual desire for other women may yet be influenced and ruined by lesbianism. Actually, this is consistent with the fear that courses through conservative Christian discussions of same-sex sexuality. Homosexuality, it seems, is preternaturally attractive, so much so that one might be forgiven for failing to understand why there are any heterosexuals left in the world. Besides disseminating propaganda about queer violence, Cameron is a rich source of depictions of the intense physical pleasure associated with queer sex.[7]

When collapsed into feminism, lesbianism is seductive because it represents the impurest of motives: a self-interest untempered by sometimes inconvenient care for others, certainly children and husbands, but one presumes, for others who inhabit the common world as well. Erasing the large numbers of lesbians and gay men who have children, queers are understood as "unencumbered selves," artists of self-indulgence whose priorities are a rebuke—and perhaps objects of envy—to traditional Americans.[8] Pat Robertson spoke to both the equation of lesbianism with feminism and the death of care when he crafted the paragraph in a 1992 fundraising letter that still surfaces from time to time on t-shirts and in parodies of the Christian right: "The feminist agenda is not about equal rights for women. It is about a socialist, anti-family political movement that encourages women to leave their husbands, kill their children, practice witchcraft, destroy capitalism, and become lesbians."[9]

Sylvia, feminist cartoonist Nicole Hollander's alter ego, responded to Robertson's broadside by noting that it constituted a "heavy schedule."[10] But those to whom the letter was addressed did not find the news risible. For them social manifestations of evil are no laughing matter, and it is the responsibility of Christians to mobilize themselves to stand firm against them.

Who're You Talking To?

All these meanings and more are packed into various venues, practices, and projects of the Christian right movement. But not all these meanings are available in mainstream media debates over gay issues. This is not mere oversight. Christian right leaders actively strive to have their political and theological beliefs misidentified by the broad public. Many students of the Christian right note the practice of speaking differently to different audiences.[11] Unfortunately, mainstream media and political commentators often collude in this strategy by delivering news reports of New Christian right religious issues that are "superficial and lacking context."[12] Throughout the period of the rise of the New Christian right, approximately the late 1970s to the present, students of politics have tended to make two basic errors: first, they fail to trace the precedents and contexts of baffling or controversial comments by Christian right opinion leaders; second, they overlook the fact that Christian right leaders tend to address subject matter of conservative Christian interest in different rhetorical styles or even with quite different arguments, depending upon the audience they are addressing. The multiple modes of address favored by Christian right leaders reflect changes in rhetorical style and emphasis, and the contents of political arguments.

This gullibility about Christian right messaging is true not only of the mainstream press and critics, but also of the lesbian and gay press, which has particular interests in understanding the deep structure of the intersections of theology and politics. To take only one example, on September 13, 2001, Jerry Falwell and Pat Robertson proclaimed the root cause of the terrorist strikes on the World Trade Center and the Pentagon as the sinfulness of "homosexuals and lesbians," among other usual suspects. The reaction that followed had liberals and conservatives alike decrying the comments. Soon after, *The Advocate* magazine featured a news bulletin entitled "News of the Year: Far Right." The bulletin asks rhetorically if "2001 mark[ed] a sea change in the right wing's willingness to demonize gay people" and concludes: "maybe so, if conservative pundits' and politicians' responses to Jerry Falwell's finger-pointing are any indication."[13] Nothing of the sort is true, but we will not know the actual state of conservative politics until we have looked carefully at antigay rhetorics in all the venues and forums where they are at home.

As we know, Christian right opinion leaders often communicate to believers and the receptive in ways that risk alienating others. They may, and often do, hone their messages so they can address different groups in different ways, just as politicians do. Politicians engage in "dog-whistle politics," signaling to their ideological constituents at a frequency that others do not hear. So do leaders of other social and political movements. In this, as in other things, the Christian right is not extraordinary.

Even so, the strategy of directing different rhetoric and argument to different audiences is never without seams, contradictions, and unanticipated consequences. One problem is that of ideology; movements do not agree on a single message, emphasis, or perspective even when members agree on broad political goals. For example, some precincts of Christian counseling or the ex-gay movement will not concur with the antigay politics of the large Christian right organizations even if they all hope for similar outcomes. But another set of issues has to do with complications endemic to movement communications with diverse audiences.

In her study of convergences between white supremacy and the Christian right, Ann Burlein notes the efficacy of the common political tools of softening rhetoric and nichemarketing. The first refers to explicit Christian right pedagogy to followers in venues such as training seminars. By softening rhetoric—for example, teaching students not to make political appeals using biblical authority—leaders hope to prepare followers for political work without inspiring charges of religious overreaching and extremism.[14] By nichemarketing, Burlein refers to the way in which organizations such as Focus on the Family and Pete Peters's Christian Identity "sell" their respective brands of ideology; "each ministry speaks an idiom to its constituents."[15] Christian right leaders combine softening rhetoric and nichemarketing to create a complex set of rhetorics that can be directed at different audiences without compromising core theological and political messages.

Both nichemarketing and softening rhetoric are strategies employed by political movements and interest groups to attain their ends in a competitive political environment. Critics of the Christian right recognize such techniques and may come to understand all instances of their use as not only deliberate but also duplicitous and disguising the absence of authentic religious convictions. In their reading, political strategy discloses pure will to power. In what follows I'll challenge that reading of strategy and disclose some of the convictions and complexities that underlie political strategy. It is also important to note that not all message tacticians understand what they do in terms of misleading outsiders. One example is John D. Woodbridge, a professor of Church history and history of Christian thought. Writing in *Christianity Today,* Woodbridge suggests addressing "society" and trying to change public opinion on matters of concern to conservative Christians by using nonbiblical language. Like many political theorists of democracy, he conceptualizes this suggestion as using the "language of the public square."[16]

A key hazard of multiple modes of address is that inevitably these movement rhetorics, like "smart" bombs, will not always find their perfect audiences, or only their perfect audiences. Christian right leaders know that messages to their followers are accessible to their political adversaries. People for the American Way, Americans United for Separation of Church and State (AUSCS), Political Research Associates (PRA), and other progressive organizations consistently monitor Christian right broadcasts, mailings, and conferences and report back to their own members. At a more spontaneous grassroots level of political activity, anyone who attends a conservative church, tunes in to the *700 Club*, surfs Christian right websites, or signs up to receive the mailings of conservative Christian organizations has access to messages that Christian right leaders send their followers. Of course, most citizens lack the time or the inclination to consistently subject themselves to political messages that have little immediate salience for them. Political organizations on the left that function as voices critical of the Christian right do not have a bottomless fund of public interest and attention on which to draw. On the other hand, public versions of these messages—including arguments about LGBT attempts to secure "special rights"—do have a political impact and may be widely embraced by those who are unfamiliar with their theological foundations and political connections.

In fact, conservative Christian life in the United States is broadly characterized by multiple modes of address, in public media as well as in other institutions and across the life span of believers. For example, Christian adolescents learn history and science as they are taught in American secondary schools, but they also learn their own versions of these and other subjects through church sermons, Sunday school, Christian literature, and Christian youth culture. The double vision of Christian conservatives forged in these social institutions is enabling and empowering. Outsiders' ignorance of their values and beliefs is disabling and disempowering. Much has been made of Ralph Reed's infamous remark that as an activist conservative Christian he intended to "be invisible," "do guerilla warfare," "paint [his] face and travel at night," and deposit his adversary in a body bag.[17] As students of the Christian Coalition know, Reed refers to political tactics in which activists and candidates for elective office hide hard right Christian positions on issues from unsuspecting voters. Unfortunately, Reed's adversaries read his electoral strategy too narrowly. They would be better off understanding Reed's comments to be as much descriptive of the relationship between the Christian right and the rest of America as prescriptive. It is not only voters in particular elections who may be briefly deceived for divine ends. As they struggle to redraw the map of American politics and policy, Christian right leaders too often can count on the apathy or ignorance of nonbelievers and of believers who are Christian, but not *Christian conservative*.[18]

Hate the Sin

Liberals and agnostics often ask rhetorically why it is so difficult for Christian conservatives to hold their beliefs, lead their own lives, and leave others to lead theirs. Such questions may indicate a variety of political dispositions (or, more negatively, betray a number of impulses): political tolerance, a commitment to pluralism or negative liberty, indifference, or mere self-interest. To know what motivates our fellow citizens, we need more information than the simple knowledge that some people approve, and others disapprove, of the morally meddlesome theological politics of the Christian right.

In this endeavor, it is helpful to learn that deep ambivalence about liberal democracy resides at the heart of the conservative Christian movement. Christian conservatives embrace democracy as the best kind of political system that can exist in a flawed temporal world. And there are moments when Christian right leaders embrace populist democracy uncritically, as when they insist that the judicial system be responsive to the expressed will of citizens whose positions on controversial issues coincide with their own. However, as a group, Christian conservatives also profoundly mistrust democracy, identifying liberty with license and with the satisfaction of individual interests through enslavement to selfish desires. There is the additional prophetic conviction that democracies are merely a stage in the irresistible historical movement toward the millennium.[19]

Neither of these aspects of a conservative Christian ambivalence toward democracy is difficult to understand. Christian conservatives have seen the role of traditional religion in policy, law, and popular culture decline over the course of American history. The decline has been especially precipitous since World War I: "In modern times, religion, or at least an agreed-upon version of it has lost its place as a prime mode of explaining reality. . . . Religion must make its way by persuasion and not by coercion. It has become escapable and has been relocated on the cultural landscape."[20] Church historian Martin Marty published these words in the year Americans elected Jimmy Carter, our first born-again evangelical president. There is irony to describing religion in American democracy today as "escapable." That irony is blunted, however, by the fact that religious elites are currently trying to relocate religion on the cultural landscape by conferring upon it a centrality that has been eroded.

The history of American democracy combines many ingredients, including deep commitments to laissez-faire capitalism and religious traditionalism. These elements have often been at odds with one another. For one thing, many Americans have embraced traditionalism and maintained a stringent critique of the excesses and consequences of capitalism. For another, the potent combination of the free market and individual cultural preferences throw up many ideas, products, and ways of life that do not aspire to any version of Christian virtue. As Lisa McGirr points out in her study of the origins of the new right, social conservatives often find themselves in the position of having to exonerate the amoral operations of the market in their critiques of contemporary American politics.[21]

There are many examples of such exonerating behavior, but consider the example of recent corporate scandals. In the summer of 2002, the Barna Group unveiled the results of a survey on the gross fiscal misconduct of many large American corporations: "Americans Speak: Enron, WorldCom and Others Are Result of Inadequate Moral Training By Families." Barna is a conservative Christian polling and information organization whose mission is "facilitat[ing] spiritual transformation in America." Barna surveys Americans—distinguishing those who meet criteria as "born again" and "evangelical" from those who don't—but the organization does not limit itself to reporting the results of its polling on a variety of values and cultural issues. It appends editorial comments on the issues for its born-again audience. In the case of Enron, WorldCom and Others, Barna confirms that the most important predictor of felonious corporate misbehavior is the failure of parents to teach their children values.[22] This conclusion is consistent with the views expressed by conservative Christian radio personalities at the time to the effect that the real gulf in corporate values lay between born-again and secular CEOs. Structural explanations that examined incentive systems and the ethos of American corporate capitalism were nowhere to be found in conservative Christian accounts of the disaster.

As a social movement, the Christian right influences and is influenced by contemporary liberal and democratic norms and discourse. At the same time, members fantasize collectively that the movement innocently embodies scriptural meaning. The Bible is the unalterable word of God, and its truths are timeless.[23] The optimistic reading of the mutual influence between contemporary liberal democracy and conservative Christian politics is that the Christian right is domesticated by the give and take of democratic politics and thereby passes into the mainstream of American political discourse and participation. In this reading, the Christian right is not a threat to liberal and democratic values. Nancy Rosenblum would seem to support such an interpretation with her claim that social groups with illiberal aims and doctrines do not necessarily constitute a threat to pluralism and democracy. For Rosenblum, such groups stimulate the development of moral dispositions that—if not constructive to, at minimum—are not destructive to the wider democratic society. Even illiberal groups encourage the cultivation of cooperation, rule following, and norms that proscribe force.[24]

However, there is a problem with the sanguine assessment of illiberal social groups: it relies on the existence of a democratic polity whose ideology and institutions are able and willing to protect the rights of those so disfavored.[25] Rosenblum is optimistic about the ability of a rights regime to empower individuals in the face of organized group disfavor. Interestingly, she does not take up the many faces of social, economic, and political exclusion suffered by queers. Her only reference to same-sex sexuality in *Membership and Morals* is one in which she notes that most violence motivated by antihomosexual bias is carried out by "unaffiliated individuals" rather than by members of groups.[26] But this narrow conception of what it means to belong to a group is surely troublesome, particularly so in light of the coherent religious beliefs that survey research confirms motivate most antigay prejudice.[27] When organized Christian right groups and opinion leaders foment antigay beliefs and these beliefs influence the distribution of rights and public goods, we must subject any theory of the pro-social effects of group membership to some specific caveats.[28]

There is a contending perspective on the relation of the Christian right to democratic norms and processes. In this view, the Christian right is not domesticated by its participation in democratic processes. It does not sublimate its activist energies into pro-social behavior. Instead, whatever the sources of its members' beliefs, the movement uses "bigoted discourse" to actively build and maintain antidemocratic values. Such discourse produces particular kinds of citizens.[29] One example of Anna Marie Smith's thesis is Dick Armey's apology for his 1995 reference to Representative Barney Franks (D-MA) as "Barney Fag." As a Republican elected official, Armey has distanced himself from the Christian right, but other examples of antigay speech are close at hand. A surprising example emerged recently at the 2006 Values Voter Summit, when Bishop Wellington Boone, of the Christian men's organization Promise Keepers, spoke of faggots and noted that gay people are "passionate at protecting their perversion."[30]

Smith points out that Christian right activists seek to redefine the liberal democratic tradition to "center" their own antidemocratic and exclusionary politics. Of course, such centering can take place in a variety of ways, including apologies for impolitic speech and careful management of public discourse right from the start. In some cases, bigoted discourse may take the truly unexpected form of an outreach of compassion. Such therapeutic ideology is central to the ex-gay movement. The payoff of redefining the center is the right's ability to occupy that position, an imaginary tolerant political center. The effects of this redefinition are many, including the rightward shift of political culture, the obfuscation of the meaning of policies and their underlying motivations, and the transformation of important ideals such as equality and tolerance.[31] The triumph of right-wing ideology is such that "the majority of the intolerant misidentify as tolerant."[32] One result is the political construction of an imaginary figure of the celibate, nonpolitically active "good homosexual." Such a character props up fictive right-wing tolerance for a kind of citizen who cannot exist as simultaneously "good" and "homosexual."

In the course of its antigay projects, the Christian right crafts some messages that merely proscribe homosexuality and homosexuals. Other messages promote the Augustinian axiom to "hate the sin but love the sinner."[33] Yet others endorse compassion for people who struggle with unwanted same-sex desires. Smith is trenchant about the new right's attempts to recode intolerance as tolerance. However, the explanation for the mixed messages is not necessarily that the Christian right "contradicts itself." Christian right leaders cultivate distinct modes of address for their different audiences, born-again followers and unbelievers as well as specific precincts of the conservative Christian movement rather than others. John C. Green confirms that different kinds of anti-gay groups specialize in different kinds of methods and messaging. So, for example, "general purpose groups" such as the Christian Coalition and Focus on the Family pragmatically "down play hostility to homosexuals" and may even criticize others in the movement for their "strident antigay rhetoric."[34]

We can distinguish the Christian right from other groups on the political right by its complicated negotiation of the terrain of tolerance. On tolerance, the Christian right plays a double game, situating conservative Christians and their political positions as tolerant on one quite specific reading of this term and righteously intolerant at the same time. Indeed, especially on themes related to gender, sexuality, reproductive rights, and family organization, Christian conservatives socialize, cultivate, and defend a virtue of intolerance that can itself be located in various forms among the multiple political traditions in American history.[35]

Being Intolerant

In the wake of the failure of the U.S. Senate to convict Bill Clinton for perjury for his testimony in the civil case of *Jones v. Clinton*, conservative activist and president of the Free Congress Foundation Paul Weyrich released an open letter to the conservative movement. Weyrich's letter caused a sensation on the right. In it, Weyrich suggested that the time had come for people of faith to concede the "collapse of [American] culture" and the loss of the "culture war." He suggested that although conservatives were able to get their candidates elected to office, they were not able to govern with a social conservative agenda; the cultural reality of Americans "tolerat[ing]" and "celebrat[ing]" the "intolerable" had finally precipitated the failure of politics. In such an atmosphere, he argued, conservatives can only withdraw from political attempts to reinstate "Judeo-Christian civilization" and separate themselves from corrupt institutions.[36]

Among those on the Christian right who responded publicly to Weyrich were Pat Robertson and James Dobson, and both rejected Weyrich's call for surrender. Robertson, as he so often does, responded in a press statement in which he denied that Christian conservatives were "ready to withdraw from the process we call democracy" and noted that the "future of America is at stake."[37] The result of the 2004 presidential election vindicated the decision of Christian conservatives not to cede electoral politics to secular elites and members of mainline Protestant denominations. However, Weyrich's preoccupation with the pernicious effects of tolerance, widely shared with other Christian conservatives, has not receded since the waning days of Clinton's presidency.

Opinion leaders of the Christian right often fulminate against religious and other forms of toleration as ideals to be upheld in American society.

For many, toleration—and especially toleration mandated by U.S. law or the Constitution—is itself an abuse of political authority. As such, it is an invitation to Christian resistance. In fact, for the Christian right, toleration is complicated and the views of the movement deserve careful treatment. It is true that some Christian right thinkers do make a distinction that permits conservative Christians to claim tolerance as their own. These thinkers defend opposition to rights claims of disfavored minorities such as lesbians and gay men by contrasting different kinds of tolerance. In "traditional tolerance," respect for others coexists with an underlying conviction that some beliefs and practices are simply wrong or sinful; public embrace of this virtue is integral to mainstream democratic politics. By contrast, "new tolerance" tries to obliterate the value distinctions between alternative beliefs, practices, and social arrangements.[38] "New tolerance" is dangerous to Christian faith, but "traditional tolerance," which is tolerance properly understood, is not.

Lest this distinction be taken as academic, a longtime leader of the Christian right, Jerry Falwell, rejected "new tolerance," and enacted that rejection in his positions on and relations with sexual minorities. In 1999, Falwell invited his ex-ghostwriter, Mel White, and two hundred LGBT members of Soulforce to take part in a dialogue with him about their issues. When Falwell later described the meeting to a *Washington Post* reporter he replied to the accusation that he did not listen to his guests in this way: "I didn't invite them in to *listen* to them. I invited them in to *talk* to them."[39] Falwell did not only rebuke the "folly of excessive tolerance" as so many conservatives do. Like many on the Christian right, he identified tolerance as itself the problem of our age, a problem so central to our contemporary condition that it can precipitate the most devastating attack on American territory.[40]

Tim LaHaye also puts this conception of tolerance in the mouth of his new action hero, Michael Murphy, biblical archeologist. In LaHaye's new, post-*Left Behind*, series, *Babylon Rising*, Murphy explains the problem of our absence of "moral absolutes" in a lecture to his undergraduate students:

> The traditional definition of tolerance is living peaceably alongside others in spite of differences. But that view of tolerance has been twisted today to mean that everyone must accept the other person's viewpoints without question because the truth is relative. What's true for one person may not be true for another person, right? . . . That was exactly what was happening in the days of Noah and in the days of Lot. Everyone was doing what was right in their own eyes. And it's the same today. Society preaches tolerance of every viewpoint and everyone—with one big exception: those people who have strong religious faith. That's where this double-standard

tolerance ends. . . . It makes me wonder if we are living in the days before the next coming judgment.[41]

Leaving aside the question of what this disquisition has to do with the teaching of archeology, it is useful to consider both the definition of tolerance that LaHaye posits and its relationship to other conservative Christian teachings on tolerance.

On the face of it, many political theorists agree with the framing of tolerance with which Christian conservatives often begin their considerations of the subject. Michael Walzer defines toleration as "the peaceful coexistence of groups of people with different histories, cultures and identities." What Walzer means by toleration, however, goes well beyond this simple formulation. Walzer describes a number of attitudes, from the exhaustion that follows social strife to enthusiastic endorsement of difference, as forms of tolerance on a continuum. And he suggests that democratic societies become more stable "if people are further along on the continuum" toward enthusiasm about the cultural differences and ways of life they find around them.

Liberal democracies can be judged in part by how well they protect minority ways of life, which "will be democratically overruled on most matters of public culture" in the absence of strong protections such as civil rights and an independent judiciary. Finally, separation of church and state safeguards toleration because it keeps those with religious objections to nonconforming groups from acting on their objections. Religious groups that hope to enact their particular forms of intolerance into law are thus "barred from seizing state power" and "confined to civil society."[42] Amy Gutmann recommends this resolution, which she calls "two-way protection." Two-way protection "recognizes that freedom of conscience can be justified only within the limits of nondiscriminatory laws and policies."[43] Like LaHaye, the political theorists are interested in maintaining a society in which citizens can live "peaceably alongside others."

One way in which Christian conservative elites and political theorists might find common ground is through the idea that tolerance is not the only value of democracies. One tradition in modern political thought, exemplified by Joseph Schumpeter, holds that most democratic citizens are little capable of tolerance and that democracy can survive this attitudinal defect. More important is the view that there are limits to tolerance, that in practice democratic societies make determinations about how to balance tolerance and other values in particular cases. What this suggests is that while for some tolerance is an absolute principle that can never be compromised, it is also possible to see a "distinction between tolerance as a principle and tolerance as prudential."[44] This distinction is crucial to understanding a Christian conservative critique of tolerance. The case against tolerance of same-sex sexuality is prudential, focusing on the harms—to marriage, the biblical family, individual salvation, and, ultimately, the nation—that follow from it. Just because such arguments are articulated in the public sphere does not, of course, mean that they become dominant in democratic discourse. Even if they don't, however, they are crucial in forging the frames of the discussion for Christian conservatives.

How useful is the version of tolerance put forth by LaHaye in broader Christian right discourse? In fact, Christian conservatives put forth disconcertingly few defenses of traditional tolerance in political debates about same-sex sexuality. More frequent is a rejection of tolerance even when the rhetoric and arguments on such issues are softened or framed in democratic terms. As examples, two quite different texts narrate the rejection of tolerance: Daniel Taylor's *Is God Intolerant? Christian Thinking about the Call for Tolerance*, and Ryan Dobson's *Be Intolerant: Because Some Things Are Just Stupid*. Taylor speaks to and for Christian conservatives in rejecting tolerance, the "pariah sin," "the only serious sin left."[45] Dobson, the son of Focus on the Family's James Dobson, speaks in a hip register to young Christians about tolerance: an "epidemic," a "broken philosophy," a "TUMOR on the American soul."

For Christian conservatives such as Taylor and Dobson, God does not call his people to tolerance, the requirement of a particular kind of secular social world, but to love; further, love is a "much higher standard."[46] The younger Dobson calls on his readers to "be intolerant—in love," and backs up his exhortation with stories of personal relationships in which he refused to compromise God's teachings when friends fell into sinful ways. Possibly overestimating his importance to "the world," the young Dobson draws this conclusion about the importance of intolerance in his life: "I am intolerant because I love. The world hates me because I love in this way, but I cannot stop. I dare not stop."[47] Pat Robertson proclaimed this principle in a reflection that has often been cited by his critics as a sign of his personal bigotry and intransigence rather than viewed in the context of a Christian conservative doctrine of tolerance: "[Y]ou're supposed to be nice to the Episcopalians and the Presbyterians and the Methodists and this, that, and the other thing. Nonsense. I don't have to be nice to the spirit of the Antichrist. I can love the people who hold false opinions, but I don't have to be nice to them."[48] It is only "new tolerance" that demands being nice to the spirit of the Antichrist, and this Pat Robertson will not do. And where's the love? Robertson's, Taylor's, and Dobson's love is tough love, reproving love. Those who disagree may well ask: what can, or should, be done to those of whom we disapprove in the name of love?

The aspiration of Robertson's love is not far to seek: Episcopalians, Presbyterians, Methodists, queers, and many other sorts of misguided fellow citizens may all take the Roman Road that leads to salvation.[49] On that road, lesbians and gay men will surely renounce their sexuality and embrace celibacy. It is well for students of the Christian right to give appropriate attention, then, to the role of love in social and political projects and forms of outreach. Love Won Out is the brand name of Focus on the Family's ex-gay project. To most observers, this brand name signals that love, not hate, can accomplish the transformation of sexuality and of lives. But it also signals something else, especially to those who are steeped in the language of conservative Christian politics: while one side of the political divide demands liberal tolerance toward those who identify as lesbian, gay, bisexual, or queer, the other side exposes tolerance as misguided and demands reproving love instead. "Love" does double duty, as the flip side of both hate and tolerance. Such a binary suggests that hate and tolerance may well be more closely related than they at first appear, and this resemblance is easily suggested by Christian witnessing that identifies tolerance as the road to hell. The message is this: those who leave you in peace and seem to wish you well are not your friends but the enemies of your everlasting soul.

This precept is particularly easy to demonstrate with regard to same-sex sexuality. For conservative Christians, tolerance is inextricably linked to all the major cultural sins, but to homosexuality most of all. In *Is God Intolerant?* Taylor employs a number of social issues and personal anecdotes to illustrate his points, but same-sex sexuality epitomizes misplaced tolerance. The book's index lists homosexuality on two of the book's 128 pages, but a close reading of the text discloses that references to same-sex sexuality outpace references to all other modern sins that often serve as occasions for tolerant forbearance.[50] Taylor contrasts appropriate applications of intolerance, for example for homosexuality, with inappropriate applications of tolerance, for example when the German people allowed themselves to be governed by the Nazis. Could it be that Taylor is suggesting a parallel between Nazism and homosexuality? Not directly, but even if he did make this connection explicit he would be in good Christian right company, for this comparison is frequent and prosaic. Whether dealing with perpetrators of genocide or homosexuals, believers are called to love individuals while struggling against their evil fruits.

The exhortation to substitute love (a private form of relation) for toleration (a potentially public form of relation) has many potential venues and implications. It reveals the real problem with the fungibility of love for tolerance. The problem is not that such harshness violates tender liberal sensibilities. Instead, it is that this substitution of love for tolerance elides a distinction that is key to informed debates on the subject. This distinction is one between *tolerance* as a subjective state, belief system, attitude, conviction, or feeling and *toleration* as a specifically public virtue and organizing principle of regimes. Distinguishing tolerance and toleration in this way does not deny that there are connections between them. Many scholars concede, for example, that it is difficult to imagine a tolerant regime that does not command the support of some broad public for its functioning. However, normative political theory does not necessarily predicate the value of the public practice of toleration on the moral impulses or beliefs of majorities. There are independent reasons to believe that toleration is a desirable value for the organization of collective life. Many of these arguments rely on some conception of human flourishing for which toleration is a necessary, if not a sufficient, condition.[51]

Daniel Taylor makes a pass at this distinction between tolerance and toleration, but it is unsatisfactory. Relying on seventeenth-century debates about religious toleration that are still relevant to us today, Taylor's distinction is historical and semantic: toleration is the early version of what is now called tolerance. In those early days, it referred to the idea that states should not force religious conformity to settle contentious social disputes. In his historical account, Taylor moves quickly from the religious wars of early modern Europe to the bargain struck with traditional believers in the twentieth century to "keep religion in the private sphere." In this analysis, early modern toleration—a matter of official state neutrality to religious dogmas—is simply irrelevant to contemporary debates about tolerance. This is so even though those who identify with "secular, progressive culture" keep raising the specter of religious wars to justify their own resistance to traditional religious convictions.[52]

As both Taylor and Dobson suggest in their treatment of tolerance, Christian right leaders routinely instruct their followers that it is they—born-again, Bible-believing Christians—who are victims of intolerance. This reversal is not simply rhetorical but reflects a conviction that the descent of America into cultural evil sets the conditions for the triumph of Satan and the decimation of Christianity.[53] What is important for critics of the Christian right to remember is that in the final analysis tolerance is "not a human conspiracy," even though it is political liberals who represent the vice of tolerance. Rather, tolerance is a satanic "grand conspiracy."[54] It is Satan's way of working in the world through either duped or enthusiastic subjects. The outcomes of political struggles over tolerance have spiritual repercussions in a world that moves inexorably toward end-times and final reckonings.

Until the End of the World

Like other aspects of Christian right politics, opposition to toleration cannot be reduced to a single cause. As historians point out, both the forms of Christian conservative intolerance and the politics that flow from them change over time, reflecting different nuances, priorities, and, in some cases, different issues. For example, there is no longer an active Christian constituency for banning the production and sale of alcohol such as the one that existed in the early years of the twentieth century.[55] Without forgetting these differences, it is still possible to investigate the doctrinal and theological roots of contemporary Christian right political positions. To do so, we must look not only at publicly articulated positions and the reasons offered on their behalf. We must supplement this knowledge with other sources of in-group information. Sometimes we'll find an identity or partial identity between these public and in-group sources. At other times the theological narratives and political goals directed to motivating and informing Christian conservatives open up strange new worlds of political reason for unbelievers.

One answer that illuminates much about Christian politics lies in contemporary end-times apocalyptic theology. Conservative Christians engage the political process for many reasons but for two reasons most of all: first is the mandate to save as many souls as possible before the end-time chronology commences; second is the desire to avert the possibility that "God would destroy our society for its wickedness." In the course of her investigation of the history of the Christian right, Ruth Murray Brown hears variations on both themes from her conservative Christian respondents. She succinctly captures these two quite different purposes in a chapter entitled "Saved People Can Save the Country."[56] Of the two purposes—saving people and saving the country—it is the second that is most frequently underestimated by outsiders to the Christian right. To understand it, we must understand at least the broad outlines of the study of last things.

Historically, Christian eschatology has taken a number of forms that include premillennialism, postmillennialism, and amillennialism. These forms persist today as variations between the belief systems of denominations, doctrinal groups, churches, and individual believers. However, this undeniable variation could easily cloak the broad outlines of end-time belief in our time. The majority of Christian right leaders such as James Dobson, Billy Graham, and Tim LaHaye, as well as the next generation to which they are now passing the mantle of leadership, are dispensational premillennialists. The doctrine to which these believers adhere teaches that Jesus Christ's triumphal return to earth will inaugurate the millennium on earth, which cannot begin until Jesus vanquishes the Antichrist and relegates Satan to the depths for a thousand years. The most popular version of this premillenial story today is found in the many pages (and over twelve volumes) of the *Left Behind* series of novels by Tim LaHaye and Jerry Jenkins.

The first book, *Left Behind: A Novel of the Earth's Last Days*, begins dramatically with the Rapture, which entails the disappearance of born-again Christians all over the earth. The plot that unspools from this auspicious opening is familiar to conservative Christians, even if such details as the operations of the "Tribulation Force" cannot be inferred from the text of the book of Revelation. In the aftermath of the Rapture, social and political hopes darken, the Antichrist arises to rule the world, mass witnessing and conversions— including conversions of God's people, the Jews—begin, and the world sinks into chaos as it moves toward Armageddon. The last battle between good and evil takes place on Middle Eastern soil. Prophesy-minded Christian conservatives scrutinize world events for insight into the unfolding of God's final plan for his creation.

Although many conservative Christians today probably believe that this formula of the end-times in the Revelation of St. John is as old as Christianity itself, it is actually relatively new. Or, rather, it is both old and new, representing a reading of eschatology that was condemned by the early church and then experienced a renaissance in the mid-nineteenth century. Our dominant "fundamentalist apocalyptic" is pretribulation ("pretrib") premillennial dispensationalism, the brainchild of an Englishman named John Nelson Darby.[57] Pretrib premillennialists expect born-again Christians to be removed from earth—"raptured"—before the inception of the seven-year "tribulation" marked by the reign of the Antichrist and well before the triumphal return of Jesus that will follow.[58] As Paul Boyer relates, Darby did not manufacture this belief system from whole cloth; in fact, major dimensions of it preceded him in the Millerite movement of the 1830s and 1840s and in other popular preachings and enthusiasms. However, it was Darby who formulated the most durable of the premillennialisms when he added the idea of a literal gathering of believers into the air, the Rapture now regarded to have been foretold by Paul. There have been many variations—pretrib, midtrib, and posttrib—of the Rapture time line since it was first set out, but Darby's version, in which believers are raptured before the suffering of the tribulation begins, has stood the test of time. Darby was not a popular preacher. Most Christians learned his interpretation of the end-time in the decades after he expounded it through other proponents or through the popular Scofield Bible, first published in 1909.[59]

The final piece of pretrib premillennialism is the centrality of the Antichrist, the leading man of the end-time. According to conservative Christian eschatology, the Antichrist will come to prominence during the first half of the tribulation and seize power at its mid-point. A man who preaches peace, he will inspire trust, gain control, and then unleash unprecedented evil on the people who remain on earth. Speculations about the identity of the Antichrist go back to the earliest days of the Christian church. A surprising number of prominent modern men (though never women) have been identified by their contemporaries as potential claimants to the position. These include George III of England, Thomas Jefferson, Adolf Hitler, Benito Mussolini, Mikhail Gorbachev (that satanic birthmark!), Sun Myung Moon, Henry Kissinger, John F. Kennedy (Catholic!), Ronald Reagan, Saddam Hussein, and Bill Clinton, as well as many others. In addition to these particular individuals, the pope has been a contender for the role of Antichrist to many—not any particular pope, though some have been suspected more than others, but "a" or "some" pope.

The idea that the leader who arises to become the Antichrist will come from the Holy See dies hard. Tim LaHaye and Jerry Jenkins have been given credit in some quarters for not selecting a pope as their fictional Antichrist. Indeed, the authors even rapture the last pope to occupy the office before the Antichrist arises. However, other astute readers point out that the raptured pope seems to have become a Protestant shortly before the saved disappear from the earth. And the execrable Cardinal Peter Matthews who takes his place at the helm of Enigma One World Church in Rome is evidence for the continuing anti-Catholicism of conservative Protestant premillennialism.[60] There is an irony to the immediacy of the setting of LaHaye and Jenkins's story: Those conservative Christian fans who hold that the well-respected Pope John Paul II may be the last pontiff before the rise of Antichrist will have to reckon with the disconcerting elevation of the conservative Cardinal Ratzinger as Pope Benedict XVI. This development seems to portend a delay in the premillennial drama.

In addition to the widely shared expectation that the pope will be the Antichrist, there has also been some support for a male homosexual in this role. Queers usually figure in conservative Christian eschatology because they practice a kind of sin that prefigures and provokes the end-times. But Paul Boyer calls attention to same-sex sexuality in a different way when he points out a not uncommon reading of a prophesy in Daniel 11:37: "Neither shall he regard the God of his fathers, nor the desire of women, nor regard any god: for he shall magnify himself above all."[61]

In *Left Behind,* LaHaye and Jenkins are evasive on this point of the Antichrist's sexuality as on their own orientation to the Catholic church (aka the religious infrastructure of the Antichrist's rule). First, it is arguable that, although Antichrist Nicolae Carpathia has a female partner in the story, he has little regard for the desire of women. More damning is the narrative of Nicolae's genesis, now told in a prequel to the original series. It turns out that Nicolae has two daddies. One, Carpathia, provides his surname as well as his wife, Marilena, as the "vessel" who will give birth to the future Antichrist. But Nicolae is genetically related only to his fathers; this "opposite god," the "victory of the people," is a direct and physical product of homosexuals. Cleverly, he is also the product of homosexual*ity* because his male biological parents are lovers.[62] Even the futuristic science behind this plot sends a didactic message about the nature-perverting consequences of reproductive technologies in the wrong ungodly hands.

In the course of this story, LaHaye and Jenkins establish a chain of associations with evil that includes humanism, academia, the occult, and possibly even multilingualism. The Carpathias are scholars of classical languages; we should have known something was awry when we realized they speak Russian and, more disturbing, *French.* But the key signifier in this chain is homosexuality.

Postmillennial teachings provide a counterpoint to the premillennial end-time narrative. In the postmillennial plan, Jesus will return to earth to close a millennial period of peace only after the world has been reconciled through Christian interventions. For postmillennialists, the reign of Jesus and the vanquishing of evil will occur after Christians have reclaimed the earth for Christianity. When compared with premillennialism, postmillennialism is, therefore, "hopeful, reformist."[63] It has been a popular belief system during optimistic periods of American history, and it consistently has been eclipsed by premillennialism when the nation is at war. Contradictory political commitments arise from the two ways of interpreting scriptural prophesies concerning the end of the world. Between these two perspectives, it is the minority postmillennialism that appears to provide more support for coercive efforts to remake societies and governments in the image of conservative Christianity.[64] God is waiting for his people to act and create the preconditions for his return. Historically and theoretically, the majority premillennial perspective underwrites a more apolitical and isolationist theology. The premillennial Christian church would appear content to save individual souls and wait for the imminent Rapture of believers.

That our current premillennialism does not function in this way requires explanation, and students of the Christian right have taken on this task. A variety of explanations have been put forward. It is no doubt true that the triumph of pretrib premillennialism is multidetermined; a variety of theological and other components constitute this belief system.

Rapture Ready

One explanation for the postmillennial political quality of our present premillennialism is that it contains residues of the postmillennialism that is also common to our religious history. In this account, the Christian right seems to have crafted from the two opposing interpretations of pre- and postmillennialism a "cloudy synthesis," a de facto consensus that born-again Christians are responsible for preparing a Christian nation and world before Jesus returns.[65]

In her ethnographic account of the evolution of the contemporary Christian right, Susan Friend Harding fills in some details of this synthesis. Its theological and political foundations are found in Bible preaching and prophesy of the 1970s and 1980s. Harding finds in these sources and in their subsequent effects the development of a new "mode of millennial dreaming" in which Christian political action expanded even as dispensational premillenialism was, at least theoretically, retained intact. An important clue to this reconciliation between political action and premillennial pessimism lies in an idea of the theologian Francis Schaeffer that is later picked up by Tim LaHaye. This is the notion of a "pre-Tribulation tribulation."[66] The pretrib trib is a time of liberal triumph and moral decline that, should it occur, will foreshadow the real tribulation. Most important, Christians awaiting rapture will be forced to live through this time that Harding dubs the "little tribulation."[67] Clearly, the hope of avoiding a tribulation of any sort makes political activism worthwhile for Christian conservatives who might otherwise concentrate on other works.

A second reason why pretrib-inclined Christian conservatives have not abandoned political activism lies with the commitment that many have to reconstructionism, a demanding form of dominion theology. Dominionism refers to the exhortation of God in the book of Genesis for man to take dominion over the earth and all its creatures. As such, dominionism is a broad orientation toward all of creation that may not signify a particular political agenda. However, the reconstructionist version of dominion theology properly is identified with a right-wing politics.[68] Reconstructionism carries this mandate to Christian dominion into activism on behalf of establishing a Christian, and especially an Old Testament, theocracy. The characteristics of such a theocracy commonly include the elimination of liberal democratic institutions and processes and the implementation of the death penalty for many sins. Homosexuality is prominent on lists of the sins that would be punished by a godly nation, but such lists also typically include abortion and sometimes adultery.

Historically, reconstructionism has been closely aligned with postmillennialism, the design to aggressively reshape America put in the service of the hopeful and reformist vision of God's return to earth. Now, however, these connections have been disrupted and reformed. If the deterioration of America is a clear and present danger, reconstructionist impulses and aspirations may make sense to many believers as a way to wrench the nation back to its faith and foundations. Indeed, as many observers point out, although it is still possible to isolate reconstructionism as a specific ideology, there is much interpenetration of "mainstream" Christian conservatism with reconstructionist beliefs. From Pat Robertson to Rod Parsley, pastor of World Harvest Church in Columbus, Ohio, Christian conservatives across the country cite reconstructionist thinkers and formulate reconstructionist political designs.

A third reason for the ill fit between political activism and pretrib premillennialism is the possibility that, influenced by many pressures, interests, and opportunities, some leaders and many rank-and-file conservative Christians simply are not consistent in reconciling their religious and political beliefs. Most political repertoires include inconsistencies, beliefs that do not add up or contradictions between beliefs and the actions that ostensibly support them. So it should not be strange to think that both opinion leaders and citizens of many ideological stripes either deny or simply do not recognize the discontinuities in their political and spiritual commitments. Another way to look at this explanation is to consider the many ways in which believers may understand themselves as called by God to perform certain acts whose relations to God's own ends are shrouded in mystery. It is an important component of faith to act and to trust God for the result. Believers often note that God, being God, (or, in a more personal vein, "my God") is capable of fulfilling and completing ends that we humans do not comprehend. In this reading, there may well be ways that political activism of the sort engaged in by contemporary Christian conservatives serves the end-times in ways that are not transparent to human understanding.

Finally, it is possible that the rapid political mobilization of the Christian right has hardened a set of theological views that primarily work to serve the ambitions of those who have emerged as leaders of the Christian conservative movement. If our dominant eschatology is off-kilter with our current conservative Christian politics, one explanation is that Christian right leaders lead with their political beliefs and shape their eschatology to fit, more or less.[69] The possibility of such a scenario has always exercised those whose commitment to religion drives their support for church-state separation. The church, it is feared, becomes corrupted by too close association with political power. A recent editorial in *Christianity Today* expresses a version of this concern, that powerful Christian leaders substitute political standards and referents for spiritual ones: "George W. Bush is not Lord. The Declaration of Independence is not an infallible guide to Christian faith and practice. . . . The American flag is not the Cross. The Pledge of Allegiance is not the Creed. 'God Bless America' is not the Doxology."[70] The editorial rebukes individual Christian right leaders and councils a turn away from what appears to be the worship of the nation to "the worship of Jesus Christ."

This last point opens up a landscape of American exceptionalism with regard to both the worship of the nation and to the worship of Jesus Christ. As Stephen Prothero traces it in his impressive history of the "American Jesus," the worship of Jesus Christ as contemporary Americans understand it is a relatively new phenomenon. The cult of Jesus, including the idea of an intimate friendship with him, was born among nineteenth-century theological liberals. Between then and now, Jesus has undergone many makeovers. These include a shift from a feminized to a masculinized persona and a shift across the theological spectrum from left—a reaction to Calvinism and the strictures of doctrine—to right.

Relatively more constant than the worship of Jesus Christ, and intersecting in important ways with it, is "the tendency of Americans to make their nation sacred."[71] Ever since colonial days, many Christians have insisted on the exceptional nature of God's relationship with the New World. For them, then and now, America is the covenant nation and enjoys an extension of the special relationship God established with the Jews. In this reading of history, God allotted the new nation and its citizens a land flowing with milk and honey, in exchange for which citizens would practice pious obedience to God's law. There is another, darker, version of the covenant story, which lies to the right of the Christian right on the American political continuum. In this far right Christian narrative, America *is* Israel and the Hebrews merely imposters. In spite of important differences such as the name of God's chosen people, there are many points of contact between these two covenant stories.[72]

Paul Boyer complicates this belief system by pointing out not only the particular nationalism of American believers but the "deeply nationalistic structure" of biblical prophesy and of the dispensational premillennialist system. Not only America individually, but the nation-state itself, is "divinely ordained." Mark Noll puts it this way: "Patriotic loyalty to America [is] more than the common affection that all peoples naturally exercise toward their native land. It is a special interpretation of divine providence and a transformation of national allegiance into a statement about the mind of God . . . called the strong, or exalted, view of Christian America."[73] Thus, nations are responsible to God for their collective character and will "face God" in judgment for their sins. Not only this, but God also uses nations as vehicles to chastise a people, as many believe he did when he permitted the Nazi genocide of European Jews.[74]

This idea of America as the covenant nation is not uncontested; even some conservative Christians push against this dominant interpretation of God's relationship with our nation. But theirs is a minority view. Today, the reconstructionist vision of American founders as a group of wise eighteenth-century born-again Christian conservatives has been duly absorbed into mainstream thought. All are assumed to share a common set of religious beliefs and political investments. Christian right leaders and thinkers communicate their convictions regarding the betrayed religious beliefs of our founders to believers in a plethora of ways. This instruction encourages contemporary believers to save from liberal corruption a set of beliefs that are crucial to the survival of America and to the nation's fulfillment of its divine mandate.

Of all the successive interpretations of Revelation and conceptions of the end-times, the one propagated by the Christian right performs another function, especially for premillennially inclined Americans. This function is to turn the attention of Americans to current events so that they may understand how God works in the last days. The bestseller that encouraged millions of Americans to speculate about the role of particular nations and peoples in God's plan for the end of the world is Hal Lindsey's prophesy bestseller, *The Late Great Planet Earth*. In fact, many specifics of Lindsey's end-time geopolitics are obsolete. Rereading the book today reminds us how much has changed since Lindsey first set down what he knew without doubt about the facts and agents of our apocalyptic age. Not only is there the preeminence of the Soviet Union in Armageddon, but there is also the African continent's "conver[sion] to Communism," a political shift that seems unlikely.[75] Those of us who grew up with Christian conservatism in the 1970s recall the equation of the European Common Market with the "beast with 10 horns" found in chapter 13 of the book of Revelation. The relationship between the European community and the tribulation was so ubiquitous that it was many years before I could hear about European integration without associating the process with the reign of the Antichrist.

What survives are not the details of Lindsey's vision—some of these have been replaced by less dated political referents—but the popular pastime of mapping end-time events onto contemporary social and political realities. Lindsey did not find a central role for the United States in end-time prophesy in his early work, but he did incorporate a wide variety of information about current events of the late 1960s. Crime data, population demographics, and even the putative existence of rampant witchcraft in American public schools, all these bring the United States into the end-times narrative.[76] Indirectly, Lindsey confirms that the United States has a central role to play in the end-times. This conviction is an open category that can be—and is—filled with a variety of events, enemies, foreign powers, and ideological currents. The puzzling absence of the United States from Revelation is replaced with an America that is the center of prophesy.[77]

Pat Robertson's prophetic writing reflects this re-centering of the United States in Christian right eschatology. Not incidentally, the fate and charge of the United States are bound up with the expected consolidation of world government with which liberals and nonbelievers are implicated. "[A] world government can come together only after the Christian United States is out of the way. . . . With America still free and at large, Satan's schemes will at best be only partially successful. . . . And if America goes down, all hope is lost to the rest of the world."[78] Pragmatically, centering the United States in the end-times encourages conservative Christians to become the agents of social and political change. What this means is that Christian conservatives are charged with working to reverse God's judgment on the American nation, even if they cannot reverse the judgment bound to be rendered on the larger world. At the least, the Christian right can take care of the church by making sure that America does not collapse into chaos and immorality until *after* the Rapture removes them to be with the Lord.

The appeal of apocalyptic thinking is not simple and is not limited to the kind of emotional comfort that comes from knowing the future and one's own place in it. There is also knowledge of the eventual triumph of good over evil and connection with communities and genealogies of belief. But the appeal of complex belief systems such as premillennial eschatology can also be found in the intellectual goods such systems deliver. Apocalyptic beliefs provide a parallel intellectual world for those steeped in its details, a world that is every bit as complex as, for example, the world of academic cultural studies. Such intellectual regimes have their own texts, jargon, and rock star–famous expositors. Anyone who doubts the intellectual complexity of premillenialism, and the time and patience necessary to master the system, should examine Tim LaHaye's nonfiction works on the subject. These texts lay out the system using scriptural exegesis, social and political interpretation, and pages of charts and graphics that provide handy references to supplement the narrative.[79]

Far from creating distance between believers and social, cultural, and political events, our present politicized premillennialism encourages its students to study and analyze the present. Reading the signs of that which is yet to come contributes to a political literacy that, in many cases, is virtually indistinguishable from the results of secular education. Indeed, in many cases, the focus, enthusiasm, and political literacy of born-again premillennial Christians are far superior to that of their less informed and curious peers. Employing a theoretical system to interpret global events provides believers with "a special sense of . . . insight."[80] Believers are not left to their own devices to make meaning from contemporary events.

Although nonbelievers might be surprised to consider it, the appeal of many forms of instructional Christian media is intellectual as well as emotional. Consider the example of the *700 Club.* The news programs that are tied to Pat Robertson's broadcasts are in many respects indistinguishable from mainstream news. Christian reporters and other *700 Club* personnel report events from locations worldwide and provide an "ultimate framework of 'interpretation'."[81] The reward for believers is a sense of intellectual mastery and integration, a result nonbelievers usually reserve for the fruit of more skeptical cognitive striving. Their convictions occupy a "domain of stigmatized knowledge" populated with ideas that are widely circulated but repudiated by traditional authorities.[82] Of course, whatever the ideas, some authorities will repudiate and others will embrace them. Unfounded ideas may not even be stigmatized when mainstream elites, such as national political figures, embrace them for their own purposes.

Know Your Audience

When the GOP lost the presidential election of 1996, Republican Party strategists began to worry about the ways in which party activists projected hatred or intolerance for minority groups. Fearing that obvious appeals to cultural boundaries and exclusions would hurt the Republican Party with swing voters, and particularly with women, strategists prevailed upon party opinion leaders to exercise caution in characterizing even marginal groups such as lesbians and gay men.[83] A benchmark for projections of intolerance was Pat Buchanan's speech to the 35th Republican National Convention in 1992.[84] Buchanan's speech is a model of defamatory rhetoric. Although Buchanan does not focus explicitly on sexual minorities, he repeatedly queers democratic candidates Clinton and Gore through references to their Democratic Convention as a "giant masquerade ball," as a display of "cross-dressing," and as a "big costume party." As Buchanan makes clear, the task of America is to reassert heteronormativity against a pervasive queerness that may slip through disguised as straight and virtuous.[85]

Although the Republican Party's cultural politics had not changed by the election of 1996, party strategists pleaded for cultural war to be muffled under the big tent of GOP aspirations. Judging from position statements, voter guides, political organizing, and political training for religious conservatives, Christian right leaders did not abandon their fundamental principles on marriage, parental rights, family authority, and sexuality: the "family values" of new right politics. While developing sophisticated political institutions and strategies, they continued to deliver jeremiads linking God's punishment on the nation with sin, and especially sexual sin. Among these new political strategies of the 1990s was a "rights pragmatism" that sought to engage the liberal rights claims of lesbians and gay men in the secular arena of liberal democratic politics. This pragmatism did not replace internal Christian right discourses of "sin and seduction" and "disease and seduction" but was turned outward toward mainstream political and legal actors and institutions.[86]

Since the mid-1990s, Christian right leaders have responded to the demands of partisan politics not only by addressing themselves in different ways to different audiences but by attempting to police the boundaries of their messaging more effectively, especially in terms of political statements in mainstream venues.[87] This phenomenon is noted, often in passing, by many observers. For example, in their journalistic account of the relationship of the Christian right and the gay movement, Chris Bull and John Gallagher note briefly that "the tune [the Christian right] sang in public [was] far different than the one it sang in private."[88] But the implications of the production and dissemination of quite different themes by the Christian right movement are less thoroughly explored.

What do messages targeted at diverse audiences of, on the one hand, born-again (and potential born-again) followers and, on the other hand, unaffiliated outsiders look like? There are many ways to begin to answer such a question. Many Christian right initiatives, organizations, and ministries may be primarily constructed, and their modes of communication primarily conceptualized, as tools of communication with followers or believers. And this can be true even though most remain aware that they are not alone, that unsympathetic outsiders are also listening and may broadcast their ideas and designs to political adversaries. Other segments of the Christian right may be understood primarily for their outreach to unbelievers or potential members. The discourse of these groups or ministries are likely to be judged by different criteria and may stimulate a kind of anxiety of representation if they do not cleave to criteria for speaking appropriately to those outsiders. We can see one example of this anxiety when Jack T. Chick's Christian cartoon publications reflect poorly on the new and politically sophisticated Christian right.

A final general kind of initiative or ministry reaches out both to insiders and outsiders, believers and those who may come to believe and capitulate to the appeals of the movement. An example of this part of the Christian right is the ex-gay movement, a set of initiatives and programs that encourage, support, and proselytize the reorientation of homosexuals to heterosexuality. Although the ex-gay movement as a whole is much too broad and varied to be captured in one chapter, what I do here is examine how the movement tries to speak and appeal to insiders and outsiders while crafting and disseminating a consistent ideology that has both political and therapeutic dimensions. As this might suggest, the tensions are sometimes too great, and the movement cannot contain them all without seams and contradictions.

The Christian right and the various ministries and programs that identify with its goals use a variety of tools to communicate with activists and the faithful. Some of these, such as direct mail, large-scale conventions, radio and television broadcasts, and websites may be vertically coordinated between different levels of the movement or horizontally coordinated between different organizations or actors. Often their consistencies may be a function of ideologies that so saturate the movement that they are taken as truths rather than as interpretations of biblical text or as dimensions of political ideology. Of course, not all political ideology is top-down or top-down in the same way. Followers sometimes choose and elevate leaders, creating them in fact if not by procedure. In a more subtle mode of relation, followers "authorize" leaders to "speak for them."[89] Bible-believing congregations proliferate leaders across the American landscape, creating pockets of deviation as well as disciplined Christian right cadres.

As ethnographers of American conservative Christianity tell us, individual believers are rich sources of diverse attitudes and "everyday theologies."[90] Students of the Christian right can, and should, focus on these differences. We can also illuminate the more monolithic political practices of the movement by focusing at another level of analysis. This is the level at which ideology is constructed and disseminated and political projects are fabricated and defended.

Four Narratives

How can we make sense of all these different stories about same-sex sexuality? Is it, as some have it, that the Christian right is hopelessly divided, a movement of idiosyncratic schismatics? Well, yes, in some respects that is true. American history has yielded up a plethora of ways to be Christian, and even Christian conservative. Ideological, theological, and rhetorical differences prevail at the micro level of individual believers, the meso level of churches and religious communities, and the macro level of national organizations and politics. We still lose much, however, if we ignore the continuities of thought and discourse, particularly the ways in which these continuities are stitched together by macro-level rhetoric, instruction, preaching, and induction into political activity that reaches down through middle-level institutions to individual believers.

In this book I argue that there are patterns of Christian right belief and politics with regard to LGBT people and queer sociopolitical issues. Further, I'll suggest that these beliefs and politics do not just comprise a number of disconnected narrative strands but, rather, that these narratives intersect and are organized in comprehensible ways. We can imagine these narratives organized along two axes: the first axis is the intended audience of communications from leaders (national leaders of organizations, televangelists, and recognized Christian conservative spokespersons) to followers. On this axis, we have messages that are intended for, and addressed to, the in-group (members of and those with an ideological affinity with Christian right organizations, Christian conservatives, and potential converts) and messages that are intended for, and addressed to, both the in-group and the national—and sometimes international—community at large. In the latter category, it is important to include both in-group and others, because group members receive key ideological instruction from messages directed to outsiders. Indeed, rhetoric directed at non-(conservative) Christians has important pedagogical functions for Christian conservatives who consume it. This is so both in situations where pedagogy is directed at the inculcation of compassion and in situations where Christian conservatives are instructed in the (real) meaning of democracy and its attendant themes of rights and choice.

The second axis describes the sociopolitical context in which the narratives are intended to function. Although it is possible that we might discover many such contexts, I think two are most central to understanding the antigay perspectives and impact of the Christian right. These contexts are the therapeutic and the political. The therapeutic context is concerned with understanding the roots of same-sex desire, healing homosexuality, and "restoring" natural heterosexual functioning. The political context is concerned with legal rights, constitutional interpretation, public policy, electoral politics, and the distribution of public goods. As the matrix below suggests, we can identify four principal narrative combinations, constituted of variations on intended audience and context.

TABLE 1.1 Christian Right Narratives of Same-Sex Sexuality

Sociopolitical Context

		THERAPEUTIC	POLITICAL
Intended Audience	IN-GROUP	(Childhood gender) development Compassion for same-sex attracted Christians and Christian families with same-sex attracted members	Abomination Homosexuality as a choice
	IN-GROUP AND PUBLIC	Healing of adults from same-sex sexuality Compassion for same-sex attracted people	Democracy (majoritarianism, choice and rights)

Keeping in mind these variations of antigay narratives, I argue in the chapters that follow that—at least at present—it is possible to discuss particular kinds of Christian right antigay ideas using the matrix as a kind of key.

The matrix of possible narratives also helps us understand some sources of conflict and instability in the narratives marketed by different segments and communities of the Christian right. So, for example, while for many Chick tracts represent a kind of Christian right understanding of same-sex sexuality that is hopelessly passé, Chick's contributions to the Christian right debate on homosexuality merely continue to reflect an in-group perspective that has not kept up with the formation of a public "democratic" narrative. Chick's obstinate delivery of this in-group perspective in public accounts for much of the discomfort with his work among Christian conservative opinion leaders. At the same time, his work remains popular with the grassroots of the movement.

The ex-gay movement represents a harder case because it involves multiple sites that are often at odds with one another. However, even here we can identify distinct narratives about recovery from homosexuality in these diverse ex-gay communities. What makes the ex-gay movement interesting from this perspective is that it employs all four kinds of narrative in its various media and contexts. Given the variety of leaders, experts, perspectives, geographic spaces, and institutional manifestations of the movement, this breadth of rhetoric is unsurprising. It does mean, however, that observers and critics of the movement must give careful attention to the internal multiplicity that rests within the appellation "ex-gay" and not collapse these multiple manifestations into a one-dimensional interpretation.

In advertisements and media intended to be consumed by the general public, the ex-gay movement sends a therapeutic message and advertises its services to gay adults who are invited to avail themselves of the chance to change their sexual orientation. Ads placed in the Washington, DC, Metrorail transport system in 2002 and 2003 employed both therapeutic and political contexts. The therapeutic message is directed at adults who may use reparative therapies to repair and reorient their sexual desire and relational aspirations.

The public political message of these same ads is that every individual has the right to make a choice to live a life free from coercion and stigma. Not only homosexuals have such a right in our democracy but also those who choose *not* to identify as homosexual. "I Chose to Change" was a Metro ad sponsored by Parents and Friends of Ex-Gays (PFOX), and its text epitomizes a brief version of public therapeutic and political messages: "I make choices everyday . . . Where to eat. What to wear. Who to see. But as a gay man I never thought I could change WHO I was. Until I realized change was a choice . . . and I chose to change from gay to straight. It may not be a decision you want to make, but you should know thousands of us already have. Please respect our choice."[91] Ex-gay ads are directed at adults who can consent to participate in reparative therapies. Ads in public contexts do not, however, contain appeals to adults to adjust the gender identity and "prehomosexuality" of children. Such appeals are reserved for literature and venues, such as Love Won Out conferences, that are geared primarily to Christian believers.

The political instruction at in-group events include not only the democratic language of rights, especially for ex-gays, but the message of homosexual abomination that is more familiar from the early public clashes over LGBT rights issues. Across all venues, "choice" is a complicated construct. In in-group contexts in which the narrative of development holds sway, the equation of same-sex sexuality with "choice" does not have the same implication that it has in other contexts in which developmental origins are not an issue. Both of these conceptions of choice differ meaningfully from the public democratic narrative that concedes that people can choose to live as gay and that LGBT people have a right to exist as long as they do not make claims on the nation for "special rights."

Queers and their allies sometimes miss this complexity when they posit that the compassion expressed in the ex-gay movement is a blind or deception that we should expose and resist. Identifying the multiple therapeutic and political narratives housed in different venues of the movement allows us to recognize how compassion can coexist with malignant antigay politics. This juxtaposition of therapeutic and political perspectives and pedagogy on gay issues creates a complex and unstable discourse. The complexity of narratives and sociopolitical contexts puts precincts of the ex-gay movement at odds with each other. It also points to some seams in the antigay discourse of the Christian right in general. These may be ignored or sutured up with various kinds of in-group rationales. I will argue that however significant these seams are in conveying and complicating the message of the movement, they do not signal its impotence or impending collapse.

Finally, there is a straightforward example of how a particular kind of message can be disseminated through preaching and political instruction without informing the general public about its meaning. It is one thing to know in a general way that there are connections between theology and politics that Christian conservative leaders do not want to disclose to outsiders. It is quite another to see a particular example of discourse between leaders and followers and to look more closely at things said and unsaid. The point of such an analysis is not to critique theology—that which is a matter of belief—but to excavate the theological roots of political arguments and designs.

As political theorists and historians can attest, political ideology and action can bear impressive amounts of contradiction. Decisive leadership can make a great deal of difference in eliding and mystifying the seams that may threaten the coherence of political ideologies.

Use Your Inside Voice

Studies of popular politics can direct our focus to many different types of political actors. In the academy today, it is less popular than it once was to focus on elites instead of on ordinary citizens or those with a more parlous subaltern existence. Of course, just as all those who speak from positions of relative vulnerability, marginality, or simple obscurity are not the same, all elites are not created equal. In one recent focus on conservative elites, David Domke analyzes White House rhetoric about the war on terror and the perils for democracy of an "echoing press."[92] The White House, all would no doubt agree, is occupied by political elites. There is less agreement about the status and influence of opinion leaders in other walks of life, from high-profile pastors to movement intellectuals, from culture entrepreneurs to organizational administrators. These actors—and their organizations or venues—may indeed have differing degrees of influence over the hearts and minds of voters and activists. Nevertheless, they control resources, including symbolic and communicative resources. And their voices may be amplified as they reinforce one another or add their own individual nuances to the ideological project.

Acknowledging the importance of learning from below, focusing on popular pedagogy often returns our attention to elites, whether formal or informal. This is not to suggest that the masses are simply credulous vessels for tales spun by elites. But it does acknowledge the extraordinary similarity and durability of particular beliefs across movements and the ways in which these beliefs can, and often do, provide the infrastructure and justifications for disciplinary norms and law/public policies. Even more fascinating as a sign of political pedagogy are the careful disarticulations that appear as we listen across the many venues in which the Christian right movement hones its messages and markets its ideological products.

It is commonplace for identity groups and political movements to try to manage what their members communicate to outsiders about the group, its ideas, its plans, and its aspirations. One version of this discipline is the exhortation not to air the group's internal dirty laundry in public. Those who identify, or are identified, with marginal identity groups are familiar with this charge, violation of which can bring harsh social retribution. But there are other versions of discipline that are not related to revealing the inner workings or dysfunctions of the group. One is significant for democratic deliberation and judgment: discipline that is dedicated to suppressing the views and aims of the group from fellow citizens. We need not pose as naively horrified that such movement pedagogy and discipline exists to find it troubling from the perspective of citizenship in a democratic regime.

Concern about the state of democracy is one motivation to excavate the relatively hidden aspects of discourse about same-sex sexuality and those identified with it. Besides this political motivation, there are also personal and intellectual ones. As to the former, it matters to me in the most personal way possible that those who work within the Christian right have to account for their beliefs and their ideas about the good society and not just the beliefs and aspirations that they might prefer to share with all their fellow citizens. Whereas I would just as soon individuals who dislike queers keep that attitude to themselves in their quotidian interactions with me at work and in social situations, I am more troubled by hidden political ideology because of its possible effects. And I like being able to talk back, an opportunity denied to those who don't hear the threat, the accusation, or the justification for punishment rendered out loud.

Finally, political ideology is an intellectual challenge, with many families of competing theories to explicate it. I enjoy applying these theories for the sheer cognitive pleasure of it. Sometimes, though, we have a less pressing need for high theory than we have a need for what passes in academic life as detective work. One question we might ask of ourselves as students of political thought is a kind of challenge to memory and to our own projections of the adversary: Do we hear what they hear? And once we listen for their vision of the good, what kind of sense can we make of it?

CHAPTER 2

The Nightmare
of Homosexuality

And when the LORD thy God shall deliver them before thee; thou shalt
smite them, and utterly destroy them; thou shalt make no covenant with
them, nor shew mercy unto them

—Deuteronomy 7:2

Blessed are ye, when men shall revile you, and persecute you, and shall say
all manner of evil against you falsely, for my sake.

—Matthew 5:11

Gay Blades

I don't recall the first time I ever saw a Chick Christian cartoon tract. In the
Southern Baptist world of the early 1970s they were always already there. But
I do recall the two tracts that had the biggest impact on me. The first was the
bestseller and jewel in the crown of Chick publications: "This Was Your Life!"
The tract features an affluent, self-congratulatory playboy to whom God shows
a frightening preview of the judgment. In the closing frames, the man receives
a second chance at repentance, falls to his knees, and accepts Jesus as his savior.
"This Was Your Life!" was a first-line weapon in the battle to bring the good
news of the gospel to a sinful world and to win souls for Christ. Yet for all its
Christian relevance, it lacked the kind of samizdat appeal that invites teenagers
to pass literature from hand to hand.

This appeal the risqué tract "The Gay Blade" possessed in abundance.
Years later I could recall vividly the one implied sexual scene between two
women. An attractive brunette runs after a blond who flees her embrace. The
blond slips from the frame, and the brunette, having lost her prey, turns to face

33

the reader. She declares: "*I cannot change*—and I don't *want* to."[1] I believed her. Well before more recent debates about the fluidity of identity, here is a lesbian who states categorically the fixity of her identity. I'm fairly certain that neither Chick nor my pastor nor any of the other members of First Baptist ever imagined that "The Gay Blade" would provoke fascination or, indeed, any other reaction than revulsion. But they were playing with fire. These cartoon gay blades only made me more curious about their real-life counterparts.

As it was, there was a dearth of popular culture information about same-sex sexuality. Indeed, the only other "text" on which I could depend in mid-adolescence was one my contemporaries will recall: Dr. David Reuben's *Everything You Always Wanted to Know about Sex but Were Afraid to Ask*. It is odd to see the encomia to this bestseller today. It appears that many early readers have fond memories of the book's helpful candor about sexuality. Not so if you were gay, or not yet gay. A gay teenager who went to some trouble to read the forbidden text would find that male homosexuals have sex in public bathrooms and that most prostitutes are actually lesbians. I found neither of these pieces of information particularly useful, but they were the pieces I remembered long into my adulthood. The straight parts simply did not stick. Hence, for me, the hip secular paean to sexual satisfaction failed utterly, and so it was back to the Baptist drawing board. I suppose I should be grateful to Fred Carter, the artist who drew "The Gay Blade" for Jack T. Chick; although he drew the gay men in the tract as grotesques, his lesbians neither embody appropriate Christian disgust nor reflect their own corrupted moral state. In addition, they aren't prostitutes.

I have one other quite fond and specific memory of "The Gay Blade," my subversive salute to all the sad, doomed, and defiant characters of the tract. As an undergraduate student at West Virginia University in 1979, I attended a Halloween party with my girlfriend at the local gay bar. We drew upon the politics of the day, electing to go as Anita Bryant and a fictitious butch bodyguard of our own imagining. As a former Southern Baptist, I knew we needed props for verisimilitude, so we rushed to the local Christian bookstore and bought fistfuls of "The Gay Blade" to pass out to our benighted homosexual friends and acquaintances. Reared an Eastern upper-middle-class agnostic, my girlfriend had rarely seen the trappings of sincere middle-American distaste for queers. But she was delighted to help me create the necessary ambience for our costumes. We were a hit as we circulated through the crowd passing out the tracts to an assortment of colorful characters. As "Anita," my girlfriend would press a tract into a reveler's hands and murmur with great intensity that she could help them overcome their homosexuality.

For these young queers, the tracts read as delicious camp. We could easily disdain their sentiments because we were young, fixed on love and sexuality, and utterly unaware that the world around us would not yield to our intensifying demands for respect. It has been over twenty-five years since I was an "out" undergraduate. As I sit at my computer in early 2004 the governor of Ohio has just signed into law one of the most restrictive Defense of Marriage laws in the nation. The president of the United States expresses his regret about the same-sex unions that are being hastily performed in San Francisco and calls for a Constitutional amendment forbidding same-sex marriage. Homosexuality, it seems, is on the lips of every American.

I only have one regret about that Halloween: I wish I'd kept a copy of "The Gay Blade" as a memento. It would not be long before AIDS would become part of our queer world. When AIDS arrived in the early 1980s, Chick Publications modified "The Gay Blade" to reflect the equation of homosexuality with disease. This revision coincided with a shift and intensification in the demonization of gays, and I'm a little nostalgic for the villainous comic-book characters of my youth.

Laying Hands on Chick

Depending upon where you are in America, it may have been difficult to avoid Chick tracts completely, and there are probably few Americans who have never seen them. Amateur evangelists place the tracts in public places, including waiting rooms, restrooms, near phones, and in laundromats. Some enterprising missionaries place them in books and magazines where unrepentant sinners will find them and be led to God. In the recent documentary film *Jesus Camp*, a child missionary reads the tracts for her own edification and hands them out to passersby when she visits the nation's capital.[2] The tracts can be ordered from the Chick Publications website at http://www.chick.com, where their complete contents can also be viewed.

The Chick Publications motto is "Chick tracts *get read!*," and those who leave them to be found by strangers clearly put their faith in this claim. Whether apocryphal or not, testimonials in the Chick Publications catalog and on the business website testify to the power of these unexpected intersections of unsaved sinner (or backslider) with God's message.

> I read a Chick tract I found while cleaning the restroom in a bank. Not long after I turned my life to Jesus for forgiveness. **Iowa**

> Two fellow employees were saved after reading your tracts. At least five others are under conviction. **E-Mail**

> We just met a Jewish teenager who was saved by reading one of your tracts that he found in a phone booth. **New York**

> My best friend had tried many time to convert me. I refused to listen. About three months ago she handed me one of your tracts. I read it. She began to bombard me with tracts at my request. I just became a born-again Christian 20 minutes ago. **Massachusetts**

When I was 10, I went Trick or Treating, and somebody inserted a SOMEBODY GOOFED tract into my bag. Thank you! I'm indebted to you and that unknown Christian for leading me to Christ. E-Mail[3]

I picked up the Chick tract that renewed my interest a few years ago in a truck stop restroom along Interstate 10 in northern Florida.[4] Its shape and comic book cover familiar to me from adolescence, I put the tract in my pocket to save for later ("Chick tracts *get read!*"). "The Death Cookie" (1988), a floridly anti-Catholic tract, features a cunning unshaven pope in league with Satan to delude humans and enslave their souls. I found myself surprised, not because I didn't know how vituperative the tracts could be but because I was no longer a reader who could absorb, ignore, discount, or satirize them. Former reluctant Southern Baptist and casual tract parodist, I now recognized the message as hateful and the comic vehicle of that message as insidious. Even if Chick hadn't changed that much since 1974, I already knew that some of his consumers had.

Others, of course, have not changed their minds about basic biblical and political convictions, which is the question Chick observers address when they speculate that Chick tracts became anathema to many Christians in the 1980s. In what follows I argue that the problem with Chick is not that the conservative Christian movement has outgrown him or that a considerable ideological gap has opened between Chick and Christian conservatives. Rather, the problem with Chick—or, at least with his standing in the Christian right—is that his tracts are intended for a primary audience that is public, mainstream, and unsaved. As well appreciated as the tracts often are by the saved and churched, they are produced to be distributed to the unsaved and unchurched. With their messages of salvation and their busy and informative back covers, they are witnessing tracts, inexpensive enough to be purchased in bulk, small enough to be used unobtrusively by those who might be uncomfortable sharing their Christian witness in person. What Jack Chick routinely takes to be the proofs of his efficacy—criticisms by uneasy Christians in addition to the attacks of tenacious sinners—are nothing more than the consequences of addressing the public in terms more appropriate to the in-group.[5] Chick's Christian social movement sin is to refuse to alter his public message in a time of increasing differentiation of these two audiences and message sophistication. For this sin, he has paid some domestic price in profits and in movement status and recognition. At the same time, both Chick's marginal status and his alleged distance from the beliefs and politics of the Christian right require close attention.

Behold, the Man (and His Time)

Through the efforts of Jack Thomas Chick's many fans, his biography has become an intrinsic part of the story of Chick tracts. As one fan website puts it,

Chick was "b. 1922, b. again 1948, still with us."[6] Dubbed the "world's most published author," Chick has not given interviews for most of the last thirty years, but information about him and his empire is available from a number of sources.[7] Jack Chick grew up in California with an interest in drama. He served in the Pacific theater during World War II, and when he returned to the United States, he did participate in some productions of a local theater company. More significant in precipitating his later fame, he married a born-again woman and soon became a born-again Christian himself. He launched his career in Christian comics in the 1960s in the Southern California "southland" that was at that very moment in the process of forging the New right coalition.[8] His first products were a handful of tracts that included "Why No Revival?" (1961) and "Holy Joe" (1964). These early tracts traded on Chick's personal experience. The artist was castigated for drawing the faces of his fellow worshippers into "Why No Revival?," a critique of his Christian peers.[9] And with its irreproachable Christian hero and his corrupt sergeant, "Holy Joe" clearly relies, however unrealistically, on Chick's military experience.

Most students of Chick repeat the provenance of the Christian comic format from Chick's own bios and from his didactic semiautobiographical tract "Who, Me?" (1969). In the story, Chinese communist agents discover the ideological potential of comic books from observing their popularity with American children. Chairman Mao used a similar format to spread communist propaganda. Chick, in his turn, takes back the genre to use in winning souls to Christ. Thus does Chick turn that tool of Godless American pop culture and Godless communism, the comic, back against Satan as a tool of Jesus Christ.

Less tractable followers of the entrepreneur's career have suggested that Chick actually modeled his tracts on small pornographic comic booklets of the early half of the twentieth century.[10] These booklets, called "eight pagers," "Tijuana Bibles," or "two by fours," came into existence in the 1920s. Popular throughout the 1930s and 1940s, the comics tended to mimic mainstream comics of the era except that they featured the well-known characters engaged in graphically and humorously drawn sex acts. According to Donald Gilmore, historian of the eight pagers, the comics were tremendously popular in their day in spite of the authorities' attempts to interdict them. It appears that one of the more influential artists was a woman, and perhaps—if the intuitions of a distributor was accurate—a lesbian. In fact, collectors today refer to her and her business colleagues, one of whom may have been her lover, as "the three gals."[11]

By the late 1940s the humor of the golden age of eight pagers had been "subordinate[d] to sex." These post World War II eight pagers remained as graphic as their predecessors but with less antic irreverence. In this mode, the eight pagers continued to be produced sporadically into the 1960s, when Chick began producing his tracts. Two years after Chick underwent his salvation experience, the eight pager format achieved its apotheosis with the publication of

an "illustrated erotic short story." "Travelin' Preacher" was a significant depar-
ture from the earlier send-ups of comics styles and characters. First, at forty-
eight pages, it was the "longest erotic comic" of the period; second, it contained
a social message of sorts: a "parody of organized religion and life in rural, middle America." In this comic, travelin' Preacher Bill sows salvation by engaging
in sex with a number of young women he encounters in his ministry. After
many such adventures, Preacher Bill delivers a sermon from the pulpit of the
church that so arouses his parishioners that they rip off their clothes and begin
to copulate. The frame that features this action announces: "the fanatical shouts
of preacher Bill have driven the place into a termoil [sic]."[12] Besides its
religious storyline, what is interesting about this pornographic comic is the
similarity between the orgiastic scene and similarly crowded (though less sexually graphic) scenes in such antigay Chick tracts as "Doom Town" and "Birds
and the Bees."

Of course, there is no proof that Chick ever saw "Travelin' Preacher" or,
indeed, any of the eight pagers. However, it would only be appropriate if the
eight pagers influenced Chick, since critics characterize his oeuvre as pornographic on its own merits. His comics are "simple, mean, and crude" with "effective artwork."[13] In fact, the tracts produced to date have been drawn by only
two artists: Jack Chick and Fred Carter, a publicity-shy African American minister.[14] The styles of the two artists could not be more different. According to
Daniel Raeburn, Chick's most perspicacious critic, Chick draws in a "traditional gag-cartoon style" while Carter, who refuses to sign his work, is the "un-
sung genius of underground comix . . . Chick's Word made Flesh." It is to
Carter's ability as an illustrator that Raeburn assigns the power of Chick tracts,
with their bodies of sinners "so vigorous, so venomous, so physical that Chick's
message seems undeniable."[15] The message plus the artwork adds up to "*hard-
core Protestant pornography*":

> This is spirtual porn, pure sadomasochistic fantasy with an empha-
> sis on the rhetorical foreplay leading up to the inevitable seduction
> and submission to Jesus Christ. The money shot, when it comes, is
> a close-up of the humiliated but grateful sinner gasping, sobbing,
> and quaking with passion. . . . All the fantasies use the conventions
> of pornography: strangers meet . . . and through a sequence of
> wooden dialogue, bad acting, and clunky transitions immediately
> establish an unrealistic level of intimacy climaxing with the words
> "gasp!" "sob," and joyous close-ups of squirting, salty body fluids.[16]

In his description, Raeburn fills in what is only implied by Chick. Of
course, by the sexual standards of the eight pagers, Chick is tame. However,
Chick's evocations of sexuality—even sadomasochistic sexuality—suggest

that coming to Jesus is not just a matter of the heart. In respect of the relation between comics and sexuality we should remind ourselves of the context in which Chick tracts were born.

An irony of Chick's conservative Christian cartoons is his relationship to the complicated history of storytelling and visual art in the Protestant tradition. As Stephen Prothero relates, American Protestants softened their disapproval of narrative and visual "works of the imagination" in the nineteenth century. This process accelerated after the Civil War and into the new century. "A new form of American popular culture"—not comics yet, but narrative tracts and illustrations of religious themes—accompanied intimate representations of Jesus as friend, companion, and moral guide, as well as the Christ.[17] In taking his place in this trajectory, Chick inherits the nineteenth-century evangelical tradition even if his progenitors could not begin to imagine the uses to which he would put it.

Not only the history of born-again belief but also the history of the comic book format itself bears on Chick's project. In 1954, the Comics Magazine Association of America introduced the Comics Code Authority as a means for the self-regulation of the comic book industry. Under the considerable influence of child psychiatrist Fredric Wertham, the Senate Judiciary Committee's Subcommittee to Investigate Juvenile Delinquency had taken up the issue of how comic books nudge young readers into delinquency. With censorship impending, comic book producers sought to keep the government from regulating comics. For a time, the code was successful in banishing certain kinds of content from the comic books. By most accounts, however, it also had unintended consequences; it stripped the comics of social relevance, confirmed that mainstream comics would be considered juvenile literature, and paved the way for the rise of contemporary underground comics/comix. Unlike the eight pagers, the new underground comics that began to flourish in the 1960s were produced and sold openly, and they were marked for mature audiences.[18] In addition, they often substituted graphic violence for the graphic sexual images of their predecessors.[19]

By the early 1970s when Chick began producing his antigay tracts the code was largely defunct. The explosion of underground comics, the increasing differentiation of target audiences for comics publications, and legal challenges to censorship in a variety of jurisdictions had done their work. But consider an interesting fact: Chick's antigay Christian comics violate the standards of the Comics Code Authority, standards put in place to protect youthful consumers from encountering the immoral shenanigans of the adult world.[20] Juxtaposing Chick's work with the code, two prohibitions stand out, both from the section of the code that details standards on "Marriage and Sex": 2) "illicit sex relations are neither to be hinted at or portrayed" and 7) "sex perversion or any inference to same is strictly forbidden."[21]

Considering "The Gay Blade" in the light of the Comics Code and the history of Protestant representation, we might come to the conclusion that in his refusal to abide by restrictions, Chick performed both a harm and a service. Jack T. Chick: purveyor of antigay propaganda and scourge of the moral nannies! However ambivalently many Christian adults may have regarded Chick tracts when they flooded Christian churches, children of the day loved them. Yesterday's children are today's Christian conservatives, and they are also today's Chick skeptics, parodists, and collectors.

Chick Lit

The Chick publications empire boasts that "Chick tracts get read." One of the ways we know this is true is because of the frequency with which the tracts and their creator appear in parodies and other media treatments. There are, it appears, three distinct categories of Chick tract readers: conservative Christians who concur with Chick's theology and see the tracts as tools to spread the gospel and win souls, readers who do not agree with the theology but are fascinated by Chick and his products, and readers who, confronted with the tracts, respond with dismay, disgust, or amusement. I often ask people I come across if they are familiar with Chick tracts. Few of my close acquaintances even know what I am talking about until I show them a sample of the genuine article. For this purpose, I have taken to carrying a copy of "This Was Your Life!" Inevitably, when people see a copy they recognize the signal size, shape, and cover of the "grisly little rectangles of pulp."[22] And they often have stories of their own to tell about their encounters with Chick. One academic colleague describes her fearful childhood conversion experience after a friend showed her a copy of "Life!" Another nostalgically recalls her teenaged letter of complaint to Chick Publications as the inception of her career as an activist.[23]

In the realm of cult media, Chick is a star. His creations inspire nostalgia, fascination, and loathing. There is even a term for people who are obsessed with Chick tracts though they do not cleave to Chick's theology: "Chicklets." Some Chicklets collect the tracts, use chat rooms to trade with other collectors, try to interview Chick, and find tracts through eBay, the online auctioneer. Chicklets write articles about Chick for indie and alternative magazines; they maintain websites dedicated to Chick arcana and maledictions; they show up at his home and business in Riverside County, California. Those who follow Chick comics compete with one another to select adjectives that describe the entrepreneur's life work: vile, hateful, paranoid, disturbing, twisted, incendiary, bloodthirsty, laughable, shameful, lurid, infamous, nasty, and vicious. And most of these terms come from readers who appreciate, even if they do not *believe*, Chick's theology.

It is not only the Chick empire that has an interest in queer themes; fans, critics, and the curious also gravitate to the antigay themes and images of the tracts. The fan term "Chicklet" seems a tad benign to describe Psycho Dave, a fan who has rewritten and redrawn some of the Chick tracts in a decidedly irreverent style.[24] In one of Psycho Dave's reconceptualizations of "The Sissy?" a buff trucker teaches two other truckers, anti-Christian bigots, to respect the manliness of Jesus. In "The Holy and the Homo," under Psycho Dave's pen, a buff gay trucker teaches two gay-bashing truckers to respect gay people, first by persuading them of the error of their ways and then by sexually assaulting them.[25] In another parody of "The Sissy?" Mirage and Psycho Dave join forces to reconceptualize the buff trucker in a way that is more consistent with the spirit of the Chick original, even as it translates the gendered message of "The Sissy?" into its implied message about sexuality. In "The Trucker and the Mind-Fucker," the trucker is a Christian who instructs his gay-tolerant companions about the evil of homosexuality. As the three sit down together over their meal at the truck stop, the Christian bows his head and prays, "Dear God, thank you for sending AIDS to kill off all the faggots," then addresses his companions: "So what makes you think fags and dykes are ok? They're evil."[26]

Psycho Dave reports that he became interested in revising Chick tracts when he began to find them tucked under the windshield wipers of cars parked in downtown Boston in the late 1980s. He had encountered the comics as a child more than a decade before when he and other parishioners routinely found them lying on benches and stuffed into hymnals in his Catholic church. The "fundies" who thus evangelized are now the objects of Dave's technical artistry.[27] Dave helpfully gives advance permission to print out his parodies of "The Sissy?" and other tracts in his collection and distribute them "to Fundamentalist Kooks on street corners" as Dave did when he completed his own early tract parodies as a teenager.[28] A look at Psycho Dave's "Prick Publications Site History" confirms that Dave has run into legal problems with Chick Publications because of his early uses of Chick's art in his parodies. Dave has engaged in a number of maneuvers to keep his material up, in many cases to no avail.[29] He now draws all his own art and encourages other parodists to join him in his enterprise.

Jim Huger has teamed up with Psycho Dave to create parodies of Chick tracts, which appear on the Jack T. Chick Parody Archives site as well as on Huger's own site, "Jhuger—'Effing the Ineffable Since 1996'."[30] In a parody of "Last Rites, entitled "Dead to Rights," Jack Chick is struck by a car in which a woman and man are arguing about who deserves the title of "greatest Christian alive." Despite receiving medical attention, Chick dies and is taken to heaven for judgment. There, a caustic God denounces Chick's theology and sends him back to earth to try again as Jackie, a "poor Hispanic Catholic lesbian." On his personal website, Huger provides a PDF file of a document suitable for framing entitled "Learn from History!" In "Learn," Huger challenges Christian conservative opponents of same-sex marriage to recall conservative stances on democracy, slavery, women's suffrage, and segregation and to ask themselves if their children and grandchildren are likely to be proud or ashamed of today's discrimination against homosexuals.

Another Chicklet tells "Jack T. Chick's Fairy Tales" on the website *Adult! Christianity: Defending the Rights of the Un-bornagain*. In this commentary, the porn motif resurfaces, this time specifically with reference to same-sex sexuality:

> The original bar scene from "The Beast" has to be Chick's most infamous work. It was cut from later editions. In a dark bar two men are kissing in a corner, everyone is drunk, the waitresses are topless, men are fighting, lovers are necking, and sin runs rampant in this strangely inviting place. It was my first exposure to homosexuality and it's ironic that I must thank Jack Chick for opening my eyes to this possibility.[31]

In the current Chick collection "The Beast" still lives, but as this comment suggests, the men in the corner no longer kiss. Today, the two men embrace, one backed against the wall while the other says, "you know you're the only man for me." Except for the general mayhem in the room—their companions are still fighting and fornicating just like before—this small scene is almost sweet. Of course, this is a matter of perspective. From Chick's perspective, it may be better to separate the homosexuals physically than suffer a depiction that leads vulnerable sinners into iniquity. As this suggests, Chick is willing to adjust his representations but not to compromise with either liberal tolerance or conservative Christian political rhetoric. If God commands abomination rhetoric as a response to heinous sin, Chick delivers it unapologetically.

The Devil and Homosexuals

"Jack Chick never gives up picking on queers."[32] Indeed, Chick was never either ambivalent or indirect about the homosexual menace and God's position on it. In tracts such as "The Gay Blade," "Wounded Children (1983), "Doom Town," "Sin City" (2001), and "Birds and the Bees" (2004), Chick addresses same-sex sexuality and its perpetrators at length. The earliest of the antigay tracts is "The Gay Blade," produced in its original version in 1972. Today "The Gay Blade" is out of print, although Chick publications will do a print run of 10,000 copies for only $700 (a savings of 50 percent off the cover price) and throw in a custom back cover—your logo, church address, or missionary contact information—absolutely free. But no matter, the essential "Blade" message is reproduced in more recent tracts. This message has two prongs: first, that the nature of homosexuality and homosexuals is revealed in the biblical story of Sodom and Gomorrah (or at least in the conservative Christian interpretation of that story) and second, that the contemporary message that God wishes to send about homosexuality is that he hates it. In the tracts, the first message is transmitted through flashbacks and archaeological evidence, while the second message is put into the mouths of a variety of uncompromising Christian characters that testify to those around them.

It might be a surprise for many consumers of "The Gay Blade" to learn that several of its frames are based on photographic images of the young Gay Liberation Movement. The tract does not advertise the provenance of these images, but their source is a photo-essay published in the December 31, 1971, issue of *Life Magazine: The Year in Pictures 1971*.[33] The essay, which is even-handed for its time, particularly when compared with the tract it helped inspire, moves from images of street protest to images taken from the daily lives of members of the movement. The first frame of the tract, in which two men stand in church before a minister in vestments and respond to the question "Wilt thou have this man as thy wedded spouse?" is a variation on a photo (and accompanying text) in which the Reverend Troy Perry, founder of the Metropolitan Community Church, joins two men in wedlock. In the original photo, shot over Perry's shoulder, we see the men looking into each other's eyes. In the Chick variation, we see the men's backs as they stand before the minister. When we do see the faces of the newlyweds in the next frame, they are strikingly disconsolate. The characters' improbable emotional reaction to their own wedding points up for tract readers the impossibility that this charade of heterosexual probity can lead to anything but despair.

Another photo in the *Life* layout appears over the headline "Experiments with different life-styles: Propagandists." The photo shows three men on a city street in what one commentator describes as "skag drag." Although they are not wearing recognizable drag, these Hollywood denizens are unusual enough to startle at least one passerby—a woman pushing a stroller—with their "outlandish" look.[34] In "The Gay Blade" rendering of the image, meaningful changes appear: the wrists of the two men depicted turn limp and interlace, and the bystander, who pushes a toddler in the photo, now grabs her older boy and covers his eyes. Many queer readers of "The Gay Blade" have ridiculed the image of these two costumed men; surely these characters can only have come from the desperate imaginations of queer haters, since gay men would never dress so badly.[35] However, the proof is in the photo.

What is interesting about the translation of the original image from a photo-essay in a national magazine to an antigay Christian tract is that the photographic image is deemed insufficient for the purpose to which it will be put. Added elements include the stereotypical effeminizing of the figures—

nowhere present in the original photo—and a reminder of the seductiveness of same-sex sexuality. The toddler in the original photo, who is not even glancing in the men's direction, is transformed into an impressionable boy whose mere glance at the oddly dressed trio might precipitate his own induction into "Satan's shadowy world of homosexuality."[36]

Besides its unremarked reliance on the *Life* photos, there is another connection between the magazine spread and the tract that followed. Both contexts place particular emphasis on same-sex marriage. In fact, 1971 saw the first legal challenge to the ban on same-sex marriage in a Minnesota case.[37] But given the relatively ambivalent political demand in the early Gay Liberation Movement for the right of same-sex couples to marry, this emphasis bears some scrutiny. The *Life* photo-essay opens and closes on the subject. Its first image is of a cake that members of the Gay Activists Alliance brought to a wedding protest at the office of the New York City Clerk. A close-up of the cake shows it decorated with a lambda symbol, a male-male couple, and a female-female couple. A heart in the foreground is inscribed in icing: "Gay Power to Gay Lovers." The essay closes with a montage of religious photos and addresses the controversy over religious blessings of same-sex relations, being careful all the while to place the words "wedding" and "marry" in quotations. Large numbers of Americans probably considered the possibility (or, if you will, threat) of same-sex marriage for the first time as a result of either *Life*'s "Homosexuals in Revolt" or Chick's "The Gay Blade." For my part, although I knew of homosexuals before I saw the tract, I had neither heard, nor considered the possibility, of gay marriage. I encountered the Gay Liberation *Movement* then and there.

In 1974 "The Gay Blade" was a common sight in my Texas Baptist church, but Dennis Brumm encountered it for the first time as a student at Iowa State University. During that academic year, the ISU Christian Fellowship passed out Chick tracts, including "The Gay Blade," at a booth in the student union. Lesbian and gay students from the Gay People's Liberation Alliance protested the representations of queers in the tract by staging a march with a gay student "Jesus" and his thirty "disciples." Because the student members of Christian Fellowship were distributing the antigay tract free of charge, protesters took as many of them as they could and destroyed them. When challenged, the minister of the ISU Christian group admitted that the tract might not represent gay people accurately, but he insisted that the tract's message was consistent with scripture on same-sex sexuality.[38]

This story of the provenance and effects of the images of "The Gay Blade" has a larger significance for analyzing Chick's place in our culture and for the politics of the contemporary Christian right. Chick observers often muse about him as a sui generis Christian salesman, which he is. However, in emphasizing Chick's tenacity, aggressiveness, and orneriness with friend and foe alike, it is easy to lose sight of the ways in which Chick tracts borrow from, and reflect, American culture, as well as influencing it. One contribution of the reviews of Chick tracts written and collected by Kurt Kuersteiner is that they indirectly document many ways in which the tracts are products not only of Chick's idiosyncratic worldview and conservative Christian theology, but also of American pop culture in the second half of the twentieth century. Besides borrowing images from *Life*, Chick Publications borrows from TV—before the more recent spate of witchcraft programming, *Bewitched* was Satan's favorite television program. In addition, Chick and Carter offer characters that are dead ringers for Sean Connery, Bill Clinton, Robert Redford, and Tom Selleck, among others. Steve Martin's "wild and crazy guy" persona from NBC's *Saturday Night Live* is translated into Chick's tract "That Crazy Guy"—a character complete with a trick arrow through the head—who loves a woman and then leaves her HIV positive.

After the phenomenal success of "The Gay Blade" came "Wounded Children," a tract that traces homosexual development in a young man from childhood to adulthood. Kuersteiner calls this one Chick's "'compassionate' attack on homosexuality," and that description is consistent with the approach toward homosexual desire that locates its origins in innocent childhood.[39] David, the protagonist, goes awry first in his gender identity and then, later, in his sexuality. When David weeps over his painful desires Satan himself stands in for the secular teacher or therapist that many in the ex-gay movement decry, telling the young man: "You're gay! So face it." After David endures the trauma of watching his ex-lover be beaten to death by gay bashers, he hits bottom. It is only then that he is receptive to the Christian witness of an ex-gay man and is loosed from bondage to homosexuality. Today, "Wounded Children" is a rare tract and a collectable item. It is the only one of the tracts with "central gay content" that is no longer available in any form from Chick Publications.[40]

The third Chick tract to focus on same-sex sexuality was "Doom Town," originally published in 1989. Unlike "The Gay Blade," "Doom Town" is a direct response not only to same-sex sexual behavior but to an organized gay movement. The tract opens with a public panel discussion led by lesbians and gay men. A highlight of the tract is the invocation of a blood libel: a member of the panel calls for "blood terrorism," deliberate poisoning of the nation's blood supply by HIV-infected gay men in retaliation for anemic federal spending on AIDS research. LGBT people have often countered Christian conservative injunctions to revere family values with the pithy "Hate Is Not a Family Value," and the phrase appears on a sign held by homosexuals in one version of the tract's first frame. It is in this second antigay tract that Chick achieves his most florid narrative of the fall of Sodom, aka "doom town." In this story, Chick extrapolates some from the Old Testament tale, for example when a fat, hairy sodomite approaches a fearful child and announces, "It's that time again!" Although the original caption for this frame read, "the children (of Sodom) were all molested at an early age," the present caption is a more qualified, "even children were not safe from their gross perversions."

Chick insinuates other points of contact between homosexuals and children, a tactic that is consistent with the kinds of political arguments that were current in antigay politics in the late 1980s and early '90s. In the first frame of "Doom Town," gay activists refer to children who will be gay in the future as "*OUR* CHILDREN." In another frame, two "perverts" share a deep kiss in the foreground while another man in a friar's robe chases a small boy. In these intersections of queers and children, Chick gives his readers both the theme of recruitment and the theme of child sexual assault.

"Sin City" (2001) is set at a gay pride parade and introduces the theme of hate speech that Chick wields in other tracts. A Christian picketing the parade with a sign that reads "HOMOSEXUALITY IS AN ABOMINATION!" is savagely beaten by police and then, though hospitalized, is charged with a hate crime for trying to disrupt the festivities. Here too, as in the other tracts, Sodom is invoked as the trumping evidence for the immorality of same-sex sexuality. As in "Doom Town," a gay character comes under conviction and turns to Christ and away from homosexuality. The "Sin City" twist on this ex-gay theme is that the repentant sinner is now also a gay minister. Reverend Ray, the gay minister, is saved in the end, but not before he is exposed as a false Christian, one who, until his conversion, did not even believe that Jesus is the son of God. Ray illustrates the Christian right belief that while people with homosexual desires may be Christians, those who claim lesbian or gay identity unapologetically cannot be.

The newest tract in the antigay line-up is "Birds and the Bees." This tract takes a gay male couple and the invisible larval demons who accompany them wherever they go to elementary school to highlight the gay agenda in public education. Fortunately, one student in the class, Susy, is available to instruct her friends that "God *hates* homosexuality," but only once they are safely off school grounds. Because she refuses to believe what she is told in school she is able to turn her classmates from the belief that "the way [the gays] live is *cool*." As she testifies, Susy narrates the ubiquitous story of Sodom, blames church-state separation for her friends' confusion over homosexuality, and, finally, leads them to Christ. Undermining one frequent complaint against public school sex education, Susy does not hear of the sin of Sodom for the first time from liberal representatives of the gay agenda. Instead, she's precociously familiar with same-sex sexuality, the biblical case against it, and the legal changes that have put the verities of the Bible beyond the reach of her peers.[41]

In these antigay tracts Chick moves through a variety of speakers, arguments, and forms of evidence about same-sex sexuality. These tracts, which appear depressingly similar from one perspective, are actually varied enough to illuminate the many shapes of antigay belief and the foundations of antigay activism. Still, they are not the only antigay messages produced by Chick Publications. There are many avenues by which consumers of Chick tracts can absorb some version of the antigay message of the Christian right.

Sin of Sins?

Many Chick tracts do not focus solely on same-sex sexuality but still include some treatment of the subject in passing. In these tracts, Chick denounces homosexuals and same-sex sexuality as one of many kinds of sin that plague a fallen world. These tracts with secondary gay content include "Back From the Dead?" (1982), "The Only Hope" (1985), "The Beast" (1988), "Going Home" (1991), "Trust Me" (1994), "Bewitched?" (2000), "A Love Story" (2002), "The Mad Machine" (2002), "God With Us" (2002), "Man in Black (2003)," and "Who's Missing?" (2003). In most of these tracts, same-sex sexuality appears only fleetingly as one of many classes of evil that confirm human degeneration and point toward the end-times: murder, anarchy, witchcraft and Satanism, pornography, drug and alcohol abuse, incest, fornication, and adultery. In most, same-sex sexuality is *a* sin but not *the* sin, not the Ur-sin that serves as a proximate cause of God's impending destruction of his creation. In conservative Christian theology, such a treatment of same-sex sexuality exists alongside one that is more familiar from political debates between pro- and antigay rights activists: the status of homosexuality as the direst of sins and the most momentous of signs.

In "Going Home," the indictment of same-sex sexuality is more circuitous than it is in most tracts with secondary gay content. The text of "Going Home" does not mention gay men, but the tract certainly points to a connection between sin and AIDS and to the salvation need of those suffering from the disease. Reading this tract through the lens of Chick's narratives and the Christian right movement, the implication of a choice between sexual sin and death, on the one hand, and salvation and death—but eternity in heaven—is not far to seek. However, Chick also accomplishes with the tract an indictment of an American government that refuses to deal with the threat of AIDS in a muscular fashion. Chick's ideology has it that the federal government—here represented by an unnamed institution that is probably the Centers for Disease Control and Prevention—is indifferent not only to the unhealed and unsaved people of Africa but also to the domestic threat posed by the propagation of AIDS. Comparing Africa and America, the Christian protagonist notes that "the U.S. could be like this is just a few years."

"The Poor Little Witch" (1987) returns to the domestic context with which Chick is most at home. The tract introduces a lonely, awkward teenaged

girl who attracts the attention of her female teacher. Mrs. White invites Mandy
to her house for an unlikely extracurricular event: a slumber party. As Mandy
approaches the house, Mrs. White warns the girls, "We have a new girl . . .
Mandy! Go easy with her. She doesn't know!" Once inside, a seductively posed
pajama-clad classmate asks Mandy if she "want[s] to learn some really neat
things." It's only then that we discover what the girl has in mind, levitation, a
demonstration of which ushers Mandy into her new (albeit short-lived) identity as a witch. Subtextually, at least, this scene connects witchcraft with lesbianism, a tried and true linkage that only occasionally surfaces explicitly, as in
Pat Robertson's fundraising letter ("practice witchcraft . . . and become lesbians"). It may hardly matter what women gathered together without appropriate masculine supervision are doing. Whatever they are doing, if it is without
God's blessing, lesbianism and witchcraft—two quintessential female vices—
may not be far behind.[42]

   A more explicit antigay message is delivered by "God With Us," a tract
that features an adult man instructing two small boys. The boys slowly realize
that the truths their tutor is delivering contradict the everyday perspectives of
the world around them. They and their tutor engage in the following exchange:
"Wow, then being gay is a no-no? *Absolutely* . . . stay away from it. It smells of
devils and death—and *God hates it*. Then our teachers are lying to us, *right*? Oh,
yes, and they're in *big* trouble with God." The Spanish language tract I found at
the Libreria Cristiana Bethesda in Atlanta, Georgia, cleaves exactly to this English text: "*Claro que sí . . . y ellos están en un gran* problema con Dios." The lead
character of "God With Us" is "Bob," a man with a receding hairline who may
be intended to be read as Latino. Bob is ubiquitous in a series of tracts drawn
by Chick himself, and Chicklets frequently comment on his appearance. As in
the other Bible story tracts, Bob delivers a brief history of biblical time. Not
only are homosexuals a central focus of this story, Bob unselfconsciously describes them to his two young companions as "perverts" and "sickos," noting
that "God created Adam and Eve—*not* Adam and Steve!"

   Such language has been commonplace on signs, and in fundraising letters,
sermons, and chants at political rallies. Today, it is precisely the kind of public language from which Christian right opinion leaders try to wean followers. At a
Focus on the Family-sponsored ex-gay conference I attended in 2004, speakers
urged members of the audience to refrain from slogans like "Adam and Eve—not
Adam and Steve" and even the more commonplace "love the sinner, hate the sin."
The injunction to "love the sinner and hate the sin" may have lately come under
critique in the movement, but it is still widely employed among conservative
Christians. As is often the case in mass movements, diversity of thought and expression often prevail even against the better political judgment of leaders. At the
very least, such pedagogy is successful if followers learn to refrain from such language in public even if it continues to circulate in more private settings.

Marketing Hate

With translations in one hundred languages and millions of customers here at home, we might assume that Chick enjoys unmixed success. Yet, those who write about Jack Chick and his tract empire agree that Chick and conservative Christians went their separate ways almost before the Christian right cohered as a new social movement. The foremost reason given for the separation is the inconsistency between Chick's theology and that of the Christian right. In this narrative, the nascent Christian right gave Chick his walking papers in the 1980s; what precipitated the break-up were his relationships with three bizarre figures: John Todd, Father Alberto Rivera, and Rebecca Brown, M.D. This thesis has some support although, as we shall see, it has been overdrawn.

John Todd ended up as a convicted sex criminal, but by his own admission he began as the scion of a multigenerational family of Druids. Todd claimed that as a member of the Illuminati he had possessed great power and influence and had sought worldwide domination. After he renounced his dynastic ambitions and was born-again, Todd traveled around the country telling his remarkable story and exposing other godless conspirators. For example, Todd revealed that Ayn Rand's novel *Atlas Shrugged* was not an objectivist tract but was, rather, a blueprint for the Illuminati's global takeover. He was championed by Chick, who for some time made excuses for behaviors that were inconsistent with Todd's status as a high-profile Christian convert.

Father Rivera was a Spanish self-professed former Catholic priest who made his living in the 1980s impeaching the Catholic Church for its sexual abominations and conspiracies with Satan. The details of Rivera's story—including his claim to the priesthood—have been called into question by diligent researchers. Nevertheless, drawn to Rivera's tales of international satanic maleficence, Chick became Rivera's sponsor and publicized his exposé of Catholicism. Using the tools of his trade, Chick initiated a series of full-sized comics that featured Rivera's adventures, including the six-part *Alberto* series that includes *Alberto* (1979) and *Double-Cross* (1981). One result of this collaboration was that the Canadian government decided to classify some of the comics as pornography under a customs law that permitted the restriction of such material. This was the first time the law was used to bar the importation of religious material.[43] By the early 1980s, some Canadian Chicklets were bemoaning the fact that antigay material could not be subjected to those same restrictions.[44]

If possible, Rebecca Brown's story is even stranger than either Todd's or Rivera's. Dr. Brown, whose real name was Ruth Bailey, lost her license to practice as a physician in 1984. By then, Brown had taken on a companion with a number of aliases but known as "Elaine." Brown tells their story on cassettes marketed by Chick and in two books, *Prepare for War* (1992) and *He Came to Set the Captives Free* (1996).[45] In these forums, Brown insisted that Elaine was in grave danger from occult forces as a result of having fled from a cult called The Brotherhood. According to Brown, Elaine had risen to the position of High Priestess, married Satan, and consummated the marriage before fleeing for her life. As for Dr. Brown, her medical license was revoked for, among other things, misdiagnosing patients, abusing drugs, and treating patients for demon possession, including conducting rituals of exorcism.

In 1991, three Christian skeptics published a book debunking Dr. Brown: *Drugs, Demons and Delusions: A Christian Investigation of the Testimony and Claims of Rebecca Brown, M.D.*[46] Originally published in journal form by Personal Freedom Outreach, the book is an indictment, not only of Brown and Elaine, but also of Brown's publisher, Jack Chick. The Christian Investigation carried out by Personal Freedom Outreach finds a number of gaps, contradictions, and suspicious claims in Brown's testimony. These include information about Elaine's marriage, Brown's legal trials and bizarre behavior as a physician, Brown's provision of illegal drugs to Elaine, the nature of Brown's relationship with Elaine (they slept in the same bed), and the details of Brown's idiosyncratic doctrine of demonic possession and exorcism. Throughout the text, the investigative team includes Jack Chick in its critique of Brown. Chick's conspiratorial and threatening persona plays a role in the Brown saga. Not only was Chick Brown's first publisher and advocate, but he is prepared to attack as Satanists those who question Brown's legitimacy. The team even gives Chick a chance to respond to their critique of Brown by including the major points of two bellicose letters Chick sent in response to the first installment of the investigation.

The cases of Todd, Rivera, and Brown are the most obvious manifestations of Chick's propensities to indulge in conspiracy theory and to lash out at putative allies who question his conclusions. Both tendencies are cited by those who attest to Chick's declining capital in the conservative Christian movement.[47] There is only one problem with the assumption of the split between Chick and the Christian right: it isn't true, strictly speaking, or at least it isn't complete. It is true that some evangelical Christians were critical of Chick's Christian cartoon enterprise in its early days, the late 1960s and early '70s. His work seemed uncomfortably close to the kinds of cultural corruption they despised. It is true that Chick resigned from the Christian Bookseller's Association (CBA) in 1981 after an event he hosted—a boisterous and, it appears, mostly well-received session between Rivera and invited attendees—caused CBA leaders to ask him to be more circumspect about some of his controversial beliefs. And it is also true that some conservative Christians were openly skeptical of Chick's credulity with regard to his protégés.

All this is true. However, the relationship between Chick and the Christian right isn't so much a divorce as it is an affair—known and relished by intimates at the same time that it is disavowed by the uninitiated. As such, Chick's views can still help us decipher the theology and politics of the Christian right, including its foundational positions on same-sex sexuality. Raeburn acknowledges this when he suggests, "examine the historical and theological forbears of little Chick and you'll find an awful, and I do mean awful, lot of mainstream beliefs. . . . Chick tracts and the violence in them are as American as apple pie."[48]

Curious about the assumption made by some Chicklets that Chick tracts are eschewed by Christians and no longer available in Christian bookstores, I carried out a casual experiment. Between 2003 and 2006, I visited Christian bookstores and found Chick tracts in many states: California, Georgia, Indiana, Kansas, Kentucky, Minnesota, Montana, Ohio, South Dakota, Tennessee, and Virginia.[49] This is an unscientific nonprobability sample, but the results were nonetheless provocative. Far from having disappeared, Chick tracts were often available. Customers may not be "flocking to Christian bookstores . . . to buy these pieces of trash," but clerks and customers alike recognize them and talk about them enthusiastically.[50] I also discovered the source of the misunderstanding about the tracts' disappearance: while they are not available in large franchise Christian bookstores such as Christian Family Stores and Lifeway Christian Stores, they are sold at many smaller and independent stores throughout the American heartland and through such online sources as Armageddon Books.[51] Indeed, when I inquired about Chick tracts in bookstores that did not stock them, clerks often directed me to the Chick Publications website so I could place my own bulk order.

One caveat: Chick tracts are sold in many Christian bookstores, but Catholic stores do not stock Chick tracts because of the anti-Catholic character of many tracts and of Chick's own convictions. In the early 1980s, Catholic bookstores and organizations led the boycott of Chick Publications because of Chick's aggressive anti-Catholicism.[52] Today, with the wide range of tracts available, Protestant stores do not always stock the anti-Catholic tracts. Indeed, when I shopped at the Pathway Bookstore in Cleveland, Tennessee—home of New Life Bible College—a young clerk assured me that the tracts are very much in demand. Then he confided spontaneously that the store doesn't stock the anti-Catholic and "anti-Islam" tracts. The Pathway Bookstore bills itself as "The Nation's Largest Christian Bookstore," and besides books, music, and a children's area, it features a central gazebo coffee bar for thirsty shoppers. Laid out like a Borders or Barnes and Noble, it provides a modern shopping experience even as it represses the unsavory dimensions of its products.

Interestingly, the same concerns with ecumenism do not prevail at many Christian shopping outlets. In Manhattan, Kansas, Christian Books and Gifts carried "The Pilgrimage" (1999), "The Traitor" (1990), "The Tycoon" (1993), and "The Last Generation" (1972), tracts that point out the satanic basis of, respectively, Islam, Buddhism, Hinduism, and Catholicism. "The Last Generation" is more coy than many of Chick's anti-Catholic tracts, but the Roman setting of the Antichrist's lair and the cult of the Mother Goddess telegraph its

meaning. Indeed, ecumenism is obviously not the trumping value to many conservative Protestants, as they continue to sell and distribute tracts that expose
the evils of Catholicism and other religious faiths. If "The Last Generation" is
indirect in its indictment, these tracts, which I purchased at Rainbow Christian
Discount in Columbus, Ohio, are not: "Are Roman Catholics Christians?"
(1981), "The Death Cookie" (1988), "The Beast" (1988), and "Man in Black"
(2003). These tracts reveal lies, blasphemies, conspiracies, "occultic murders,"
and diabolic abuses of power committed by the Catholic Church and its min-
ions throughout history. Everything old is new again.

Politics and Witness

The related beliefs that Chick tracts are no longer sold in Christian bookstores
because Chick's views are too extreme are widespread among those who comment on the tract phenomenon. How accurate is the second of these assumptions? I think the evidence shows that Chick's views do not lie outside the
boundaries of polite Christian right politics. Further, a close examination of the
political content of Chick tracts suggests that Chick—ostensibly a pariah—
is actually a prescient contemporary Christian conservative. Chick's politics line
up with the core agenda of the Christian right without remainder, a feat that
might suggest coordination but most likely just permits students of the movement to trace the emergence and maturation of its politics and rhetoric.

It is not tendentious to refer to the political agenda of Chick tracts.
Although they are witnessing tracts, intended to bring the good news of the
Gospel to unbelievers, the tracts collectively construct a body of beliefs that are
social and political as well as theological. One difference between Chick and
the Christian right, and not a small one, is that Chick does not urge his consumers to engage in political action. Throughout the 1970s, political activism
was already being pressed as a responsibility of Christian conservatives, but this
aspect of new Christian right formation has largely passed Chick by.[53] However, reading Chick tracts in retrospect, students of political ideology can see
the political agenda of the new Christian right coalescing. In the virtual world
of Chick commentary, those who have followed the tracts for decades attest to
their didactic potential in suggesting, repeating, confirming, and consolidating
a set of viewpoints on key social and political questions of recent times. Here is
political instruction beneath the radar of political elites, parties, and mainstream political institutions.

Chick's relative indifference to political action mitigates against too
much specificity in the views he expresses in the tracts. Indeed, on first blush, it
might be difficult to derive *political* positions from these cartoons at all. The
cartoon frames include intimate set pieces and dialogue between characters, not
just editorial jeremiads on public issues. In reality, it is the intimacy of the

medium that lends itself to a particular kind of indirect political pedagogy, delivered by godly characters in the context of personal relations with which the reader can identify. Constituting a political believer at the moment when a religious believer is born (again) is powerful pedagogy. It is moral instruction of a sort that is perfectly consistent with recent public conversations about how a real Christian should—or should not—vote.

Because the tracts are not in the first instance political, it makes sense that they express political views not as specific issue positions or policy recommendations but as general categories whose terms can be filled in by more activist movement partners. Chick's categories are refined and operationalized by the Christian right today, but they are not substantially altered. Another way to express this relationship is to say that none of Chick's political categories has become obsolete to the conservative Christian movement today. What are these political views that are so closely shared between Chick and the contemporary Christian right? Chick's political views fall into five categories that I express in negative terms because Chick frames them all as indictments against an essentially corrupt and libertine social reality. They are opposition to: abortion, gay rights, evolution, social provisioning, and separation of church and state.

In noting the remarkable agreement between Chick and the Christian right on these broad categories of political concern, I do not mean to suggest that we should be surprised by this agenda. Indeed, it is the agenda of a long, potent, and tenacious conservative strain in American life and politics. Yet three things are striking and worthy of close consideration. First, although he has not received credit or recognition for it, Chick quietly primed the conservative Christian political agenda for many years for his millions of readers without engaging in overt political discourse. Second, whatever differences of opinion there are between Chick and the leaders of the Christian right movement, they do not put Chick tracts and conservative Christian political opinion at odds with each other. On the contrary, they expose incontrovertible agreement, if not deliberate coordination. And finally, it is possible for at least some well-informed observers to mistake Chick's refusal to engage in contemporary forms of message discipline for substantive political disagreement. I don't doubt that some Christian right leaders and activists are exasperated with Chick, but it is not because they do not share his politics. Rather, it is because—an old school Christian in a focus group world—he does not share their commitment to strategy and tactics.

It is not difficult to demonstrate the tight links that prevail between Chick's political categories and their contemporary Christian right manifestations. Chick's opposition to abortion, expressed in "Baby Talk" (1995) and "Who Murdered Clarice?" (2000), is today evident in a range of policies supported by the Republican Party. On his first day in office, George W. Bush reimposed the Reagan-era Mexico City Policy (aka the global gag order) that prevents international family planning groups and facilities that receive U.S. federal funding for any programming from giving women information about abortion. The administration also created obstacles to the availability of the emergency contraceptive drug, Plan B, and has supported a multitude of antiabortion laws and policies that aim to reverse the right to legal abortion established by *Roe v. Wade*. Immediately after the 2004 election, Christian right leaders announced their expectation that Bush court appointees would share their opposition to legal abortion. Nor is Chick unaware of these political currents. In "Clarice," it is not only the "butcher" who is judged in heaven, but also a member of the Supreme Court, who asks a hovering angel, "*Uh*, I was a Supreme Court Justice, *am I involved*?"

Chick is well known for his opposition to same-sex sexuality and gay rights; indeed, he was an early expositor of many arguments associated with the issue. Today, same-sex issues are on the front burner of state legislatures, federal courts, Congress, and federal bureaucracies. These include the military's "don't ask, don't tell" policy, same-sex marriage, civil unions, and domestic partnerships; and family policies regarding child custody and adoption rights. The June 2003 Supreme Court decision in *Lawrence v. Texas* that reversed the court's 1986 decision in *Bowers v. Hardwick* was read by the Christian right as "America's moral 9/11."[54] One effect of this movement loss was to energize a variety of electoral initiatives as well as the Christian right's long-standing campaign against judicial independence. In part as a response to the decision in *Lawrence*, Pat Robertson launched an initiative he called "Operation Supreme Court Freedom" to encourage followers and other Christians to "cry out to our Lord to change the Court."[55] Other influential Christian right leaders, such as James Dobson, Gary Bauer, and Tony Perkins, routinely link court judgments favorable to LGBT rights to the need to transform the judiciary so that judges rule in accordance with God's will.

With regard to Chick's opposition to evolution science, the first of the creationist tracts is "Big Daddy?," originally created in 1970. In the tract, a polite and well-groomed student confronts a biology professor over the evidence for evolution. Barred from discussing his faith, and forced to fight with the weapons of the adversary, the student systematically undermines each piece of the increasingly hysterical professor's evidence. In the end, no longer able to defend his science, the professor abdicates, and the student leads the class to Christ. "Big Daddy?," "perhaps the most popular and widely distributed piece of creationist literature ever," is still around thirty-five years and many revisions later.[56] Since its introduction, it has been updated many times, both to shed anachronisms (such as the students' "far out") and to include more putatively lethal rejoinders to evolution. The student's case for divine creation is premised on Fred Carter's recasting of the *Ascent of Man*, an illustration in a 1968 Time-Life book.[57]

Chick's opposition to evolution as an explanation for human origins is no longer tainted with its history of know-nothingism and anti-intellectualism.

New think tanks, educational institutions, and activist organizations demand an end to the monopoly of agnostic science—otherwise known as the "philosophy of Naturalism"—on the education of children through the rewriting of science standards and the institutionalization of Intelligent Design. Intelligent Design is the version of creation science that has been crafted by proponents of creationism to circumvent decisions such as the one in the 1987 Louisiana case, *Edwards v. Aguillard*, that prevent the teaching of creationism in public schools. A variety of state and local political projects concerning the origins of life have recently become visible to mainstream publics. In Kansas, where I have consulted on a National Science Foundation grant for gender equity in university science and engineering departments, the struggle over evolution and creation science heated up in the 1990s. Scientists there have boycotted hearings held by the State Board of Education to highlight the naturalistic bias in traditional science education. The attempt in Dover, Pennsylvania, to mandate the teaching of Intelligent Design was curtailed in 2005 by the federal court ruling in *Kitzmiller v. Dover*. However, activists in many states continue to profess confidence that changes in the judiciary and broad public support for the teaching of alternatives to evolution will eventually bring the movement success.

Chick's opposition to social provisioning and Christian social justice is less evident in his tracts but present nonetheless. Daniel Raeburn points out that Chick's gospel of salvation is indifferent to "works" and to the well-being of the world. He gives as an example "The Poor Pope," a tract in which Chick repudiates "social welfare" and "social justice problems" as appropriate concerns of Christianity.[58] There is little in Chick's work to suggest that he is as enthusiastic a supporter of market fundamentalism as is the contemporary Christian right. But there is still common ground in these repudiations of government intervention in the economy on behalf of the vulnerable. Chick repudiates "liberation theology" as well as communism in "Fat Cats" (1989). In this tract, the protagonist, Juan, is introduced to Father Dominic, "a good communist." Juan asks the priest how he can "be a follower of Jesus and be a communist"; Father Dominic's response begins with Chick's trademark, "Haw, haw, haw!"—an interjection much beloved of Chicklets that Chick usually puts into the mouths of demons—followed by the claim that "Jesus was a communist." Here, Chick identifies the social justice orientation of many Catholics and mainline Protestants with despised Cold War communism.[59]

Finally, Chick is no respecter of church-state separation. In "Birds and the Bees," children receive corrupt moral instruction because God has been driven from public schools. Certainly, Chick's perspective on church and state is crude and uninformed by sophisticated legal and rhetorical strategy. Having failed in many efforts to eradicate boundaries between church and state, the Christian right now employs a more effective legal strategy that relies on the Free Speech Clause of the First Amendment.[60] Individual battles that receive media attention include displaying the Ten Commandments and Christian symbols in the public square, vouchers for religious school education, as well as the older and still venerable battle over prayer and religious instruction in public schools. In March, 2005, the Presidential Prayer Team posed a survey question on its website that asked if American citizens should be permitted to pray in public. Not surprisingly, over 90 percent of respondents said "yes." I agree; Americans should be able to pray in public. Of course, we already have the right to pray, in public and in private. But such deceptive locutions as these reinforce the claim—common in post-*Engel v. Vitale* conversations—that as a nation America has rejected God and must bear the consequences.

Of the positions Chick proselytizes most forcefully, there is one—theological rather than political—that does not anticipate the platform of the Christian right. This is his opposition to other faiths besides born-again Protestant Christianity. For those who pay attention to Chick tracts today, the buzz centers mostly on his unapologetic anti-ecumenism. This public anti-ecumenism is more unusual today than it was thirty years ago, but there is more at stake in these new coalitions between disparate faith communities than tolerance and comity between believers. What is more, the tenets of faith that drive Chick's adversarial relations with Catholicism, Mormonism, Islam, and other faiths continue to be central to conservative Christian theology today. What has changed is the success of political coalitions and the need to cultivate productive relations between conservative Protestants and the unborn-again of other religious traditions.

Pure Rapture

Chick's positions on other faiths—particularly his convictions regarding Catholicism and the pope—make his work a dirty little secret of right-wing Protestant born-again evangelicalism. Chick's anti-Catholic tracts are without question shocking in their bigotry. They hark back to a time in American history when Protestants aimed the most vile anti-Catholic sentiments and violence at undesirable immigrant groups; when conspiracy theories linked the pope with international financiers and satanic cabals; when pornography about the prurient habits of nuns and priests circulated through underground pop culture.[61] What survives of these views and acts in mainstream political culture today is the residue of Catholic and Protestant theological discord and a general continuing Catholic wariness toward Protestant conservatives.

Conservative Catholics are an important faction of the Christian right coalition. Prominent Catholic government officials often speak for that coalition as they express their own convictions. What these convergences suggest is that either conservative Protestant Christianity has jettisoned its theological opposition to the Catholic faith or there are more complicated dynamics afoot between the two traditions. In Protestant bookstores today, a silence prevails on the subject of the Catholic faith. Not only is there little residue of earlier denunciations of Catholic beliefs and forms of worship, even resources that specifically list cults and false doctrines are careful to exclude Catholicism from censure. In these precincts, Chick finds no allies.

However, in Catholic bookstores such discretion is not as much in evidence. There, one finds a multitude of resources for Catholics anxious to respond to conservative Protestant attitudes, arguments, and attempts at conversion. These include such titles as: *Born Fundamentalist, Born Again Catholic*; *Nuts and Bolts: A Practical How-To Guide for Explaining the Catholic Faith*; *Where's That in the Bible?*; *Answer Me This!*; *Strangers at Your Door: How to Respond to Jehovah's Witnesses, the Mormons, Televangelists, Jimmy Swaggart, Cults, and More*; *Answering a Fundamentalist*; *Catholicism and Fundamentalism: The Attack on "Romanism" by "Bible Christians"*; and *Will Catholics Be "Left Behind"?* The Catholic faith that is itself known for expressing an exclusive claim to God's favor is plainly on the defensive. What motivates these defenses? The sheer numbers of such titles suggest that in spite of the decreasing political differentiation of traditionalist Catholics and Protestants, Catholics remain wary about the dominance of evangelizing right-wing Protestantism. Unlike the triumphal silence of conservative Protestantism, Catholics are more likely to exhibit a defensive and didactic faith. The "culture of life" that embraces Terry Schiavo and challenges to *Roe* has not yet eliminated all the meaningful differences between these religious traditions.

It would not have been true throughout much of American history, but Chick's anti-Catholic impiousness is shocking today. However, the anti-Catholic quality of Chick tracts allows other aspects of his theology to go relatively unnoticed. One fruitful reading of Chick tracts highlights conservative Protestant eschatology, an aspect of his theology that both departs from Catholic teachings and confirms his location in the mainstream of the Christian right. Chick tracts are advertisements for premillennial dispensationalism; they "make the Rapture the central hope of the Christians in these times."[62] Well before Tim LaHaye and Jerry Jenkins sat down to plot the *Left Behind* franchise that has held much of America in thrall to Christian conservative beliefs about the end-times, Chick was elucidating premillennialism. It turns out that Chick's eschatology is indeed key to understanding his convictions and obsessions, including his orientations toward the Catholic heresy and same-sex sexuality.

Politically, conservative Muslims and Catholics often concur with the antigay positions of their conservative Protestant brethren. At the same time, there are significant differences in the ideologies and goals that motivate these positions. For conservative Protestants, including Jack Chick, antigay politics are consistent with a particular kind of soul-saving mission: the requirement that all sinners accept Jesus Christ and become born again. However, even though Chick tracts appear to eschew every purpose but witnessing to those in need of salvation, Chick also has another mission that corresponds with that of the larger Protestant Christian right. This is stamping out large-scale sinfulness, the kind of sin that prevailed in Sodom and Gomorrah and that persuaded God to destroy mankind while saving Noah and his family. In "The Missing Day" (2005), Uncle Mortimer is an awkward guest at a Thanksgiving Day family dinner. He reminds unrepentant family members that "when any nation stops being thankful and forgets God, it's headed for judgement. The Bible says that . . . 'The wicked shall be turned into hell, and all the nations that forget God.' Psalms 9:17." In "Sin City," the character who voices Chick's theology asks, "Tell me, Ray, of all the sins, lying adultery, stealing, etc., can you think of any other sin . . . where God Himself wiped out entire cities, to remove *that* sin?" We learn from reading the various versions of the Sodom story in Chick tracts that homosexuality can precipitate the pouring out of God's devastating wrath.

Same-sex sexuality is central to Chick's theology and to the political implications that follow from it. Chick's response to same-sex sexuality reveals important dimensions of a premillennial case for the end-times. And so does Chick's response to other religious traditions, especially Catholicism, the tradition that is most threatening to the version of American Protestantism for which Chick speaks. In an array of tracts—such as "The Last Generation" (1972), "The Only Hope" (1985), "The Last Missionary" (1987), "The Beast" (1988), "The Great Escape" (1991), "Here He Comes" (2003), and "Who's Missing?" (2003)—Chick rehearses a response to Catholic faith and sexual sin that is geared primarily to an end-times vision. This vision is consistent in its details with the premillennialism of, for example, the *Left Behind* novels and other nonfiction treatments of the theme.

"The Only Hope" is representative of the genre. "Hope" opens with a vista of the sins that drove God to destroy the world with a flood. Introducing a small motif that recurs in the antigay tract "Doom Town," one man warns another, "Take your hands off him. @*#! He's my wife." The tract brings this sinful scenario up to date, confirming that our contemporary landscape of sin mirrors that of biblical times. It outlines the institutional infrastructure of the last days as centered around the Catholic Church and the Antichrist who arises from it. Chick cites authorities to bolster his eschatology, noting the "leaders of major Protestant denominations [who] *all* called the pope ANTICHRIST": Luther, Calvin, Wesley, Knox, and Cotton Mather. "The Blessed Hope"—including the Rapture—is God's promise to his Church (the true body of believers, not the false universal Church) with regard to the wicked and secular world.

Besides the close identification between pope and Antichrist, there is an additional wedge between Catholicism and conservative Protestantism that Rapture theology illuminates. This is Catholic amillennialism. Amillennialists, including most members of mainline Protestant denominations, reject what premillennialists take to be the literal reading of Revelation and read that book as symbolic instead. They deny the Rapture and locate the millennium in the present and past rather than in a future time to be preceded by a dreaded tribulation. For the church, the social hegemony of premillenial dispensationalism requires a rejoinder that stakes out the Catholic doctrine of Last Things. In this version of the end-times, the Antichrist is not a feared political dictator, and the Rapture does not catch believers up into the air.[63] Neither do believers await a seven-year tribulation that is the direct fruit of national deviations from God's will. There are many differences that bisect the beliefs and practices of different constituencies of the Christian right coalition. Differences are important to catalogue, but how about an irony? As Lutheran theologian Barbara R. Rossing demonstrates, there is no reasonable biblical support for the doctrine of the Rapture. Indeed, Rapture belief requires remarkably convoluted interpretations of key proof-texts, all of which assume the accuracy of the premillennial timetable.[64] Since Protestants expend much energy cataloguing the ways in which the Catholic Church develops doctrines that are not grounded in scriptural texts, the Rapture seems to be an excellent case of imitation, projection, or both.

Chick's eschatological tracts clarify two important points that educate their readers about the contemporary Christian right. The first is that the critiques of same-sex sexuality and Catholicism are not independent but connected through the conservative Christian interpretation of the last days. Second, these tracts gesture toward a goal other than the one that is most obvious in Chick's oeuvre. Chick tracts are witnessing tracts and thus are one means to the goal of saving individual souls, an end that remains important to the Christian right today. The soul-saving mandate is evident in the eschatological tracts; Chick begs sinners to give their lives to Christ before the onset of the tribulation signals that it may be too late. But it is also possible to read the end-times tracts as frenzied calls to avert the wrath of God by turning from sexual sins and corrupt faith. Ruth Murray Brown's pithy phrase "Saved People Can Save the Country" is nearly as appropriate as an account of Chick tracts as it is of the contemporary politics of the Christian right.[65] If premillennial eschatology is central to the politics, including the antigay politics, of Christian conservatism, the rejection of this eschatology always threatens to disrupt the stability of the conservative Christian coalition.

Framing Chick

Mainstream Christian conservatives today are often abjured from indulging in public utterances that begin with the phrase "God hates." This proscription is consistent with the public narrative about same-sex sexuality that emphasizes

TC·
chick

democratic norms and standards of argument. In continuing to violate this proscription, Chick is a brother-in-arms of the Reverend Fred Phelps of Topeka,
Kansas's Westboro Baptist Church. As many Americans know, Phelps's motto
is "God hates fags"; indeed, he is so wedded to the phrase that it is the address
of his website: *http://www.godhatesfags.com*. The difference between Chick's
and Phelps's rendering of this sentiment is the object, which corresponds to the
distinction between status and conduct. This has been a key distinction in, for
example, debates over gays in the military. However, in distinguishing between
forms of political rhetoric, we should shift our attention from the variable objects of such sentences to the consistent subject and verb. There is a reason why
Christian conservative leaders now proscribe the phrase "God hates" in public
discourse regardless of its object. Such a phrase exposes both the religious roots
of political argument and the assumption that its proponents can speak for
God's attitudes with confidence. Of course, such beliefs are common bases of
religious discourse, but they are more unpredictable in their effects as bases for
political arguments in liberal democracies. Even so, Chick perseveres in disseminating God's messages, and the attention he gets from friend and foe alike
testify to his success in attracting an audience.

Christian conservatives resist the social, cultural, and political changes of
the last few decades, especially changes in mores and their implications, by tes-
tifying that God is the same yesterday, today, and tomorrow. Chick takes pride
in the unalterable convictions he conveys in his tracts, comic books, and other
Christian products. And he protects his creations through threats of legal action against trespassers. As timeless as his religious convictions are, however,
Chick is not unaware of the social and political changes of the New right period. In several tracts Chick notes that he has been accused of hate speech and
names his accusers: Catholics and queers. Chick first began to receive hate mail
and threats in the years after he published "The Gay Blade." However, he believes that he has made his most lasting and dangerous enemies among the
Catholics whose faith he excoriates. It is they who organized to execute the
bookstore boycott of the early 1980s that has gone down into Chick lore. And,
in keeping with Alberto Rivera's sordid accusations against the Church of
Rome, Chick suspects them of so much more. In his turn, Chick refuses the ecumenism that is key to strategic cooperation between the Catholic Church and
the Protestant Christian right.

"The Trial" is Chick's rejoinder to charges from gay and Catholic activists,
as well as other critics, that he engages in "hate speech." In this 1996 tract, the
Word of God is taken to court as hate literature, and a small girl is indicted for
pushing the literature to a friend in the schoolyard. In the course of the "trial," a
Catholic bishop, a Muslim, a rabbi, and a theology professor testify against the
Christian child, "Annie," and insist that the text of John 14:6 ("I am the way, the
truth, and the life: no man cometh unto the Father, but by me") be expunged

from the Bible. The victim's hysterical mother gives Chick the opportunity for a parody of his own, directed at those like lesbians and gay men who point out the emotional costs of being objects of hatred; "The emotional stress of this *hateful* attack has almost caused me to have a breakdown," she wails.

As ugly as it is, here is a rare example of deliberate tract humor. From another perspective, this focus on pain is widespread among theological liberals and conservatives on the issue of same-sex sexuality. Dawne Moon not only documents the variations of the theme of "gay pain" but also points out the costs of such a focus to lesbians and gay men.[66] This is not a concern that gay objects and consumers of Chick tracts need to have. The tracts don't really explore gay pain, which leaves the LGBT targets of Chick's opprobrium without the particular dilemma of being reduced to, and defined by, the unhappiness that flows from the reception of their sexuality by censorious heterosexuals.

Many Chick tracts have been revised over the years in which they have remained active Chick products. One example is Chick's de-coupling of the amorous men in "The Beast," but there are others. In his massively researched book, Robert Fowler documents these individual changes for collectors. These changes fall into a number of categories, five of which seem most useful for deciphering Chick's relationship to Christian right politics. First, there are revisions that take account of actual historical change.[67] A second category of revisions consists of those that add evidence for Chick's propositions or bring his claims up to date. The addition of AIDS to the final frames of "The Gay Blade" falls into this category, as do extensive changes to the antievolution tract, "Big Daddy?" Third, Chick sometimes alters tracts to remove anachronisms, although most Chicklets would no doubt agree that some of the unintentional humor of the tracts is associated with anachronistic elements that are not expunged. Clothing, hairstyles, cultural touchstones, and language all fall into this category of graphic elements that do not age well.

Contradicting assumptions about Chick's resolute fidelity to the most extreme expression of his beliefs, he has sometimes changed the text and images of tracts to soften them for anxious readers. This he has done with tracts such as "Somebody Loves Me" (1969), "The Visitors" (1984), "The Poor Little Witch" (1987), and "The Royal Affair" (1990), among others. These revisions constitute the strategic softening of a message to abet its reception. Although they are not tantamount to the multiple modes of address practiced by other Christian right opinion leaders, their existence alerts us to the strategic component of Chick's enterprise.

Finally, Chick has reached out to African American Christians in a way that's consistent with the outreach of the broader Christian right movement. For example, "This Was Your Life!" has now been "adapted for black audiences" and renamed "It's Your Life" (2006). The "black" version of the popular standard doesn't just substitute black characters for white ones; instead, Chick's original gag cartoon tract is completely redrawn by Fred Carter with illustrations that suggest African culture. In fact, the African American "It's Your Life" merely substitutes English for the Zulu version of "This Was Your Life!" and the subsequent African-language versions of the tract that followed. Cultural infelicities occur in Chick's attempts at Christian conservative multiculturalism. One is that the black child in the tract's flashback is seen naked and beating a drum, a slight change from the naked child beating a section of tree trunk with sticks in the African versions (the white child in the original version wears pajamas and plays with dolls). Nevertheless, one significant difference between Chick and the conservative Christian movement in which his ideas are embedded is that Chick does not have a history of deliberate racist discrimination and exclusions to overcome in order to make common cause with African American Christian conservatives.

Chick's theological message has not changed over the decades. Even so, he is willing to change and compromise in small ways in order to produce Christian conservative ideology and to close the deal with receptive sinners. Chicklets and occasional critics alike might conclude from the outré nature of Chick's tracts that he is not interested in grounding his ideology in any evidence but, instead, grounds it in biblical literalism. But this would be a misunderstanding of the tracts in important respects. In fact, in however unorthodox a fashion, Chick looks outside scripture to compose his Christian narratives. And here is an exception to the general rule that Chick tracts do not adhere to Christian right standards of public address. In the area of Chick's resort to objective standards of authority, his work prefigures and reinforces the modes of address of the Christian right.

Although it would surprise readers who see the tracts as mere expressions of religious dogma, Chick is interested in nonbiblical authority in his texts. It is not only the "facts" of the Bible that are summoned to lend authority to bias but also the other side of Christian right discourse, the "use of statistics and the language of the social sciences."[68] It is typical for critics of the Christian right to cite Christian conservative indifference or hostility to science as a foundation for their own considered opposition to that movement. Just to be clear: the agnostic and liberal Christian charge that Christian conservatives ignore scientific theories, methods, and standards isn't false; but it is incomplete. In fact it is important for critics of the Christian right to understand that Christian conservatives, like members of many other social movements, are not hostile to science per se. Instead, they want to control how science is defined, funded, performed, taught, and reported, as well as how science informs public policy.

Even Chick, propagandist and provocateur of the simple comic-book medium, relies upon a relation to science. Chick's reliance on science and its mantle of legitimacy is most evident in his tracts on creationism. How important is scientific legitimacy to Chick's antievolution project? It is significant that in "Big Daddy?" Chick does not fight science with scripture but, instead, fights science with "better" science. One impulse that animates the move from creationism to Intelligent Design is the desire to make better—more persuasive, as well as more politically sophisticated—science.[69] The movement's success relies on two pillars: supportive members of the political establishment, including state and federal legislators and other influential actors; and a redesign of the public script. Central to rescripting is a willingness of the Intelligent Design movement, and the larger Christian right movement to which it belongs, to sacrifice openly religious language and justification. But the rescripting also incorporates terms and concepts identified with American liberal democracy, including pluralism, free speech, and the rights of individuals to hold diverse beliefs. Those who would restrict students to one account of the origins of life on earth—evolution—or who protest the democratic rewriting of science standards are bullies, the new totalitarian antidemocrats.

Of all the Chick tracts that critics cite for their group-based bigotry, those that deal with issues of same-sex sexuality best exemplify the orientation of the contemporary Christian right toward science. The anti-Catholic tracts trade in conspiracy theories, doctrinal deconstruction, and historical and scriptural interpretations. The difference between the anti-Catholic and antigay tracts is that the antigay tracts invoke more of the authority of science to ground their repudiation of same-sex sexuality. This difference should not surprise us. Scientific speculations regarding a "gay gene," same-sex animal sexual behavior and differences between gay and straight brains, fingers, and earlobes have become part of everyday discourse about sexuality in recent years.

Let's return to the tracts themselves for examples of Chick's interest in antigay science. In "The Gay Blade," archeologists discover carvings that depict religious practices in "Canaanite ruins" that, it is implied, show some kind of homosexual activity. The archeologists' reactions to this discovery—one covers his mouth and expostulates, "*I'm going to vomit!*" while the other covers his eyes and says, "*Good Lord,* I can't believe my eyes, we *can't* publish this. It's filthy!"— are ridiculed by Chicklets. How long would scientists this fragile be able to pursue their vocations? But humor about Chick's dainty scientists obscures their role as representatives of scientific authority. In addition to archeological evidence, Chick introduces demographic science to confirm the very corporeal effects of homosexual activity. Unfortunately, Chick relies upon the statistical work of the delegitimated psychologist Paul Cameron to instruct that AIDS lowers the life expectancy of gay men from 42 years to 39. The difference, according to Cameron, reflects the added effect of AIDS-related morbidity to the violence and venereal diseases that plague those who engage in homosexuality. Cameron's work has been debunked by social scientists, but it remains influential science for many Christian conservatives.[70]

In his antigay work, Chick employs a strategy like that of the larger Christian right movement. Far from eschewing science and belittling its conclusions, Chick lauds science, as long as science undergirds the moral and social regime of

Christian conservatism. When it does not, so much the worse for science, which is after all the domain of godlessness and an undemocratic will to power. In this schizoid view, Chick is like the prophesy popularizers of the twentieth century, "jeering at the learned while simultaneously invoking the prestige and name recognition of secular experts."[71] As we shall see in chapter 3, Dr. Joseph Nicolosi could not have better comrades for his own antigay science than today's partisans of Intelligent Design. And Chick helped lay the foundations for their success.

Standing in the Gap

Christian conservatives are often exhorted to "stand in the gap" between God's will and requirements and particular unbelievers or a recalcitrant world.[72] Sometimes this means praying for those who err or for God's will to be done. At other times, it can mean acting in the way that God demands and trusting him to bring about an effect, changing minds, hearts, and lives or turning away a feared outcome. Conservative Christians stand in the gap when they evangelize and bring the "good news" of the Gospel to those who have not yet accepted Jesus as their savior.

For over four decades, millions of believers around the world have evangelized with Chick tracts. In the beginning, the tracts were the product of a social movement that was marginal to mainstream political institutions and leaders. They were born in the 1960s, a time when rock-ribbed social conservatives who shared Chick's beliefs were vying for power but still regarded as outsiders to a liberal political consensus. By the 1980s, with a coalition of social and economic conservatives in ascendance, Chick was already perceived as a partial liability. There was no question that his positions on salvation, eschatology, and human behavior and relations were extremely popular among conservative Christians. However, Christian right opinion leaders understood that, in his tracts and other publications, Chick telegraphed too much information—in far too coarse a fashion—to the readers for whom his tracts were intended. Ever since the Reagan years, Chick has doggedly continued his mission to evangelize to the world's unsaved regardless of his standing with the institutional Christian right.

The result is that throughout the 1990s and today, Chick can be disclaimed by the Christian right while he continues to represent the social and political positions of the movement. And he can continue to be enormously popular with the grass roots. This grassroots popularity appears to be a liability for the Christian right, seeding and revealing positions on controversial issues that are better kept among the in-group. It may be, however, that this liability is balanced by a proportional asset. On the negative side of the ledger, it is difficult for elites to manage grassroots followers with message discipline that is appropriate to collective goals. On this side, Chick's propensity to talk out of turn is an irritant to a sophisticated national political movement and may always threaten to undermine the pluralistic democratic rhetoric that attracts those beyond the activist core. On the positive side of the ledger, Chick stokes the ideological fires in ways that are essential for keeping grassroots movement activists attentive and active. Respected or reviled, he stands in the gap between the Christian right and those the movement hopes to either convert or control.

Of the many projects of the Christian right, the ex-gay movement also counsels believers to stand in the gap for the lost, in this case, those struggling to rid themselves of their sinful same-sex desires and impulses. There are many similarities, as well as differences, between the political pedagogy of Chick tracts and that of the ex-gay movement (and the particular manifestation of that movement which is Love Won Out). Chick tracts and Love Won Out are alike in disseminating a political message of queer abomination; however, while Chick broadcasts this message to all, Love Won Out targets the message to conservative Christians. Unlike Chick tracts, Love Won Out skillfully combines a therapeutic message— one that encourages the treatment of gender-nonconforming children and sexually deviant adults—with its political instruction. After the antigay rhetoric of Chick tracts and other Christian right media has done its work, consumers of Love Won Out are prepared for its depictions of struggling young gender-confused prehomosexuals, sordid and miserable gay lives, and a defiant and demonic gay movement bent on destroying Christian America. Still, the careful nichemarketing of antigay political rhetorics puts less of the abomination rhetoric on display today than in an earlier period of Christian right politics. After Chick blazed a rhetorical trail, it's no wonder that the public rhetoric of today's Christian right seems almost to turn the other cheek.

CHAPTER 3

Origin Stories
(with Jyl J. Josephson)

There hath no temptation taken you but such as is common to man: but God is faithful, who will not suffer you to be tempted above that ye are able; but will with the temptation also make a way to escape, that ye may be able to bear it.

—1 Corinthians 10:13

And have no fellowship with the unfruitful works of darkness, but rather reprove them. For it is a shame even to speak of those things which are done of them in secret.

—Ephesians 5:11–12

Becoming Queer

In the typical coming-out narrative, it is not how the story goes. In the beginning, I did not decide, realize, or announce my homosexuality. Instead, when I was 15 years old I determined—based on all the available data—that I was not heterosexual. By then, I had consumed all the books on adolescent development I could lay my hands on. Because I was not attracted to men, I was particularly curious about the possibilities for asexual development, but the few books in the intellectual marketplace at the time did not sustain this possibility. As it turned out, I maintained my negative reading of the evidence of my sexuality for two years until, with a little help from a senior class athlete, I turned the evidence on its head and read it the other way. Ah! Not heterosexual equals homosexual. It was as simple as that.

It would make a better story if I could say now that, having come out as a lesbian, I worried about the etiology of that developmental outcome. But in spite of my nascent interest in psychology, I didn't. It wasn't a *choice* in the sense that many conservative Christians have regarded it; in other words, I hadn't—in the sardonic words of one lesbian I knew in my undergraduate days—rolled out of bed one morning and announced that I was tired of God and goodness and was now going to be *gay*! But I also perceived quite early that trying to find some awful event on which to pin my queer desire was a risky business. I did not have a disease, contracted in some moment of trauma or frustration. I was not entertaining an imp of the perverse. I simply was.

Fortunately, my mother helped solidify my resistance to ferreting out the cause of my sexuality. Wielding a convenient Christian perspective on my sexuality, she pronounced my sexuality a choice and refused any responsibility in its genesis. This position disappointed me; of the young queers I knew, many had parents who responded to the first news of their deviant sexuality with guilt. This reaction had the virtue of providing a buffer between the queer child and the crushed—and often furious—parent. It's not that most of us wanted our parents to feel guilty; we didn't think there was anything wrong to feel guilty about. We just wanted them to calm down and begin to come to terms with it. A little worry about their own complicity often facilitated that process.

For myself, unwilling either to trace my desire to developmental trauma or to concede that my sexuality was elective, I held my ground and asserted my lesbian identity. My mother warned me that as long as I made such choices, God would never leave me alone. And in a way, she was right. It's been thirty years since my mother prophesied that God would never stop campaigning to change my sexuality and—if the indefatigable activity of his servants is any indication—he's still trying. Sadly, as I predicted even then, my mother remains today as immovable as she ever was. Like the ex-gays in the glossy ads, my mother stands for the truth that homosexuals can change.

Saving Homosexuals . . . and America

Jean Hardisty calls the ex-gay movement "the right's kinder and gentler anti-gay campaign."[1] This characterization captures important dimensions of a movement that is dedicated both to ending homosexuality—hence, "antigay"—and to dealing respectfully, indeed, compassionately with what it defines as the "struggle" against homosexual desire and temptation. As we shall see, "compassion" is a key term of this campaign, and while it is easy for many observers to discount this emphasis as a clever political ploy, we should take it more seriously than that.

The stated goal of the ex-gay movement is encouraging and supporting people with a same-sex sexual orientation in an abiding reorientation to heterosexual desire and sexual functioning. The movement began as a reaction to the 1973 decision of the American Psychiatric Association to reclassify homosexuality from a mental disorder to a sexual orientation. With this revision of the Diagnostic and <u>Statistical Manual of Mental Disorders</u> (DSM), homosexuality merited a category only to account for individuals who experienced conflict with their sexuality.[2] The revision of the DSM was preceded by the declining verisimilitude of antihomosexual psychoanalysis and a lobbying campaign by queers and their allies. It coincided broadly with the rise of the contemporary LGBT movement. As a result of these currents, ex-gay proponents uniformly represent the decision as politicized cultural decline rather than as a professional decision driven by intellectual and ethical considerations.

The first ministry aimed at queers who wanted to change their sexual orientation was founded in the San Francisco Bay area in 1973. The founding coincided with the counterculture Jesus movement that began in the same place in the late 1960s. From this modest beginning, the ex-gay movement has diversified to a network of publishing enterprises, tailored therapies, residential facilities, support groups, and activities such as conferences that deliver support and information for same-sex attracted people, their families, and members of the community.[3] The movement's infrastructure is composed of overlapping groups of allies: mental health professionals who disapprove of the APA decision, Christian activists, and "strugglers"/ex-gays. These groups have created a network of organizations and therapies, of which the National Association for Research and Therapy of Homosexuality (NARTH) and Exodus International (EI) are prominent.

In turn, the movement has called into existence its opposition; exposés of the ex-gay phenomenon by gay civil rights organizations like the Human Rights Campaign (HRC) and the National Gay and Lesbian Task Force (NGLTF) and support groups and therapies for ex-ex-gays. These "ex-ex's" are veterans of some facet of the Christian ex-gay movement who now embrace a gay, lesbian, bisexual, or queer identity.[4] The testimonies of ex-ex-gays are rarely amusing. However, as an apocryphal "news" article from *The Onion* demonstrates, the spectacle of unhappy individuals laboring to reorganize their sexual desires is irresistible to the humor industry. Here, Dennis and Diane stand in for the sexual struggles of ex-gays everywhere:

> "While it is true that Dennis and Diane may still harbor homosexual desires deep within their hearts, this is all right, because God forgives them for it," said [Reverend] Spottiswood, who had numerous homosexual encounters during his teenage years but has never allowed himself to consciously acknowledge them. . . . The important thing to remember is that this is not about what Dennis and Diane want. It is about what God wants for Dennis and Diane.[5]

The tools of the ex-gay movement are conservative Christian religious doctrine, ex-gay groups, and long-term "reparative therapies" intended to suppress homosexual behavior even if full heterosexual functioning cannot be achieved. The APA and other associations of mental health professionals oppose the therapies employed by the ex-gay movement, noting that "potential risks" of reparative therapies include "depression, anxiety and self-destructive behavior, since therapist alignment with societal prejudices against homosexuality may reinforce self-hatred already experienced by the patient."[6] On the other side are therapists and mental health professionals who use a democratic political narrative to support the right of patients to choose ex-gay therapies. They rebuke mainstream mental health professionals by representing them as biased against the proven success of ex-gay therapy and as heedless of the suffering of those struggling with same-sex desire. It is worth noting that not all therapeutic interventions with same-sex attracted people are framed in voluntaristic democratic terms. When Pastor Ted Haggard's involvement with a male prostitute was exposed in late 2006, he was sent into therapy by a group of conversative Christian leaders. However, Haggard's case was unusual because of his eminence in the Christian right movement.

For ordinary Christians afflicted with same-sex desire there is Love Won Out. On September 18, 2004, Jyl Josephson and I attended a Focus on the Family-sponsored ex-gay conference and reported our experience and conclusions in an NGLTF policy brief.[7] FOF's ex-gay ministry is not representative of the ex-gay movement as a whole, but it does provide a window into the movement's integration with the broader politics of the Christian right.[8] Not only this, the attempt of FOF to blend an ongoing therapeutic discourse about same-sex sexuality with cutting-edge antigay politics exposes discontinuous narratives within the antigay Christian right. Finally, Love Won Out (LWO) is a public event whose function is educational. Even so, with its Christian prayers, born-again testimonies, and theological literature, the conference is heavily oriented toward conservative Christian insiders rather than outsiders. For this reason, it provides a look at the services and instruction Christian right organizations provide to believers about same-sex sexuality.

My interest in Love Won Out is both personal and intellectual. Although I have never participated in an ex-gay therapy, I have often been encouraged to trust Jesus to remove my romantic and sexual interest in other women. Thus, the discourse of the event held fewer mysteries for me than it might for the truly uninitiated. Fortunately, there were still some surprises. Jyl is a PFLAG mom who is active in safe schools work and in LGBT activism generally. We've been friends for many years, and although we aroused the curiosity of one young ex-lesbian volunteer, we managed to keep our noses clean and to avoid being ejected from the event.

FOF holds LWO conferences four times a year in different cities across the country. The conference we attended was held in Minneapolis. Minnesota is an interesting location for a LWO conference because of its political history as a state that historically has been fiscally conservative but socially liberal. This was the second such conference held in Minnesota; according to conference organizers, the first attracted some disapproval and the host church received "threatening" phone calls. Both events were held at North Heights Lutheran Church, a very large suburban church once affiliated with the Evangelical Lutheran Church in America (ELCA) but now affiliated with the more conservative Missouri Synod. As a result of the movement among some churches and members in the ELCA for greater inclusion of LGBT people, a conservative movement has arisen in the church, and Minnesota has been one center of that movement.[9]

Minnesota Republican State Senator Michele Bachmann—now a member of the U.S. House of Representatives (R-MN)—opened the conference with a greeting and blessing, underscoring the alliance of the Republican Party with antigay Christian right projects. Among the other participants were volunteers, staffers of a book exhibit, representatives of chapters of national ex-gay organizations and affiliated local groups, and purveyors of ex-gay therapeutic services. The conference was organized with alternating plenary and small breakout sessions for the several hundred attendees. It relied upon the expertise of a number of featured speakers, including five who identified themselves as ex-gay or ex-lesbian: Mike Haley, Melissa Fryrear, Joe Dallas, Jane Boyer, and Alan Chambers. Two other featured speakers, Joseph Nicolosi and Dick Carpenter II, did not so identify. All of these featured experts are or have been employed by FOF or an ex-gay organization, and most have written books on the subject of their recovery from same-sex sexuality. The personal testimony of ex-gays, delivered in a variety of settings, is a lynchpin of the ex-gay movement. They testify to FOF founder James Dobson's claim that "prevention [of homosexuality] is effective. Change is possible. Hope is available."[10]

The optimism of the setting does not, however, remove the necessity to prevent deviations, disruptions, and disagreements. LWO conferences are constructed to obviate any kind of dissent from attendees or outsiders. The plan of the conference itself discourages disruption. Unlike many similar events, which provide opportunities for questions during large group sessions, at LWO audience participation is limited to small group breakout sessions. There, any conflict that emerges can be more easily contained than it would be in full sessions.

More significant than the structure of the conference is the code of conduct, provided to enrollees in preconference materials. The code of conduct warns that not only disruption but also the dissemination of alternative viewpoints and distribution of non-FOF literature are grounds for dismissal from the conference. The conferences are held on private property so that inconvenient protesters or disruptors can be ejected. At the Minnesota conference a few isolated protesters stood and interjected criticisms of the proceedings during plenary sessions, and they were quickly removed by security officers while the presenter led the group in prayer. During the lunch break, a handful of young silent protesters walked through the church courtyard bearing signs with slogans such as "Focus on Someone Else." This silent protest prompted a heated discussion between one conference organizer and a uniformed officer; the organizer demanded that the protesters be arrested, while the officer patiently explained that those who left the property after a warning could not be taken into custody. When this group was ejected, two female members staged a brief impromptu kiss-in in front of the church doors. Passing conferees studiously ignored the pair.[11]

In fact, it is useful to call attention to the designation "conference" for LWO. In my experience as an academic, a conference is an event that invites and presupposes constructive intellectual conflicts rather than proscribing them. From the perspective of intellectual—indeed, ideological—give and take, it is useful to ask what LWO is and how it is related to the preexisting movement with which it is aligned.

Although the ex-gay movement is nearly thirty years old, LWO is a late-arriving brand in the movement. It was only in the late 1990s that activists introduced the movement to the American public through mainstream media. This introduction began in 1998 when well over a dozen Christian right organizations, including the Center for Reclaiming America, the Christian Coalition, the Family Research Council, and Focus on the Family, purchased a series of full-page ads in the *Washington Post* (July 14, 1998), *New York Times* (July 15), *USA Today* (July 15), and *Washington Times* (July 15). Entitled "Truth in Love," the ads in the first three mainstream venues claimed success for reparative therapies in converting homosexuals into heterosexuals and carried a message of religious redemption. They also illustrate an important distinction between this public face of the ex-gay movement and even the closely related LWO initiative. While the message of "Truth in Love" is directed to adults, LWO, and the development literature upon which it relies, understands same-sex attracted teenagers and their families as an important audience and target population.

On the other hand, the "Reggie White/In Defense of Free Speech" ad published in the conservative *Washington Times* took an aggressive rhetorical stance. The ad accuses "the activist homosexual lobby" of using "its free speech privilege to promote its own ideas":

> believing they've captured the culture's ear, they [activist homosexuals] have become a jealous lover . . . demanding the culture hear no other view but theirs. . . . [A]ll Americans should shudder when homosexual activists routinely use the tactics of threats, intimidation, blackmail and deception to strangle a free and open exchange on homosexual behavior.[12]

Unlike other ads in the series, the *Washington Times* ad explicitly embraces a political narrative of choice/abomination and is aimed at an audience that is assumed to be religious, conservative, and antigay. Notably absent in the "Reggie White" ad is the therapeutic discourse familiar both to readers of the mainstream "Truth in Love" ads and to participants in LWO. Besides appearing in newspapers, the "Truth in Love" ads continued on television in 1998 and 1999. Ads aired in the Washington, DC, market in an attempt to influence policymakers on lesbian and gay political issues.[13]

In most ex-gay discourse the emphasis is on sexual desire and behavior, rather than on love or orientation. In conservative venues, newspaper ads excoriate "homosexual behavior," "self-destructive behavior," and "yielding to temptation."[14] Accordingly, success is counted as persuading lesbians and gay men to change sexual behavior or to become celibate. But there is also a tacit goal associated with the ads and with the ex-gay movement as a whole, crafting a distinction between two categories of persons: those who experience same-sex sexual desire and those who live, either openly or in the closet, as gay, engaging in same-sex relationships. This distinction complicates the idea of "choice" that is central to the movement, though not always in the ways that critics believe. It is true that one primary objective of the ex-gay movement since the 1990s is to "reinforc[e] the 'No special rights' argument. If lesbians and gay men can change, their sexuality is not immutable. The ex-gay movement rebukes gay rights by asserting that gay sexuality is a choice. As such, the right argues, it is not a candidate for civil rights protections."[15]

Commentators extend different readings to the Christian right's "no special rights" agenda formulated in recent political battles in Oregon, Colorado, Hawaii, and Vermont. For many critics, conservative Christian "special rights" rhetoric is meretricious; it is strategic to its core, reflecting Christian right prejudice and political interests. "Special rights" rhetoric is undeniably politically strategic, deployed as it is in the context of specific debates over rights claims. However, Christian right hostility to homosexuality as unnatural and ungodly is also consistent with a range of other Christian right positions: on "the family," on gender roles, on leadership and authority, and even on the market economy and entrepreneurship.[16] It's counterproductive to conclude that antilesbian and antigay rhetoric is purely malign and strategic, that it expresses no authentic, and even complicating, theological convictions. This may even be true when practitioners of such rhetoric apologize, equivocate, elide, and counter-accuse when they are caught engaging in the more blatant forms of it before a broad, national audience.

Being of Two Minds

Equal rights for people with a same-sex sexual orientation remain fiercely contested in the United States. Indeed, the recent court decision in *Lawrence v. Texas*, far from settling the citizenship status of lesbians and gay men, has exacerbated political differences and propelled support for constitutional amendments to prohibit same-sex marriage. However, if we look beneath the surface of antigay social attitudes, we find different strains of antigay belief that have different effects on the framing of political issues and political activism. Two quite different artic-ulations of the origins of same-sex desire and identity circulate within the Chris-tian right. As different as these articulations are—and in some respects as inconsistent with one another—they forge crucial foundations for different kinds of organized antigay politics. To make matters even more complicated, an inter-nally contested compassion operates within antigay projects that rely on a narra-tive of development for their moral and political force.

Why do the origins of homosexuality matter to conservative Christians? The existence of people who self-identify as gay, lesbian, and bisexual consti-tutes a significant challenge to conservative Christian believers.[17] After all, if God made everyone naturally heterosexual, as ex-gay proponents believe he did, why did he make some people who seem only or primarily to experience same-sex sexual desire? Are some people "damned from birth, morally black-ened" as a result of their sexual desire?[18] Since the Bible is not helpful in offer-ing an explanation for the origins of homosexuality, conservative Christians must turn to other sources. Besides condemning homosexuality as immoral, a great deal is at stake for conservative Christian activists in producing a com-pelling story about the origins of homosexuality.

Why should members of the LGBT community care about these origin stories? We should care about these stories because in large measure popular politics arises from the stories we tell about the world we share in common. Stories about homosexuality are not only riveting tales, but they have a variety of political uses. However, it is a mistake to assume that the origin stories of Christian conservatives are purely utilitarian. Rather, the two principal origin stories are both founded in deeply held beliefs that have great emotional reso-nance for Christian activists. This is evident both in the conflict between those activists who adhere to narratives of choice and development and in the narra-tive of the ex-gay movement as one enactment of Christian compassion.

Those who criticize the Christian right for its support of a wide palette of antigay projects usually focus on one conservative Christian narrative of ho-mosexual origins: the narrative of choice. Arguing that same-sex sexuality is a "choice" subtends a range of political positions. In many contexts, it effectively neutralizes both queer claims of discrimination and public support for poten-tial legal remedies. For example, this narrative is particularly effective in white conservative Christian efforts to join forces with African American religious leaders in opposition to such gay rights issues as same-sex marriage.[19] On the other hand, critics of the Christian right often neglect a second narrative, a narrative of development. This is so even though one or another version of such a narrative has been in force throughout the formative period of the Christian right. What may account for the relative visibility of one kind of narrative to critics of the Christian right and the relative invisibility of the other is the nature of the political struggles in which major lesbian and gay civil rights organizations have engaged. Because the narrative of choice has been such a potent tool for the Christian right, both in mobilizing its own members and in persuading others to support its political positions, critics have rightly given it more attention.[20]

Even though some of its political functions are not immediately apparent, and even if it does not have a singular political provenance, the narrative of development also has political functions. Indeed, it circulates tacitly through a different set of public debates than those usually associated with the narrative of choice. Yet the fact that these narratives about homosexual identity serve political functions for Christian right organizing and issue negotiation does not mean that they are, as some critics suggest, merely expedient grounds for pre-existing biases or political formulations. Progressive critics of the right are more accurate when they describe the narrative of choice as an expedient political strategy than they are when they collapse these different narratives together and treat them as one. This said, even narratives that are largely or exclusively created as political strategy may simultaneously reflect genuine—even if new and evolving—affective and theological commitments at the same time that they underwrite minoritizing and discriminatory forms of politics. Political advocates tend to position their opponents as cunning and meretricious, not as earnest and well meaning, and this debate is no different. However, even if both sides of the pro-gay/ex-gay debate honestly understand their opponents as evil on their own understanding of that concept, we should look more closely at the complexities that exist within our adversaries' positions.

Choice Point

Most critics of the Christian right's antigay politics recognize the political significance of its conception of homosexuals as those who exercise free will and engage in sexual acts with same-sex partners. This dominant narrative of choice with regard to sexuality is widely recognized as central to a variety of Christian right political initiatives in the 1990s. In the debate over Colorado's Amendment 2, the conservative group Colorado for Family Values (CFV) argued that "homosexuality is a willful behavioral choice, not an identity."[21] The political function of such a position is not far to seek: "If gay sexuality is a choice . . . it is not a candidate for civil rights protections."[22] In terms of public opinion, scholars also find that Americans are more likely to support gay civil rights when they believe that same-sex sexual orientation is immutable and, conversely, less likely to support civil rights when they believe that same-sex sexuality is a "lifestyle choice."[23] Therefore, we are not surprised to find that antigay political activists advocate a narrative of choice for same-sex sexuality and that lesbian and gay civil rights activists more often have been likely to endorse a narrative of immutability.[24]

The narrative of choice is a powerful weapon in the Christian right arsenal, one that serves to anchor and justify antigay political activism. This is so even at the cost of some internal contradictions in conservative Christian political discourse. One contradiction is between conservative Christian positions on sexuality and gender. As Didi Herman points out, it is not consistent for conservative Christian leaders to simultaneously insist on the essential nature of gender identity and roles and the voluntaristic nature of sexual identity.[25] A second contradiction is between Christian right positions on the origins of homosexuality itself, the narrative of development ("'psy' theories") versus the "preferred" narrative of choice.[26] However, these two lines of argument—although clearly inconsistent with one another—are more fruitfully seen as products of different, and sometimes conflicting, periods and projects in the trajectory of the Christian right.

This perspective is supported by Herman's observations about Christian right activists' own ambivalence about the usefulness of "anti-immutability arguments." Jyl and I noted this ambivalence at play even within the single LWO conference: some speakers bluntly stated that homosexuality is not a function of biology, but one pointedly qualified the claim by noting that even if biological roots of same-sex orientation are someday discovered, it doesn't matter: homosexuality remains a violation of God's will for his people.[27] Herman traces how, starting in the 1990s, many cutting-edge rights pragmatists preferred to drop the emphasis on the origins of same-sex sexuality as unimportant and concentrate on gay wealth and power to nullify lesbian and gay rights claims.[28] This pragmatic perspective can be very useful, as it has been during recent campaigns against same-sex marriage. However, neither anti-immutability arguments nor other narratives explaining the origin of same-sex sexuality have been jettisoned from Christian right discourse. Either activists in certain sectors of conservative Christian politics have not received the message that the emphasis on the origins of same-sex sexuality is now counterproductive, or such an emphasis continues to be useful for some kinds of political projects.

The Narrative of Development

The narrative of development appears in a variety of venues, from literature on reparative therapies and counseling of repentant homosexuals to literature on Christian parenting and childhood. Accounts of the development of homosexuality do not vary significantly from one context to the next however much the focus—on adults in the case of reparative and ex-gay therapies and on children (and their parents) in the case of family counseling—gives the arguments

a somewhat different tone. In both contexts where the narrative of development occurs the emphasis is on the continuity and force of same-sex desire over
time in certain individuals.

Most authors of the development literature disarticulate same-sex desire
from gay identity. They thus fix identity at either the point of behavioral capit-
ulation to desire or at the point of willful entry into a "homosexual lifestyle."
One blunt articulation of this distinction comes from "Love in Action": "There
is no such creation as a 'gay' or 'homosexual' person. There is only homosexual
attraction and behavior; accordingly, there can be no change from a sexual identity that never existed in the first place."[29] The word choice here is significant;
the fact that there is "no such *creation* as a gay or homosexual person" emphasizes that God made no such persons or, if you will, that God made persons in
no such way. The lie that gay identity constitutes a particular kind of being and
orientation toward love and sexuality is the "homosexual myth."

This conception of identity is found in the work of many Christian right
clergy, activists, and academics. Mark Yarhouse is a psychologist who makes a
systematic theoretical and empirical set of arguments about sexual identity
using diverse psychological, Christian, and gay/lesbian/queer literatures.
Yarhouse may not be widely read among Christian conservatives. His work is
certainly more careful and sophisticated—and hence less representative of the
genre—than most ex-gay literature. Nevertheless, his work can inform critics of
the ex-gay movement about its most rigorous manifestations. Like other
thinkers with antigay commitments, Yarhouse follows his "LGB-disidentified"
ex-gay subjects, including active strugglers, in reporting their sexual identity as
"heterosexual."[30] However differently they might express it, those who embrace, theorize, or advocate a narrative of development certify that heterosexuality is already the sexual orientation of all people and the way they were created
by God. Thus, (to name only some possible positions) those who exclusively
experience opposite-sex desire, those who actively struggle against same-sex
desire, and even those who exclusively experience same-sex desire are, either
by nature, moral fiat, or aspiration, heterosexual.

The narrative of development of conservative Christian ministers and lay
authors is not a new phenomenon. Its major themes were well developed in
mid-century psychoanalytic works. In the 1970s and 1980s antigay psychotherapeutic literature was absorbed into a literature that mixed Christian moraliz-
ing and political attunement with developmental psychological theory. By the
1990s, such works almost uniformly offered critiques of scientific studies on the
biological origins and immutability of same-sex sexuality. These are intended to
counter the popular understandings of provocative scientific research on biological, especially genetic, roots of same-sex orientation. The repudiation of immutability in Christian right developmental works is indistinguishable from the

more popular versions circulated in the Christian right political activism of the last fifteen years, and it serves one shared purpose: to undermine credibility and public support for the queer rights movement.

In addition, however, the developmental literature has other purposes. These include responding to the fears of Christian families about child rearing, affirming the possibility that swift intervention can interrupt pernicious developmental processes, protecting (or rescuing) young people from homosexuality, and teaching children and adolescents a conservative biblical account of sexuality.

It would be impossible at this point to document exhaustively the developmental arguments of conservative Christian writers over the last thirty years, but it is useful to examine the most salient dimensions of the narrative and to introduce some prominent examples of the literature. Three arguments predictably are present in these Christian developmental accounts of homosexual identity. First is the claim that homosexuality is forged to some degree in emotional responses to poor or damaged relations between adult(s), and especially parent(s), and child. In the conservative Christian literature on the development of same-sex desire, there are many variations on this theme. Two of these variations are absent same-sex parents and trauma—sexual or otherwise—to the child. However, the more usual psychological narrative of homosexual development implicates what readers might otherwise understand as good-enough parenting. Here, the variations are nuanced, and perhaps more frightening for their prosaic quality: failures to mirror or model appropriate masculinity or femininity, a lack of appropriate attention to a child's emerging gender nonnormativity. Otherwise good-enough parents may be doubly to blame, both for setting in motion the psychological development that culminates in adolescent same-sex desire and for failing to arrest that development through proper interventions.

The second dimension of the narrative of development is the principle that, although the onset of same-sex desire does not sentence individuals to a life of homosexuality, predispositions and homosexual desires are not easily reversed once they are formed. Here, proponents of the development narrative indirectly allude to the development and consolidation of "identity."

Third is the claim that damaged proto- or "prehomosexuals" can nonetheless decide not to engage in same-sex sexual behavior and to further entrench their dysfunctional sexual identities. The rubric of addiction that circulates in many of these developmental texts is apropos of this point. For those who embrace the developmental origins of homosexuality, sexual repetition alone does not *cause* same-sex sexuality. Instead, repetition entrenches desire and identity, the sense of oneself as lesbian or gay. One surprising piece of information we learned by attending LWO is related to this theme of addictively creating *identity* out of desire. For Christian conservatives on the front line of the ex-gay movement, those who do embrace their same-sex attraction and name themselves as "gay" become, ceteris paribus, "gay activists." My confusion about the use of this common term at LWO stems from my own understanding of what constitutes "activism," some deliberate intervention aimed at influencing political beliefs and/or realities. By this definition, many queer people, like many of our fellow citizens, are quite apolitical. Some may not vote, contribute resources, or work for any political cause or organization. They may simply wish to be left alone by all political causes and interests.

However, by the definition of Christian conservatives in the ex-gay movement, anyone who claims a gay identity is already a *gay activist*. It is in this sense that the ex-gays who spoke at LWO in Minnesota spoke of having been gay activists. They had gone to gay clubs, attended gay pride events, and generally considered themselves to be gay people. It is a low bar for activism, but such a standard has two effects. First, it reinforces the threat of gay activism for worried Christian conservatives (they're not just *gay*, they're gay *activists*). And second, it reinforces the often-neglected idea, rightfully identified with feminism, that simply being gay in an antigay society is, indeed, a form of action with political significance.

There is a connection between the choice to engage in same-sex sexual behavior and any developmental story about same-sex sexuality. At some point in the trajectory of desire, many people who are attracted to those of their own sex do choose to act on that desire. However, although the choice to have a sexual and/or romantic relationship with a same-sex partner clearly enters into the developmental paradigm at some point after the formation of desire, the two narratives of choice and development still must be distinguished from one another. In spite of some overlap and similarities, these two narratives arise within different contexts, are frequently championed by different political actors, and are used for different purposes.

What Went Wrong?

Tim LaHaye is best known today as the first author of the enormously popular *Left Behind* series of novels. But he also penned one early example of the developmental genre, *The Unhappy Gays: What Everyone Should Know about Homosexuality*, published in 1978. In this book, the conservative Christian author and entrepreneur argues that to understand "people who are sexually attracted to those of their own sex, we must look beyond their biological and chemical composition to an even more complex area, their psychological makeup."[31] For LaHaye, one dominant cause of same-sex sexual desire is a psychological "predisposition to homosexuality," which includes "ingredients" such as "temperament" (most homosexuals are melancholics!), "inadequate parental relationships," and "insecurity about sexual identity."[32] LaHaye is forceful about his perception—formed, he says, in interactions with numerous homosexuals—

that a predisposition to homosexuality does not guarantee adult homosexual experience or self-identification. Predisposition "is not homosexuality *per se*," but "it may lead a person into homosexuality," and it certainly defines the nature of an individual's sexual desire even if it is not acted upon.[33]

In 1979, Frank M. du Mas followed LaHaye's *Unhappy Gays* with *Gay Is Not Good*, a general exposé of homosexuality and gay life. Du Mas's is a social-scientific approach to "children who are beginning to show signs or trends of future homosexual development." He warns that parents should be concerned if symptoms of homosexuality (presented in appendices to the book) persist over a long period or increase in "frequency and intensity."[34] Du Mas intends his checklist appendices—E for males, F for females, and G for use with both males and females—to be used and scored by clinical professionals with adult patients. However, many of the checklist items are framed as questions asked of children rather than questions about a distant childhood, a framing that strongly suggests a disclaimed agenda for therapy with children. Items for males include: "particularly fearful of playing baseball, especially the 'fast ball'" and "has had an extreme and long-standing crush on a playmate, teacher, or adult of the same sex." Items for females include: "is tomboyish coupled with a strong desire to *be* a boy" and "does not wear attractive girlish clothes."[35] Both du Mas's phrasing and his use of the term "prehomosexual" to describe such children suggests that he believes that both parents of prehomosexual children and adults in therapy to treat their own sexuality will benefit from his model.

In the 1980s a slightly different approach to the conservative Christian psychology of homosexuality begins to appear. An example is *Counseling the Homosexual: A Compassionate and Biblical Guide for Pastors and Counselors as well as Non-Professionals and Families*. The central tenets of Michael Saia's compassionate approach are by now well known to many critics of the Christian right. They include reaching out to homosexuals in love, confronting the "revulsion" that many heterosexual people experience toward queers, telling them the truth about God's commandment against same-sex sexuality, and helping them to develop a personal relationship with Jesus Christ. In a chapter entitled "What Went Wrong?" Saia notes that gay men tell the "same old story" about their childhood and concludes that "the homosexual man has had some kind of relationship problem with this father."[36] Although Saia concedes that there is no "iron-clad explanation of the development of homosexual tendencies," he finds patterns that allow him to build a simple syndrome model of gay male development and an even simpler one of lesbian development. Like others, Saia takes "rejection by the father" and subsequent "rejection of the male image" as key pillars in the construction of gay male identity.[37] His much briefer account of "The Female Homosexual" posits trauma, particularly sexual or other physical abuse, as a key cause of lesbian orientation.[38]

By the late 1980s to early 1990s, it is common for authors in the genre to respond to the possibility that homosexual orientation is innate and immutable. Saia briefly addresses and rejects this argument, as do Marlin Maddoux and Christopher Corbett in *Answers to the Gay Deception*. Like their predecessors, Maddoux and Corbett conclude that "homosexuality is the *sexualization of deep emotional needs which develop in childhood*."[39] It is only after development has done its work that the "decision to act upon the desire is in their hands."[40] In contrast, in his medicalized account of the origin of homosexuality, Jeffrey Satinover suggests that genes, environment (intrauterine and social), and choice all play a role. Nevertheless, in *Homosexuality and the Politics of Truth*, Satinover follows other authors in the development genre to make psychological disposition a precursor to the choice to engage in same-sex sexual behavior. Markers of male homosexuality are "sensitivity," a distant father, "defensive detachment" in the boy, and a longing for love.[41] At the time of publication, Satinover was a medical advisor for FOF, and the book is endorsed by conservatives of many faith traditions.

If many conservative Christians who write on the origins of homosexuality are unfamiliar even to informed readers, James Dobson is a familiar and influential Christian right leader. In his bestselling book *Bringing Up Boys*, Dobson subscribes to a developmental account of homosexuality, many features of which are familiar from earlier works. For Dobson, adult male homosexuality is prefigured by "a condition we might call 'prehomosexuality.'"[42] The "disorder is not typically 'chosen'," but this does not mean that it is "inherited" (although a "biological predisposition" may exist). Citing both John Paulk's "momentary setback" in Mr. P's in 2000 and Robert Spitzer's controversial recent research on the consequences of reparative therapy, Dobson builds a case for overcoming homosexuality.[43] Throughout, Dobson strives for a respectful tone that blends psychological developmental facts with empathy for those afflicted with same-sex desires. To parents he offers direct advice:

> If you as a parent have an effeminate boy or a masculinized girl, I urge you to get a copy [of Joseph and Linda Ames Nicolosi's *A Parent's Guide to Preventing Homosexuality*] and then seek immediate professional help. Be very careful whom you consult, however. Getting the wrong advice at this stage could be most unfortunate, solidifying the tendencies that are developing. . . . [M]ost secular psychiatrists, psychologists, and counselors would, I believe, take the wrong approach—telling your child that he is homosexual and needs to accept that fact. You as parents would then be urged to consider the effeminate behavior to be healthy and normal. That is exactly what you and your son don't need![44]

As this passage suggests, Dobson relies extensively on Joseph Nicolosi's work on homosexuality. A longtime contributor to debates over same-sex sexuality, Joseph Nicolosi is, with his wife, author of *A Parent's Guide to Preventing Homosexuality*. The Nicolosis market the book as a scientific account of development. However, they sustain close intellectual and institutional ties to more familiar Christian right figures through NARTH and related activities. Dobson relies on Nicolosi for his own formulation of the developmental narrative, citing him at length in *Bringing Up Boys*. In turn, the Nicolosis offer a prefatory blurb by Dobson, with others by such antigay luminaries as Charles Socarides, John Paulk, and Lynn D. Wardle.

A Parent's Guide certainly reinforces the stigmatizing antigay perspective of the Christian right. But it does so by reinforcing compassion for children with damaged gender identities and for the parents whose sex- and gender-related hopes for their children are disappointed. Noting the smaller percentage of women than men who identify exclusively as lesbian, the Nicolosis concentrate more on the prevention of homosexuality in boys. They emphasize parental anxieties about gender nonconformity and the specter of adult homosexuality, including the details of communication between parents (mostly mothers) and Joseph Nicolosi.

It is interesting to note that *A Parent's Guide* is similar to many pieces of Christian right development literature in holding fathers, rather than mothers, responsible for the development of homosexuality. This emphasis deviates from the more familiar mother-blaming of much early psychoanalytic—including antihomosexual—literature on which Christian writers in the movement draw. It is not that Christian ex-gay literature ignores mothers and the unconscious forms of mothering that may precipitate especially male homosexuality. And as in much socially conservative literature on child development, women who parent children without men in the household are implicitly, if not explicitly, held responsible for poor outcomes associated with single-parent family arrangements.[45] However, most Christian literature on homosexual origins makes more of fathers' than mothers' influence on the adult sexuality of children. Indeed, early examples anticipate the discourse of Promise Keepers, the Christian men's organization, in charging men with the care and authority of the household. At the same time the Nicolosis note with sadness that even when parents are apprised of the parenting strategies necessary to intervene and prevent same-sex orientation in a child, it is the mother who often takes responsibility for performing them rather than the irreplaceable father.[46]

At the Minnesota LWO conference Joseph Nicolosi, a psychologist by training and practice, provided much of the psychological infrastructure for the event. It was he who communicated the key ideas that particular gender and family dynamics cause homosexual desire, that all people are heterosexual by nature, and that, contra the major psychological professional associations, homosexuality *is* an illness. These ideas did not originate with Nicolosi. After Freud's ambivalent theorizing of same-sex sexuality—progressive for his time—a number of psychoanalysts took up the issue in a decidedly negative way. Among those who established the key points of antigay psychodynamic theory that Nicolosi now disseminates were Sandor Rado and Irving Bieber, as well as Charles Socarides.

Jack Drescher trenchantly notes that as the gap between antigay, "reparative," psychological theory and the mainstream mental health profession has deepened, the organizations that represent antigay views embrace "religious organizational practices themselves, preaching dogma and stifling dissent."[47] The comparison between antigay psychology and fundamentalist faith is appropriate for more than one reason. Joseph Nicoloi is a conservative Catholic, and although in his writing he adopts a largely secular and professional demeanor, at LWO he spoke in an explicitly Christian register. He indicted his own profession as "basically taken over by gay activists" and defined the conceptual parameters of ex-gay discourse. While gay is a "social identity, homosexual is a psychological condition." "Gay activists"—that is, people who think of themselves as gay—hold on to the "androgynous fantasy" of infancy that it is not necessary to have, and thereby exclude, a single gender identity.[48] "Homosexual behavior" is an attempt to "repair childhood emotional hurts" by compensating for what is missing in the self. In particular, as Nicolosi details in cases from his therapeutic work, it is a man's way of embracing "idolatry" of masculinity in other men instead of enacting that masculinity himself. At least Nicolosi's theory of homosexuality is consistent and easy to grasp. This is not true even of all developmental origins literature.

A recent example of the genre, and one that deals specifically with lesbians, is Anne Paulk's *Restoring Sexual Identity: Hope for Women Who Struggle with Same-Sex Identity.* Paulk, who is active in the LWO ministry, bases her account of lesbian development on her personal contacts with ex-lesbians and lesbian strugglers and on a survey of same-sex attracted women she distributed through EI referral ministries in 2000. Leaving aside here the problems raised by Paulk's reliance on her survey of ex-lesbians and aspiring ex-lesbians, Paulk both follows and departs from the contemporary model of a Christian right narrative of development. She follows the model by offering a compassionate account of lesbian strugglers and by identifying herself when it is appropriate with these strugglers. She also challenges the scientific studies that, for some, provide support for the immutability of homosexual desire.[49] However, unlike many narratives of development, Paulk's contribution does not have the virtue of consistency. Instead of telling a consistent story about the developmental processes that are likely to culminate in lesbian desire, Paulk borrows liberally from a number of developmental and other scripts. So, for example, unavailable or narcissistic mothers and unavailable or (sexually) abusive fathers, seduction by girls or women, gender nonnormative behavior, and positive portrayals of same-sex sexuality in schools and the media are treated alike as possible causes of lesbian attraction.

However multidetermined the developmental trajectory that Paulk presents, central to her book is her personal and professional commitment to the well-being and flourishing of women who "struggle with same-sex attraction." Paulk and other writers in this genre are stern about the conservative Christian precepts concerning gender, marriage, family, and sexuality. But their attitude to those struggling with same-sex sexuality is neither harsh nor punitive. For those, like Paulk, who claim to have once identified as gay or lesbian, the sympathy and compassion for gender nonnormative young people and for adults who work to resist their own same-sex sexuality is palpable.[50]

Such developmental accounts may be flawed, theologically determined, and prejudicial. The compassion projected and aroused by the narrative of development may not extend to lesbians, gay men, bisexuals, and transgender people who refuse to resist their same-sex sexuality and gender nonnormativity. And the compassion generated within such a narrative may be deployed cynically against the interests of a wide range of sexual minorities. Nevertheless, it remains important for critics of the Christian right to understand the ways in which narratives of development and expressions of compassion can operate as political strategy, not be reducible to political strategy, and disrupt other forms of Christian right political work.

From Development to Compassion

Christian conservatives who work in the developmental genre urge compassion for the pain that same-sex sexuality inflicts. Compassion is a key concept and motivation of the ex-gay movement. Compassion follows from a developmental understanding of the origins of same-sex sexual desire. In this understanding, people do not choose same-sex attraction but are conditioned for it by failures (or perceptions of failure) in their early relationships. Because dysfunctional family dynamics and relations create same-sex attraction, those with same-sex attractions are not responsible for their desires but only for the ways in which they may act on them.

However, the emphasis on compassion creates a gulf between the ex-gay movement and other segments of the larger Christian right on gay issues. It also creates fault lines within the ex-gay movement itself. One fault is a distinction between how the movement treats and regards repentant "struggling" gays and teens and how it treats lesbian and gay adults who do not seek to change their sexual orientation. At a deeper level, a focus on the developmental model of same-sex sexuality reveals a striking aspect of ex-gay literature and teaching, an implicit distinction between its own conservative Christian audience and the outside realm of fallen culture and politics.

The ex-gay movement is oriented toward "strugglers," those who ask God to remove their same-sex feelings and desires to form romantic relationships with people of the same sex. Although it is certainly open to converts, there is a tacit, and sometimes explicit, understanding in the ex-gay movement that the movement primarily serves those reared in Christian families. Jeffry G. Ford addresses this aspect of the movement in his first-person account of his own decade in various reparative therapies and ex-gay groups. Among the many benefits of enrolling in these therapies, Ford highlights the love and support in ex-gay communities and the ability to attribute one's own sexual desires to satanic attacks that originate outside the self.[51] If the majority of consumers for ex-gay services are motivated by their own and family members' Christian beliefs, the compassion touted by the developmental model is primarily turned inward toward members of the Christian community. This means that the appropriate targets of compassion are not only same-sex attracted people who foreswear homosexual lives but also their families and congregations.

All ex-gay speakers at LWO spoke in their testimonies about their Christian families of origin and/or their childhood salvation experiences. Their testimonies focused on the misery and depravity of their gay lives and on the joy of reuniting with their biological families as ex-gays. Of course, this post-gay celebration of family life is difficult to reconcile with developmental psychologies. In the developmental model, family life creates the problem of same-sex attraction, and Christian families seem as likely as non-Christian families to generate that outcome. But even though same-sex desire emerges from the cauldron of family life, LWO teaches that it's important not to blame family members of same-sex attracted people for their condition. It is not only critical observers of LWO who note this dilemma; presenters address it directly, if not satisfactorily.

In addition to serving same-sex attracted individuals who hail from Christian families of origin that reject their sexuality, LWO also serves the family units themselves. Speakers cite the pain and sense of loss that parents and family members experience when they learn that a loved one is gay. Parents and family members are important consumers of ex-gay literature and a key constituency for LWO. Their anguish is recognized, as well as reinforced, by the advocacy of the ex-gay movement, which reminds them not only of their own loss but of the pain and degeneracy of life as a gay person. With regard to families, LWO engages in a careful narrative that always threatens to collapse under the weight of its own contradictions. On the one hand, parents are responsible for the condition of a gay child; on the other, it is important not to blame parents who, it is understood, love their children even as they reject their children's immoral sexuality. As one speaker noted, there is "no such thing as a perfect parent." At the LWO we attended, Melissa Fryrear tried to resolve this contradiction by suggesting the possibility of healing in families. She spoke of mothers and fathers going to a son or daughter to ask forgiveness for not giving the child what she or he needed in the developmental process. But it is difficult to maintain such a benevolent therapeutic perspective. In the same session, Fryrear described mothers whose characteristics may lead to lesbianism as "doormat[s]," "manipulative," "domineering," and/or "self-consumed." It might be difficult to persuade any parent so indicted of the compassion at the heart of the ex-gay enterprise.

At the same time that LWO speakers work to maintain the delicate balance of blame and exoneration, they also work to keep families together. In distinction to earlier Christian pedagogy that was likely to council separation of the gay child from a Christian family, today the movement emphasizes the importance of keeping both a gay child and even the child's partner within the family circle. Fryrear made the distinction between actively loving a gay child and her partner and accepting or advocating same-sex sexuality. Indeed, not only does compassion require a continuing relationship with gay loved ones, but such a stance is also a pragmatic necessity. Gay adult children and their partners are more likely to eventually accept Christ and "leave homosexuality" if they are treated with kindness by family members. The danger of such proximity is not far to seek, however. Speakers note that gay loved ones so embraced may act in a manipulative fashion to try to alter their Christian family member's perspective on homosexuality. Family members must be on their guard not to be taken in by such designs. Antigay Christians must stand strong against same-sex sexuality and the threats it creates, even if that threat resides in the bosom of their own family.

Moreover, as valuable as compassion is, it does not extend to those who refuse to renounce their same-sex attractions or who embrace a public *identity* as lesbian or gay. If the ex-gay movement directs compassion toward strugglers, LWO targets unregenerate queers for political intervention and punishment. The political intervention at LWO begins with the claim that Christian and homosexual identities are mutually exclusive, repudiating the existence of LGBT Christians. Once queers are located outside the Christian community, other forms of political instruction follow. At LWO—as in the developmental literature—there are no happy homosexuals or satisfying same-sex relationships. And as many observers of the ex-gay movement point out, accounts of homosexual disease and misery constitute a mendacious baseline of information for those who struggle to transform their sexual desires.[52]

Movement leaders swear that lesbians and gay men cannot lead happy or satisfied lives. At the same time, these leaders call on participants at LWO to examine and challenge their own attitudes of disgust and outrage toward homosexuals. Those who identify as ex-gay speak movingly of the costs of such stigmatizing attitudes. Joe Dallas recalled bemused conversations between gay men in the 1970s about misleading descriptions of gay male sex produced by antigay Christians. Mike Haley made an even more personal plea to eliminate slogans such as "love the sinner, hate the sin." Haley explained that gay people, self-defined as they are by their behavior, experience the hate as directed at them rather than at their "sin." Gay people so admonished are unlikely to turn to the god of their antagonists for healing.

Love Won Out juxtaposes therapeutic discourse with brass-knuckled political instruction for a conservative Christian audience. In this setting, the narrative of development and the call for compassion at its core easily can be read by critics as hypocritical window dressing. It is true that some authors and ex-gay leaders are more successful than others in projecting compassion for the plight of strugglers and same-sex attracted people. Still, compassion remains a central dimension of the developmental project. In this narrative, the fault of same-sex desire does not lie in the wounded themselves but in their histories and, particularly, in their family relations. Hence, the narrative contains a powerful indictment of many Christian families even when it denies that families are to blame. To be fair, not all participants in this tradition practice such indirection: one claims that parents of children who refuse to renounce their same-sex sexuality should accept "a proper measure of guilt [to] foster humility and sensitivity."[53] Generally, however, the narrative of development eases up on Christian families. It also relieves homosexually afflicted people of responsibility for their condition, although it charges them with what they make of the condition, most notably the choice to avoid or act upon same-sex desire.

The Political Work of Compassion

When they undertake to respond to the Christian right, lesbians, gay men, and their allies do not always appreciate the compassionate dimensions of the narrative of development. It is not uncommon for queer activists (using the more traditional definition of "activist") and intellectuals to reject and deride the very idea that anything about the conservative Christian antigay agenda can be compassionate. After all, today's ex-gay movement does not only offer therapeutic help for those who seek reparative sexual reorientation. It also involves antigay political work that threatens the economic welfare and legal status of LGBT people. The movement is at the center of political activism to limit the rights of queers; FOF sponsors not only LWO but also a variety of antigay initiatives through its sister organization, FRC, and through the more recent lobbying arm, Focus on the Family Action.

One piece of critical literature on the Christian right's ex-gay movement helps to illustrate this problem. In 1998, PRA, the Policy Institute of NGLTF, and Equal Partners in Faith jointly sponsored a report on the ex-gay movement. Rigorously researched and written by Surina Khan of PRA, "Calculated Compassion: How the Ex-Gay Movement Serves the Right's Attack on

Democracy" explains the movement and its connections to the broader antigay agenda of the Christian right.

Khan concludes that the ex-gay movement "lends political cover to the Right's hostile political campaign against gay/lesbian/bisexual/transgender people" by helping the right to reframe its "attack on homosexuality in kinder, gentler terms."[54] This is a trenchant account of how the Christian right has functioned politically, especially since the late 1980s and early 1990s, but it overlooks two important distinctions. First, such a conclusion does not distinguish the ex-gay movement as a whole (including the psychotherapeutic ideas on which the ex-gay movement relies) from the 1998 media campaign coordinated by prominent Christian right organizations and from other manifestations of Christian right politics such as LWO. The "Truth in Love" media campaign was undeniably politically strategic and those who executed it can rightfully be accused of "calculated compassion." However, it obscures our political understanding to collapse such a media spectacle with the movement and the therapeutic literature from which the public campaign ostensibly springs.

In 2001, Tanya Erzen concluded a study of the ex-gay movement that consisted in part of ethnographic fieldwork at New Hope, the first residential ex-gay ministry.[55] Erzen points out that at the time of the 1998 ex-gay ad campaign many ex-gay participants at New Hope regretted the association between the movement and the larger scope of Christian right antigay politics.[56] Many disapproved of the way in which the ad campaign and other Christian right political initiatives pushed the idea of a "radical homosexual conspiracy." These ex-gays were "sympathetic to gay rights" and believed that they and their movement were being used as compassionate cover for the more punitive parts of the Christian right agenda.[57] This critique contributes to our understanding of the disjunctions within Christian right politics by highlighting the conflicts between many ex-gays in the movement and the political leaders of large Christian right organizations. It also confirms that different sectors of the Christian right borrow and rely upon the narrative of development and its association with compassion for (ex) gays and their families.

Ethnographic attention to the ex-gay movement suggests that it may be hazardous to assume the perfect coordination of the internal operation of even this one segment of Christian right antigay politics. However, one key to understanding the internal dynamics of Christian right antigay politics may be taking seriously diverse conceptualizations of the origins of same-sex sexuality. In fact, the PRA report on the ex-gay movement simultaneously highlights and neglects this important distinction. In different sections of the report, Khan points out that the ex-gay movement treats homosexuality as a "lifestyle choice" (a "voluntary lifestyle choice," in the words of the Executive Summary) and as "caused by childhood circumstances."[58] It is certainly not impossible for a movement to be actuated by two quite different beliefs about the source of a social problem. But it is more accurate to say that the ex-gay movement (as opposed to other political projects of the Christian right) has been constructed through a narrative of development than that it is grounded in a narrative of choice. If this is so, and taking into account the deep sense of betrayal that some "ex-gays," "strugglers," and their allies felt during and after the "Love Won Out" media blitz, it is inaccurate to conclude that Christian right politics as a whole employ a "mask of compassion." It is more accurate to assume that compassion is itself a contested dimension of Christian right politics. This does not obviate the possibility that compassion, tolerance, and democratic rights discourse are used strategically as packaging for antidemocratic forms of antigay politics. And it does not require us to agree with the conception of compassion that is at play. But it does encourage us to judge these projects in the full knowledge of the affective and theological commitments of their proponents.

One way to judge what is at stake in divergent formulations of the origins of same-sex desire and sexuality and the politics of compassion is to listen in on the conversations of parties to the debate. An issue of the *Family Research Report* published by Paul Cameron's Family Research Institute (FRI) is revealing. In this issue, Paul's son, Kirk Cameron highlights the disagreement between antigay critics who concede that same-sex sexuality is developmental and those who deny the existence of such a developmental sequence. Citing James Dobson's leadership in the "pro-family movement," and noting that Dobson "ought to know better," Kirk Cameron refers to Dobson's comments in a March 2002 segment of Larry King Live and passages in *Bringing Up Boys* to demonstrate Dobson's dangerous infatuation with a developmental explanation of same-sex sexuality. Placing Dobson and the Nicolosis in the same baleful category, Cameron denounces the developmental arguments as "Freudian" and suggests this substitute thesis: "homosexuality is a choice"; "it is about rebelling against and trying to corrupt society." And Cameron reverses the causal direction suggested by developmental arguments: "while we would not deny that 'loneliness, rejection, self-hatred, and a search for belonging' are part of the price for rebellion, these are not the fundamental causes of homosexual behavior, but instead some of its consequences."[59]

How illuminating is such a dispute between those who represent a narrative of development and those who insist on a narrative of choice for homosexuality? As the Camerons obviously know, invocations of unchosen desire or orientation have the potential to produce compassion for those who find themselves saddled with same-sex desires. And in fact, in the FRI report's attack on Dobson, Kirk Cameron expresses anxiety about this potential outcome. Cameron repeatedly works to preempt compassion for the putative injustices visited on LGBT people by sampling stories of antigay incidents from Washington, DC's *Washington Blade* newspaper and creating counternarratives that position the queer "victims" either as "victimizers" or as recipients of appropriate consequences. His rhetorical questions—"how is [sexual exhibitionism] to be explained by familial child-rearing practices?" "Are we really to feel sorry for [a man caught in a police sting operation]?" "But isn't this the kind of tragedy that one would expect to visit the rebellious . . . ?"—clarify Cameron's interest in foreclosing any possibility that a developmental argument can be used to underwrite compassion for homosexuals.

On the farther edge of the Christian and political continuum, Kansas minister Fred Phelps brings the repudiation of compassion evident in Cameron's debate with Dobson to a logical conclusion. Phelps has a national reputation for ambitious antigay bigotry. His activism includes picketing the funerals of AIDS and hate crime victims, funerals of American soldiers killed in Iraq, and gatherings such as those of PFLAG with signs that read "God Hates Fags," "Fag Enablers," and "God Is Not Mocked." Phelps's Westboro Baptist Church website is replete with explicit antigay sentiments and images, including Matthew Shepherd's face enveloped in the dancing flames of hell. Phelps also rejects the compassionate approach to same-sex sexual sin advocated by many Christian conservatives who subscribe to the narrative of development. Disparaging compassion, Phelps's message to members of PFLAG who met in Salt Lake City, Utah, in October 2004 was: "God hates PFLAG and the filthy fag/dyke kids PFLAG encourages to continue in vile lives of sin, shame, misery, disease, death, and Hell."[60]

Always unstable in its political effects, compassion can undermine the message that homosexuals are unregenerately evil corruptors of society and manipulators of a democratic political system. This is just the effect the Camerons hope to subvert by insisting on the rebellious and contemptuous nature of homosexual choices and behaviors. However, just as compassion can have this "liberal" effect, it can also perform another kind of conservative political work. Compassion can work to shore up support for "mainstream" antigay initiatives by assuaging the suspicion that these programs are driven by group-related bias or defended by arguments that are pretexts for bias. In this way, compassion helps to "center" cultural and political actors.[61]

Much has been written in recent years about the effective coopting of left politics and issues by the American political right and the dubious "centering" of right-wing political culture. Critics such as Angela Dillard and Didi Herman trace the transformation of such lynchpins of the left as the Civil Rights movement and rights-based political discourse.[62] Others reconstruct the rightward shift of the political center since the end of the Cold War.[63] Nor have students of American politics ignored "compassion" as a legitimating factor in political discourse, if not in actual policy. Critics have concentrated on the ideals, pretensions, and policy aspirations associated with "compassionate conservatism" and have criticized Republican claims to any such label.[64] It would be inadequate to dismiss compassionate conservatism as mere public relations both because of the complex ways in which such an understanding can do its work and because of its devastating political consequences. The right-wing claim on compassion is a culmination of the right's coopting of left political projects in combination with the construction of a new kind of "centrist" political identity.[65]

Compassion has a utility for the political projects of the right, including the Christian right. In fact, the compassion for homosexuals that often is explicit in the narrative of development provides foundations for Christian right advocacy in relation to LGBT issues affecting minors and addressing the needs of family members and friends of LGBT people. On the other hand, critics of the right may inappropriately impute instrumental motivations to right-wing political actors. Not all political formations rest upon self-consciously laid foundational assumptions, rhetorics, and practices. The factors that gave rise to a narrative of development are no doubt multidetermined and include anxieties about parenting in an age of changing social mores and enhanced parental responsibility for the character development of children.[66]

Proponents of development do wish to stigmatize and prevent same-sex sexuality. Indeed, these spokespersons regard the continuing social stigma attached to same-sex sexuality as essential to sustain the impetus for lesbians and gay men to give up their sexuality. In this, they do not differ much from other antigay Christian right activists from whom they might otherwise be distinguished. Both may practice a version of what Angelia Wilson, in her study of sexuality and Southern Christianity, calls "conditional love."[67] The difference is that the narrative of development provides support for particular kinds of antigay political projects, especially those like LWO or struggles over Safe Schools that are oriented to minors and to parental control over children. The Christian right doesn't go to war against children who may be, or think themselves, gay. But extending compassion to the young does not make these projects any less political; indeed, however authentic, compassion may still successfully camouflage an antigay agenda.

Our Parents and Friends

PFLAG was formed in the early 1970s by parents who supported their self-identified gay or lesbian children. The organization has a national office and more than four hundred local affiliate chapters; its policymaking process is grassroots; representatives and policy changes are approved through a process of elections and referendums. PFLAG's current mission statement includes three elements: supporting LGBT persons and their families and friends, educating society about LGBT people and issues, and advocating for social and political inclusion. Local chapters provide a local help line and hold meetings that provide opportunities for information sharing and discussion by members and new attendees.

As part of its educational mission, PFLAG produces informational brochures intended for different audiences. Brochures like "Our Daughters and Sons" and "Be Yourself: Questions and Answers for Gay, Lesbian, Bisexual, and Transgender Youth" are written in a question and answer format and are intended to help parents and young people reflect on issues related to how a family member's sexual orientation will affect family relationships. Unlike LWO, PFLAG publications for parents emphasize that parents are not "to blame" for their children's sexual orientation. These materials also emphasize that being gay, lesbian, bisexual, or transgender is normal for some people just as being heterosexual is normal for other people. Early PFLAG materials offered the analogy of the stages of grief for parents trying to understand and come to terms with their children's sexual orientation. Newer materials emphasize that parents might have a variety of reactions to their children's sexual orientation, and that the stages of grief—grieving for the expectations of a child's heterosexual life—might not fit all parents' responses to a child's same-sex sexuality.

At one time, PFLAG had a policy statement that refuted the idea that sexual orientation is a choice. During the 1990s PFLAG retracted this position in favor of a statement that the etiology of sexual orientation is some combination of nature and nurture. Here is "Our Daughters and Sons":

> For years, psychology and psychiatry have bandied around theories that homosexuality is caused by parental personality types—the dominant female, the weak male—or by the absence of same-gender role models. Those theories are no longer accepted within psychiatry and psychology, and part of PFLAG's work focuses on erasing these myths and misconceptions from our popular culture. Gay people come from all types of families.[68]

Today, PFLAG takes the position that the cause of same-sex sexuality is not important. Instead, the organization refocuses attention on how discrimination harms LGBT people and their families.

> Many parents wonder if there is a genetic or biological basis to homosexuality. While there are some studies on homosexuality and genetics, there are no conclusive studies to date on the "cause" of homosexuality. . . . Although we may be curious, it is really not that important to know why your child is gay in order to support and love him or her.[69]

The purpose of PFLAG is to help people cope with the harms caused by discrimination and to try to eliminate discrimination through education and advocacy.

Parents and Friends of Ex-Gays (PFOX) is the ex-gay movement's answer to PFLAG. PFOX is a support group for parents who wish to change, rather than support or affirm, their children's LGB or T identity. On its website, PFOX "support[s] the right of homosexuals and lesbians to change." The group's mission statement includes the goals of educating the public about ex-gay men and women, and supporting the "ex-gay community" and "those families whose lives have been affected by homosexuality." PFOX also has a brochure for youth, as well as a brochure entitled "Can Sexual Orientation Change?" but the contents are very different from those distributed by PFLAG. The teen brochure prominently features a narrative of development and rejects immutability by emphasizing that being gay or lesbian is not genetic, that there is no gay gene, and no single biological explanation for gay, lesbian, and bisexual sexual orientation. The brochure for teens appeals with hip prose: "Feelings Change. They are only one part of you! Get Smart! Get the Facts! . . . If only one part of you has gay feelings, should your whole life be gay identified?"

"Can Sexual Orientation Change?" provides "facts" regarding sexual orientation, including citations to the American Psychological Association. Ignoring the position of that association and other professional organizations, the brochure disingenuously notes that psychologists "support sexual reorientation." The text that follows includes quotations from selected spokespersons such as the recently controversial Robert Spitzer and antigay researcher Warren Throckmorton. The brochure also helpfully defines several terms, including "sexual orientation" and "transgender." According to PFOX, sexual orientation "is a combination of sexual attractions/feelings and behavior associated with those feelings. *It is a developmental process not genetically determined.*"[70] The brochure identifies a transgender person as "someone whose gender identity or expression differs from conventional expectations for their physical sex" and concludes, "This is a *gender identity disorder.*"[71] This brochure also lists a series of heightened health risks for "homosexual and bisexual behavior."

"Can Sexual Orientation Change" recommends "reorientation therapy" that "supports people's objective to change their orientation from gay or bisexual to straight." In a letter to the editor, the executive director of PFOX affirms the position of PFOX regarding the treatment of teens with same-sex attractions:

> Teenagers' same sex attractions do not automatically mean that they are homosexual. Many teens go through temporary episodes of idealization of same-sex peers and should not be urged to prematurely label themselves as gay as GSA encourages them to do. For those teens who do actually show gender-identity confusion, we support the availability of gender affirming therapy.[72]

This brief statement includes a simplified developmental model of same-sex sexuality, a repudiation of same-sex sexual identity, and a recommendation to parents of a therapeutic fix for nonconforming teens.

That the ex-gay movement insists upon the congruence between gender identity and sexuality is well known by critics. Indeed, the simplicity of this gender equals sexuality equation is virtually a pop culture joke. It is the running gag of the 1999 film *But I'm a Cheerleader!*—a film in which teenaged hostages in an ex-gay academy are subjected to campy training in gender-linked forms of dress, deportment, and activities.[73] In *Cheerleader*, the parodied pedagogy fails and the young people end up in sinful pairs. In real life, ex-gay experts continue to highlight the risks of gender nonconformity for anxious parents and then prescribe gender stereotypes for sexual healing. PFOX also provides materials and recommends therapy for transgender-identifying teens to reorient them to their correct gender and sexual orientation. Conversely, the PFLAG informational brochure on transgender issues, "Our Trans Children," provides a description of gender identity disorder that indicates that, while GID is "the only diagnosis under which trans people may receive treatment" it has also been "used inappropriately and harmfully by some psychotherapists to treat *gender variant* youth."[74]

Like other parts of the ex-gay movement, PFOX uses a compassionate developmental narrative to persuade adolescents to repudiate same-sex attraction and to persuade parents to reject their children's same-sex sexuality. Materials produced by FOF, ex-gay experts, and Christian talk radio programs across the country counsel teens and their parents on how to address LGBT tendencies and identities in young people through interventions and reparative therapies. These materials teach that if intervention comes expeditiously enough, the progress of queer identity formation can be arrested.

The FOF website features a series of informational brochures in the series "Helping Boys Become Men, and Girls Become Women." This series provides information for parents about when to be concerned about their children's possible prehomosexuality and how and when to intervene. While parents need not be concerned about gender inappropriate behaviors in preschool children, children aged 5 to 11 may exhibit behaviors that should trigger parental anxiety and action.[75] What's more, the brochures instruct parents how to intervene. As the Nicolosis emphasize, fathers must intervene to teach their sons how to be men. Spouses with a troubled marriage are urged to get marriage counseling to help their children become heterosexual. And single mothers should "recruit a trustworthy male role model." Parents should take care to consult a psychologist who believes in the possibility of sexual conversion, which is to say one whose practices do not reside in the therapeutic mainstream. The brochure includes contact information for EI and NARTH as sources for "a qualified therapist."

PFOX responds to the gay affirmative ideology of PFLAG with developmental narratives that support sexual reorientation in adult children. Similar narratives undergird Christian right activism against Safe Schools programs. At stake is the ability to absolve children of their sexual feelings, to hold adults responsible for preventing the formation of LGBT identity, and to stigmatize same-sex sexuality.

Safety First

A second arena where the narrative of development provides foundations for Christian right social and political activism is in battles over "safe schools." The Safe Schools movement consists of programs across the nation that address sexual orientation–based discrimination and harassment in schools. These programs have been implemented in part due to the advocacy work done by gay and other civil rights organizations, including PFLAG, the Gay, Lesbian, Straight, Education Network (GLSEN), the American Civil Liberties Union (ACLU), and Lambda Legal Defense and Education Fund. Christian right organizations such as FRC, Concerned Women for America (CWA), and the American Family Association (AFA) oppose Safe Schools programs. These groups urge their supporters at the state and local levels to fight programs that teach faculty or other school staff how to stop antigay harassment, support tolerance for LGBT youth, or address the needs of these youth.

One dilemma Christian conservatives encounter when they oppose safe schools work is that such opposition appears to defend bullying in schools. Christian right advocates respond to the charge that they defend bullying by clarifying that bullying is wrong, but that opposition to bullying, and school policies to address it, should not specifically address sexual orientation. And they rely on a developmental narrative to argue that addressing sexual orientation specifically is a way for advocates to talk about and thus to promote homosexuality to children. Furthermore, for Christian conservatives, any assumption that some teenagers *are* or may be lesbian, gay, or bisexual reifies sexual identity instead of compassionately challenging and treating it. For these activists, opposing Safe Schools programs is a major grassroots strategy, and many national organizations have produced anti-Safe Schools materials for local activists to use in their communities.[76]

In spite of concerted activism, not all opposition to Safe Schools programs is successful. Conservative Christian opposition is more difficult in states where civil rights or school safety codes include sexual orientation and gender identity as protected categories.[77] By contrast, in states where there are no such provisions, political arguments grounded in a narrative of development are often more successful. One tactic that Christian groups have used to oppose Safe Schools initiatives is to urge local activists to argue for equal time in schools for their position. If a school plans to show the film *It's Elementary* for a teacher's training, Christian conservatives might advocate for a screening of *It's Not Gay* to ensure balance and fairness in presentation of views about homosexuality.[78] In cases like these, the Christian conservative activists use a civil rights framework to gain a hearing for the Christian right viewpoint, including the developmental narrative of gay origins.

The message of compassion, and the narrative of development in which it is nested, resonates more clearly when the issue at hand concerns gay teenagers rather than adults. This is especially true given the common anxiety that adults recruit young people into their lifestyle.[79] A narrative of development also speaks to the tentative and emerging nature of adolescent sexuality and sexual identity. PFOX teaches that LGB teens might identify their same-sex attractions or feelings without necessarily acting on those feelings, telling them that their feelings need not be their destiny. Christian conservatives argue that it is more compassionate to provide reparative therapy and ensure that LGB youth do not act on their same-sex attractions than to support or affirm a same-sex sexual identity. In this way, they can be saved from the homosexual lifestyle and live lives in keeping with God's will for sexuality. For Christian conservatives, celibacy and sexual reorientation come recommended as alternatives to a homosexual lifestyle.

Feeling Sorry for Themselves

When they develop and deploy a narrative of development, Christian conservatives contest the idea of "identity" even as they acknowledge identity-like processes. From this perspective, it is appropriate for compassionate adults to acknowledge the sexual feelings and gender patterns of young people who identify as gay, lesbian, or bisexual. However, neither compassion nor an understanding of the etiology of homosexual attraction authorize accepting and legitimizing these feelings and patterns *as* sexual orientation or identity. At the center of a variety of antigay Christian social and political positions is the conviction that sexual identity is not a settled fact beyond God's power to heal. Sexual minority and other tolerant adults put young people—and those adults who wish to change their sexual orientation—at risk by insisting upon the legitimacy and/or immutability of same-sex sexuality.

At the LWO conference, Alan Chambers instructed the audience that we must enshrine the prohibition against same-sex marriage in our laws in order to support those struggling against their homosexual desires. Strugglers with the option available to them might marry; he suggested that he would have availed himself of such an opportunity during his own struggle with homosexuality and that it is imperative for society to help those in the grip of their desires abstain from this choice. Since his appearance at LWO in 2004,

Chambers, who is president of EI, has called into question the appellation "ex-gay" and suggested that the struggle with same-sex desire is never complete. However, such doctrinal defections do not change the position of the Christian right on same-sex sexuality and marriage. To conservative Christians, gay activists bear the blame for the risk presented by same-sex marriage because of their disproportionate influence on social attitudes and political processes. Prohibiting same-sex marriage to protect those struggling against homosexuality from themselves is consistent with Christian arguments that equate self-determination with license and true freedom with submission to God's will. It is also an argument that betrays a profound indifference toward the individual rights of gays at the same time that it deploys a kind of rights argument on behalf of those struggling with same-sex attraction. This dual quality of the argument appears to make it appropriate for both in-group and public venues and, indeed, the argument has appeared in public advertisements in states undergoing debates over same-sex marriage bans.

It is no doubt true that much antigay thought and activism is the fruit of deeply rooted biases that are widely shared within affinity groups such as the conservative Christian right. However, there is no reason to believe that the sexual disgust and revulsion that many feel toward queers—even queers who emerge from within conservative Christian families—cannot coexist with compassion and a developmental explication of same-sex sexuality. Indeed, many conservative Christians may understand both their feelings of sexual disgust and their willingness to extend compassion to those who inspire it as divine mandates on the issue of same-sex sexuality as well as personal virtues. The political philosopher John Stuart Mill articulates powerful arguments against reading our own feelings as indicators of some reality external to ourselves.[80] What occasions such forceful dissent is the frequency with which we are tempted to take feelings as signifiers of natural law, right and wrong, or godliness and sinfulness. The fact that God might use feelings to "tell different people different things" is discomfiting.[81]

What this suggests is that the purpose of investigating the political narratives, strategies, and rhetorics of various Christian right projects is not to persuade these political adversaries that they are misguided. Rather, the purpose is to understand the complexities of Christian right political projects: their constitution from diverse, and sometimes contradictory, motivations and from complex combinations of affect, theology, and political strategy. Important tasks for critics of Christian right projects are distinguishing political strategies, including the deployment of compassion and more explicitly political talk about choice and abomination, from genealogies of affective and theological commitment. Even if it is never possible to disarticulate these strands of meaning and motivation completely, we understand the Christian right as a social and political movement best when we try.

LGBT scholars and their allies can also investigate how compassion works through narratives that conservative Christians tell themselves. Like identification, compassion and empathy do not have only one shape. Compassion can select and construct its objects with great flexibility. For example, we may take not only very specific others as objects of our compassion but also ourselves. Indeed, this is in one important respect what the narrative of same-sex sexual development does: it encourages its audience to take themselves—and others with whom they identify most closely—as objects of compassion. Thus, parents who dread the disappointment of a homosexual child and young people who dread the dismay of their parents, friends, and religious communities become the objects of compassion that narratives of development serve.

These narratives also protect particular objects by vividly contrasting them with the unredeemed and unregenerate. However, as the conflict between James Dobson and Kirk Cameron reveal, the two conservative Christian narratives of homosexual origins do not just quietly coexist. Even if outside critics do not call attention to their seams and contradictions, the narratives threaten to undermine each other. The narrative of choice can devastate the hopes and aspirations of conservative Christians with same-sex attractions and those who dedicate themselves to helping them. The narrative of development can foster compassion (or pity or perhaps even social toleration) toward those whom conservative Christians believe it would be better to punish. Neither of these origin stories is entirely a political strategy. But to the extent that both narratives are political strategies, they continue to make both benefits and trouble for those who produce them.

As Love Won Out is intended for in-group Christian conservative audiences, so abomination rhetoric that links queers with a variety of malignant social enemies is also targeted to the in-group. Radio and television shows, organization newsletters and websites, sermons and lectures, all these media are delivery systems for a discourse that links same-sex sexuality with the worst evils of our civilization. One of these evils, with which same-sex sexuality is now consistently linked by the Christian right, is terrorism. While most Americans are probably aware of one infamous disclosure of the linkage in the days after September 11, 2001, fewer are aware of the ubiquity of these arguments and the theological meanings they invoke. Today, the unassuming political pedagogy of the Christian right mobilizes Christian soldiers with the refrain that America faces two enemies: "radical Islam" (or "Islamo-fascism") and "radical secular humanism," usually most easily invoked by the gay agenda, and particularly the horror of same-sex marriage.[82]

In LWO, compassion rhetoric mixes easily with abomination rhetoric as the objects of discussion shift from children to adults and from repentant to unrepentant. In more exclusively political settings, such as the Family Research

Council's Washington Briefing: Values Voter Summit, held in Washington, DC, weeks before the 2006 midterm election, abomination rhetoric holds sway. In these settings, the children to be protected are innocent of gender abjection and sexual desire; they are preheterosexual and endangered not prehomosexual and candidates for compassion. The adults who insist on flaunting same-sex sexual identity are safely outside the doors and on the far side of moral boundaries of concern. And for good reason: their grotesque violations of the laws of God endanger not only themselves but all who do not labor to wrest the United States of America from their sinful grasp.

Chapter 4

Getting What "We" Deserve

Shall I not visit them for these things? saith the LORD: shall not my soul be avenged on such a nation as this?

—Jeremiah 9:9

Be sober, be vigilant; because your adversary the devil, as a roaring lion, walketh about, seeking whom he may devour.

—1 Peter 5:8

Pick an Enemy

The Christian right considers homosexuals and terrorists in the same breath, and this connection wasn't made for the first time when foreign terrorists hijacked airplanes to attack the World Trade Center and the Pentagon. To understand the connection between homosexuals and terrorists, we must return to the late 1980s and early 1990s, the period of the decline and death of the Soviet Union. After the unexpected collapse of the Soviet Union, Christian conservatives and other members of the New right coalition had to reorient themselves to a global system without the traditional communist foe. By the early 1990s, Christian conservatives and even some other elements of the New right, including many neoconservatives, had revived earlier discourses of domestic subversion.[1] The broad category of enemy consisted of liberals who coddled those who refused to work, subverted the natural operations of the free market, celebrated all manner of socially corrosive behaviors, and jeered at real Americans and their values.

Many observers of American politics suggest that once the communist empire collapsed before the astonished eyes of the West, the search was on for a single enemy that could continue to unite the conservative coalition and vindicate concerns for the moral degeneration of America. The enemy would also

101

have to bear the burden of rerouting anxieties about values away from the depredations of market fundamentalism.[2] With our violations of values, our presumed secular humanism, and our putative wealth and self-indulgence, LGBT people seem perfectly fitted for this status. What remains to be mapped is how queers become associated with terrorism.

First, before we were terrorists, we were Nazis and communists. Instead of a single narrative of the Christian right's attitude toward lesbians and gay men there are multiple narratives, depending upon where and when you look. As a result, there are also multiple tropes and comparisons, serving many different purposes of warning, rebuke, exhortation, and retribution. One prominent theme has been that of Nazis and Nazism. In the simple sense of historical context, the comparison between queers and Nazis makes sense. The men— virtually all men—who built the Christian right as a political movement shared the touchstone of World War II and Nazism as their youthful confrontation with evil. In spite of the Cold War, and perhaps in large measure because of the efforts of Jewish communities to represent the Holocaust and commemorate its victims, Nazism has until recently remained our collective public exemplar of evil.

What do queers have in common with Nazis? After all, during their regime of terror, the Nazis arrested and imprisoned people for homosexuality. Homosexuals, especially gay men, made up small percentages of those imprisoned in concentration camps during the war. Lesbians were marginally safer only because of their relative invisibility in a vociferously pro-natalist society that could not seem to imagine their agency and existence.[3] In the world of public discourse, whether theological or explicitly political, such historical considerations pale before the political and psychological effects of the comparisons. From mainstream to far right, other Christian right leaders use the Nazi analogy as a convenient way to provoke a set of associations that are deeply engrained in popular culture as a synonym for evil even among those who are innocent of many details of Nazi ideology and atrocities.

On the far right, Fred Phelps has long maintained the link between Nazism and same-sex sexuality on his Westboro Baptist Church and God Hates Fags websites. Several years ago Phelps kept a curious page that linked the two through the juxtaposition of visual symbols. Alone on a white page, a large pink triangle and swastika superimposed without accompanying text asserted the equivalence of Nazism and same-sex sexuality. Without explanation, and given the critique of queers, gay sexuality, and social tolerance on display elsewhere on the website, Phelps could incite a range of associations with this minimalist page: suffering, brutality, godlessness, death, and perhaps even genocide with present-day Christians as potential martyrs for their faith. Today, this simple page is gone, and it is replaced with a link to a website that connects gays and Nazis explicitly and in detail. "The Pink Swastika," by Scott Lively and Kevin Abrams, does the same kind of work as Phelps's earlier page except that it provides more information about this putative connection and less startling visual imagery.[4]

If this seems a far-fetched reading of the juxtaposition of these two symbols, it is useful to listen to Pat Robertson on Nazism and same-sex sexuality. One oft-cited quote from Robertson has him linking Nazis, Satanists, and homosexuals: "many of those people involved with Adolph Hitler were Satanists, many of them were homosexuals—the two things seem to go together."[5] Most critics who have cited this declaration over the years assume that "the two things" that go together are Nazism and homosexuality, although it may be that Robertson's colloquial delivery disguises some other meaning. Perhaps the safest interpretation is transitive: Satanism and Nazism go together, Nazism and homosexuality go together, and Satanism and homosexuality go together. In a 1993 interview with journalist and author Molly Ivins, Robertson expanded the scope of his indictment. There, he pointed out that Democrats in Congress, the liberal media, and homosexuals were doing to Christians in America just "what Nazi Germany did to the Jews."[6] As Nazis must have their victims, so must liberals, and especially homosexuals, have theirs. For Robertson, as for Phelps, the result is Christian martyrdom in America.[7]

Likewise, James Dobson equates Nazis and queers throughout *Marriage Under Fire,* his polemic against same-sex marriage. A chapter entitled "How Did We Get In This [same-sex marriage] Mess?" begins "When Nazi Germany marched its troops into Austria. . . ." Later, Dobson grounds the comparison in Nazi and queer aggression which, left unchecked, is devastating for any society: "this is why we are in the state of peril that faces our nation today. Like Adolf Hitler, who overran his European neighbors, those who favor homosexual marriage are determined to make it legal, regardless of the democratic processes that stand in their way."[8] In passages like these, Dobson and other Christian right leaders inscribe charged connections between gay "activists" (for example, lesbians and gay men seeking the right to marry) and murderous totalitarians at the same time that they position themselves and their cause on the side of the democratic angels.

Nor is the association between queers and Nazis dying out of public discourse with the passing of the movement torch from older leaders, such as Robertson and to a lesser extent Dobson, to the younger and more media savvy. At Love Won Out, political panels that concentrate on halting and reversing the gay rights movement rely on the comparison to arouse listeners, politically and emotionally. During my visit to LWO, Joe Dallas, ex-gay author and speaker, equated the gay rights movement to Nazism in two ways. First, he invoked the experience of Christian writer Corrie ten Boom, who fought the Nazi occupation of the Netherlands, noting that the Nazi tyranny descended on its victims by slow degrees until resistance to it was futile.[9] Then, invoking the notorious early British response to Nazi aggression, he warned that the church often settles for practicing "appeasement" with proponents of gay rights. Given its pernicious history, it is unnecessary for speakers to linger on the likely consequences of this particular tactic.

By calling attention to the ubiquity of the Nazi trope, I don't mean to suggest that it's the only enemy formation that works for antigay politics. Indeed, almost any enemy may do as a metaphor or metonym for homosexual. The enemy of choice really depends upon how homosexuals are being conceived at a particular moment and by particular groups. Besides the Nazi trope there is also a durable set of narratives that link queers with communists, and not only because of the notoriously antireligious ideology of communist states. The East-West spy game gave rise to particular concerns about manliness and resistance to political seduction, from homosexual Brits who spied for the KGB in the early years of the Cold War to decades of American government concern that gay intelligence officers might constitute weak security links against the Soviets. During the Cold War, both communists and homosexuals were "subversives," and the American climate of fear in which many gay men and lesbians lost their livelihoods has been well documented.[10] In addition to the putative risks and similarities of queers and communists, yet another connection: a narrative of "containment" that seeks to fight both internal and external threats to the American homeland by cordoning off the danger until it can, finally, be extinguished.[11] The problem is that, unlike communists, queers have neither been contained nor extinguished. We remain a vital enemy, one might say, an enemy for the twenty-first century.

And Now We Are Terrorists

Terrorism did not begin, even in the United States, on September 11. Yet, in spite of a long history of terrorism the link between terrorism and same-sex sexuality is relatively new. Nor is the attractiveness of this link too outrageous to understand. Consider the common elements of rhetoric about terrorists and queers. They: slip through our defenses disguised as normal citizens; take advantage of our goodness or openness to wreak havoc on us; undermine our way of life and the most innocent among us; serve darks gods; threaten us with large-scale social chaos; owe their allegiance to others of their kind rather than to a lawful nation; have allies that live among us; are few but disproportionately powerful; will only be able to be dealt with effectively by a national government wielding its most powerful weapons. We must be willing to sacrifice our own liberties to end their reign of terror, the war against them is binary and total: you're either with us or against us.

Even the belief that they are not really of *us* is common to rhetoric about terrorists and homosexuals. The terrorists originate outside our society; therefore, those who carry out what might otherwise be regarded as terrorist acts—for example such domestic terrorists as Eric Rudolph and Tim McVeigh—are not terrorists but ordinary criminals. Indeed, some of these—Eric Rudolph is certainly one—may receive tacit, if not material, support on the extreme edges of the Christian right for their holy acts against abortion providers, queers, and the government that shelters them.

Christian conservatives treat lesbians and gay men as a satanic fifth column within America, attempting in a variety of ways to negotiate the inside/outside distinction. On the one hand—and in the more rare of narratives—queers may originate from outside and try to penetrate our borders. This has been a commonplace narrative about same-sex sexuality in many parts of the world. It is also a narrative that has obviated the effective treatment of AIDS. If AIDS is a function of decadent capitalism or Western values, to say nothing of mere godless voluntarism, it is likely the disease will not be treated forthrightly as a community, national, or global health threat.[12]

This narrative becomes more resonant in the age of anti-American terrorism. One example helps to illustrate both the usefulness of the trope of terror and the anxieties about audience and effect that come with the political territory. In 2003, a news article from CWA commented on the attempt of a recently wed gay Canadian couple to enter the United States as married. The article referred to the couple as the "latest pair of domestic terrorists" and linked the men's attempt to enter the United States using a single U.S. Customs form to the porousness of American's borders to potential terrorists. The language of the article in CWA intern James Kimball's "Homosexuals Pose New Threat to U.S. Border Security" was widely reported by progressive news and information sources. Five days after the original article appeared on its website, CWA amended it to remove the language equating the gay men with terrorists. The freshly scrubbed article, "'Gay' Activists Not Allowed to Enter U.S. as Married Couple," was published on the CWA website, where it still resides.[13]

James Dobson is also preoccupied with the threat of terrorism. In *Marriage Under Fire*, Dobson offers his perspective that the goal of defending the boundaries of heterosexual marriage is more important than prosecuting the war on terror. He thus manages to link terrorism and same-sex sexuality for his readers while elevating the status of homosexual enemies above that of conventional terrorist threats.[14] In his Focus on the Family mailings, Dobson entrenches the connection between terrorism and same-sex sexuality and sexual rights, using the language of "cultural terrorism." Dobson gives appropriate credit for this stirring term to the Heritage Foundation's Rebecca Hagelin, the author of *Equipping Parents for the Culture War* and *Home Invasion: Protecting Your Family in a Culture That's Gone Stark Raving Mad*.

In these narratives, queers are outsiders poised to strike against the impressionable minds, if not the bodies, of innocent victims. In a more common set

us & them

of narratives, queers are among us but not *of* us. The slipperiness of the inclusive pronoun creates the possibility of many different narratives. These begin with the boundaries of the nation-state and telescope to the level of "the family," particularly the Christian family. Even when lesbians and gay men are nominally members of the American community they are not part of the "us" that needs protecting but rather are part of the "them" that precipitates danger. At the level of family life, most accounts of the threat of same-sex sexuality feature queers threatening "the family." As with all these narratives, contradictions abound. In the various versions of narrative of development that have been created over the past four decades, conservative Christians often attribute same-sex sexual identity to familial dysfunction. Here, dysfunction includes, though it is not exhausted by, the rearing of children in families with lesbian, gay, and other kinds of subobtimal parents.

But like members of other affinity groups, conservative Christians do not publicly grapple with the wrenching intragroup realities that destabilize public discourses. Usually, advocates of lesbian and gay rights react to the juxtaposition of homosexuals and families by pointing that lesbians and gay men also form and have families. These are both "natural" families and families of choice. Another kind of response is to note that homosexuals emerge from childhoods in all kinds of families, including conservative and Christian families such as the (Tim and Beverly) LaHayes, the (Phyllis) Schlaflys, the (Dick and Lynne) Cheneys, the (Alan) Keyeses, the (Randall) Terrys, and countless others. It is instructive to reflect on the recent public dialogue between Randall Terry, the founder of Operation Rescue, and his gay adopted son. After Jamiel Terry gave an interview to *Out* magazine in 2004, the elder Terry engaged in a public campaign to impugn his son and blame his sexuality on the young man's pre-Terry family upbringing.[15] In this way, the father offered an unusually venomous, although still recognizable, developmental explanation of homosexuality while acquitting himself of any responsibility for the son's sexuality. Although homosexuality appeared to occur on his familial watch, it actually originated outside and insinuated itself into a moral domestic space. By engaging in such a public meditation about the source of his son's sexuality, Randall Terry reminds us of one public service that some ex-gay programs perform. These programs unintentionally teach that although lesbians and gay men come from every kind of family, those reared in conservative Christian families are more likely than others to try to extirpate their sexuality.

Although Christian right leaders dispute the connection, public and private rhetoric that equates lesbians and gay men with Satan and evil does much the same kind of cognitive work that the equation of Islamic terrorists with evil does. Such rhetoric authorizes aggression. Indeed, the complicated but unmistakable relation of aggressive rhetoric to aggressive action is a principal reason why potential victims may appeal to opinion leaders to speak more reparatively about their putative adversaries. Former Falwell speechwriter Mel White certainly had this goal when he took a lesbian and gay group to visit Jerry Falwell in 1999.[16] And to his credit, Falwell agreed to moderate his rhetoric about homosexuals even if he could not in good conscience change his views.

Ironically, the dispute over fiery rhetoric aimed at identity groups may subvert appropriate dialogues about the political ideologies of groups. Sometimes it is difficult to perceive the difference between rejecting a particular set of beliefs or acts and disdaining the kinds of people who may be loosely, contingently, or partially responsible for them. Conversations about the troublesome nature and consequences of fighting words are not limited to those between secular and Christian adversaries. Sometimes they take place between putative allies and, when they do, they can be even more revealing about the internal workings of ideology than when they occur across impassable fault lines of belief. A telling debate of this sort took place between John D. Woodbridge and James Dobson in the pages of *Christianity Today*. In the debate, Woodbridge decries the polarizing and destructive culture-war rhetoric, fretting that "war talk" creates enmity and enemies, even among evangelical Christians themselves, and makes it more difficult for Christians to preach the gospel of Christ. He warns that warfare may cause warriors to distort the positions of their opponents and even to "become evil." In his turn, Dobson notes that the current culture wars are merely an extension of the "age-old struggle between the principles of righteousness and the kingdom of darkness," and he accuses Woodbridge—and others who might be concerned with the consequences of culture war on Christianity—of undermining the work of the people of God against Satan's kingdom.[17]

Woodbridge warns Dobson and other Christian conservatives that hateful rhetoric has, and can, provoke religious violence, and in this he is clearly correct.[18] It is careless to speak of a simple causal connection between demonizing rhetoric and violence against hated groups. Clearly, all those subject to heated public speech do not pick up weapons and assault those they perceive as members of the group in question. However, this caveat about causality does not mean there is no connection between demonizing rhetoric and continua of hatred and violence. In the aftermath of the U.S. government's identification of the September 11 hijackers, reports of assaults against those perceived to be Muslim or of Middle Eastern origin rose precipitously. In "'We Are Not the Enemy': Hate Crimes Against Arabs, Muslims, and Those Perceived to Be Arab or Muslim After September 11," Human Rights Watch reported on the spike of "backlash" violence against those perceived to belong to the group associated with the September 11 attacks. The HRW report recognized the efforts of the president and his administration to sow tolerance at the same time that it criticized the infrastructure for enacting ethnic and religious tolerance against the groups associated with terrorism. Indeed, the report includes a section entitled "A History of Backlash Attacks Against Arabs and Muslims in America" that puts the post-September 11 violence into perspective.[19]

It is useful to look more closely at President Bush's widely praised attempts to avoid scapegoating Muslims or, more broadly, people perceived to be of Middle Eastern descent. On the one hand, Bush attended interfaith services after September 11 and spoke of Islam on many occasions as a peaceful religion. As is obvious from internal Christian right opinion, many conservative Christian leaders begged to differ on this point. However, for the most part they did not publicly criticize the president for taking this position. On the other hand, Bush described the American anti-terrorist war project as a "crusade" and made a numbingly repetitive series of statements that framed the war on terror as a war of good against evil. I am willing to believe that the president did not realize what he was invoking when he spoke of a Western Crusade in the Arab Middle East. However, the speechwriters responsible for the president's visionary war speeches were not neophytes communicating with the Christian right. They well knew that conservative Christians easily would translate Bush's "good vs. evil" rhetoric into their own grammar of Christianity vs. Islam and God vs. Satan.

The Bush administration was not alone in constructing the stark binaries that distinguished "us" from "them" and "good" from "evil" after September 11. The president's public performances were shadowed by similar rhetorical performances from Osama bin Laden and other Islamist spokespersons. Thus, it is edifying to consider the rhetorical and political struggles to fix certain ideas, impressions, and "symmetric dualisms" in the minds of different publics. Bruce Lincoln does this by comparing and contrasting Bush's and bin Laden's speeches of October 7, 2001, and he finds surprising symmetries between the two. There is, however, one quite large difference that must be accounted for: while bin Laden speaks in an overtly religious register in which Americans are "infidels" (making Bush "the head of international infidels"), Bush confines himself to a secular register in which the September 11 attackers are "murderers" and "killers." As Lincoln makes clear, however, Bush sends more than enough signals to Christian conservatives, even in this one speech, to gesture toward a "vast subtextual [religious] iceberg" beneath his secular rhetoric.

One of these references is to Revelation and the horror of the end-time, a reference that Lincoln notes is "likely to go unheard by those without the requisite textual knowledge":

> [Bush's] statement "the terrorists may burrow deeper into caves and other entrenched hiding places" reduced his adversaries to hunted animals, but also gestured toward a climactic scene of the Apocalypse. This is the moment when the Lamb of God (i.e., Jesus in his character of eschatological hero and avenger) opens the sixth seal on the scroll of doom. . . .[20]

"Double coding," of which this is only one example, recuperates Bush's speech as religious and as religious in a particular fashion that bows to the theology of the Christian right. But Bush did not speak openly of religious war and satanic foes. It fell to Jerry Falwell and Pat Robertson to tell that story and to be overheard mapping homosexuals and other liberal enemies into the narrative of terrorism and God's vengeance.

Setting the Straight Story

When the World Trade Center and the Pentagon became terrorist targets on September 11, 2001, two conservative Christian leaders agreed on an interpretation of the attack that emphasized American culpability.[21] As we shall see, their interpretation was not unusual among conservative Christians. Indeed, the interpretation would have gone unremarked except that critics made it visible to mainstream publics, and, as a result, it underwent a brief notoriety. On September 13, 2001, Jerry Falwell made a guest appearance on Pat Robertson's *700 Club* by remote satellite and commented on the bombings of the World Trade Center in New York City and the Pentagon in Washington, DC. Falwell noted that "God continues to lift the curtain and allow the enemies of America to give us probably what we deserve." In response, Robertson explicitly agreed: "Jerry, that's my feeling. I think we've just seen the antechamber to horror. We haven't even begun to see what they can do to the major population." Falwell continued: "I really believe that the pagans, and the abortionists, and the feminists, and the gays and the lesbians who are trying to make that an alternative lifestyle, the ACLU, People for the American Way—all of them who have tried to secularize America—I point the finger in their face and say, 'You helped this happen.'"[22]

Falwell's comments blaming perverts and liberal elites for the suicide attacks were quickly assailed from different positions on the ideological spectrum. Predictably, liberal groups denounced the hatefulness of the claims, but President Bush also used proxies to distance himself from the comments. Responding to the linkage of homosexuality with terrorism, Elizabeth Birch, at that time the executive director of HRC, immediately spoke out against the comments. In a speech delivered on October 6, she compared the pair's political ideology to that of the terrorists. Falwell and Robertson, she said, "chose to blame blindly, motivated by prejudice and fueled by the very brand of zealotry and hatred that has put America in danger." The ministers' comments were "a difficult reminder of the challenges we still face within our own borders. Our community knows all too well the devastating effects of hate."[23]

Responding to the avalanche of negative publicity, Falwell apologized for his comments on September 18, calling them "insensitive, uncalled for at the time and unnecessary."[24] As pundits pointed out, he was careful not to say he was wrong. Cartoonists and comics picked up the controversy and made it yet another chapter in the long-running mainstream joke on the man who only a few years before had warned American parents about the dangers posed to their children by androgynous Teletubbies.[25] For his part, Pat Robertson remained defiant, and his subsequent statements help to clarify what is at stake in the original comments and in the controversy that followed.

By early October, journalists, newspaper editors, talking heads, and public intellectuals had weighed in on the Falwell-Robertson remarks, calling them "despicable," "obscene," "divisive," and "hateful."[26] On October 14, Robertson responded in a press release. In it, he answered his own rhetorical question about public tragedy—"why does this happen?"—by referring to the sinfulness of American society and repeating claims familiar from the original *700 Club* interview: that "it is happening because God Almighty is lifting his protection from us" and that "this is only a foretaste, a little warning, of what is going to happen."[27] In his press release, Robertson did delete the list of domestic groups responsible for the terror attack, although sexuality and self-indulgence continued to figure as causes of terrorism. However, even more revealing, both as doctrine and defense, is Robertson's open letter to American newspaper editors.

Responding to the criticisms of himself and Falwell, in the open letter Robertson deplores the "misinformation, misstatements of fact, snippets of conversation wrenched out of context, and vicious criticism of sentiments attributed to me which I never articulated."[28] Robertson points out in the letter that he had "never expressed the statements that are attributed to Dr. Falwell." However, Robertson ends the letter by quoting Abraham Lincoln in a way that undercuts his demurral. Referring to the Civil War and the struggle over slavery that precipitated it, Lincoln's words in essence recapitulate the theme of cultural sinfulness followed by the visitation of divine wrath. The apology ends with these reflections: "Why has a statement that was so universally acclaimed in 1863 become the object of scorn and ridicule when made in a slightly different form in the year 2001? I do not know what others will do, but I choose to follow the advice of Abraham Lincoln."[29] In the open letter, Robertson turns the accusation of intolerance back on the media, reiterates the content of his and Falwell's original statement, and seizes the moral high ground from his adversaries.

Although the public controversy over the Falwell-Robertson interview had died away by the end of October, a postscript appeared in the mainstream press. An October 4 fundraising letter for Jerry Falwell ministries had accused "liberals of all stripes" of "seiz[ing] this opportunity to trash Dad's deeply held Christian beliefs and to literally attack him day and night."[30] The letter was signed by Falwell's son, Jonathan. In a November 18 interview, a *Washington Post* reporter tried to induce Falwell to reconcile his earlier apology with the text of the fundraising letter. Falwell successfully frustrated the reporter's attempts to clarify his position by invoking Jonathan's right to react to attacks on his father and by coyly pointing out that he received many more complaints from Christian followers about his "apology" than he received complaints from critics about his original statement.[31]

Transcripts of televised *700 Club* conversations are posted to the Christian Broadcasting Network website as a matter of course. However, if Falwell's controversial comments about the cause of the terrorist attacks were ever posted in their entirety, they had been edited by October 9 to remove the controversial statements and reflect merely the "brokenness [and] tears" appropriate in the aftermath of tragedy. In the abbreviated comments, Falwell notes that the "most optimistic thing" he can find in the devastation is that "only God could bring it upon us."[32] This is one central element of the message that Falwell and Robertson broadcast to their followers on September 13. However, in order to decipher the complete meaning of the message, we must consider the intersection of theology and politics with regard to tolerance and particular categories of sins and sinners.

In their public statements, Falwell, Robertson, and other Christian right actors complain that secular responses to incidents such as the *700 Club* interview are a sign of pervasive anti-Christian sentiment and religious intolerance. These charges confuse religious prejudice with vigorous political disagreement over the terms of democracy and citizenship. In addition, they often successfully derail substantive responses to aspects of the Christian right political agenda. In fact, Falwell and Robertson's statements were neither misspoken (as Falwell later claimed) nor merely signs of capricious malice against disfavored groups (as many critics assumed). Rather, they are long-standing theological and political claims. These are claims so commonplace to those who share the assumptions and convictions of leaders like Falwell and Robertson that challenging them or casting aspersions on those who carried the message could function effectively as evidence of their accuracy.

The fact that Falwell and Robertson's claims about the linkage between terrorism and tolerance of sinfulness were intended for an audience of born-again Bible-believing Christians and not for others does not diminish their political significance. Since the early years of the Christian right movement, leaders have become more effective at parsing their public statements so that some aspects of political beliefs and theological foundations for political beliefs are misidentified by the broad public.[33] Commentators who speak the language of conservative Christianity are able to translate Christian right rhetoric and ideas for mainstream audiences. Those who do not often either rely on vague conceptions of Christianity for their interpretation or bypass any mention of theological foundations for the political positions they report.[34] Although it was not widely identified, a conservative Christian politics of desert quickly emerged into public view after September 11. This reading of the attacks contextualized them in terms of God's will and plan for America.

A politics of desert is related to what one anthropologist labels a "theology of blame": the belief that "God may allow bad things to happen without necessarily causing them, and when he allows bad things to happen, it is for reasons that are transcendent and often punitive, though ultimately redemptive (however unfathomable that seems to those who suffer immediate consequences)."[35] Moving beyond this formulation, a politics of desert fuses theological criteria and agendas with political ones. It is characterized by the general conviction that God punishes nations that refuse his criteria for righteousness, and the more specific conviction that tolerance and forbearance of particular kinds of sins—and groups of sinners— are responsible for God's decision to bring scourges such as terrorism upon the United States. Although many opinion leaders and secular Americans condemned the most notorious expression of a politics of desert in the days after September 11, few seemed to grasp the theological roots and political implications of such a conviction.

So let us return to the *700 Club* interview. One reading of Falwell and Robertson's conversation is consistent with the mandate of Christian conservatives to propagate the gospel of Jesus Christ to the world. On this interpretation, the ministers sought to bring conviction and an understanding of the need for salvation to those who precipitated the withdrawal of God's protection. A second reading is that the statements attributing blame for the terrorist strikes were not intended to speak *to* feminists, abortion providers, lesbians and gay men, and the rest; they were not intended to persuade these actors to accept Christ or to change their sinful ways. Rather, the message was consistent with the mandate to urge Christians toward large-scale social and political change as a way to divert God's wrath away from the nation. In this second reading, the intended audience for the comments would be the Christian followers of Falwell, Robertson, and other conservative Christian ministers, those for whom messages of this sort are both commonplace and credible. In fact, Falwell, Robertson, and other Christian right leaders have consistently delivered such messages to their followers as a way of constructing the "cultural exodus" of fundamentalists and other Christian proponents of biblical inerrancy from political separatism to political engagement.[36]

Examples of this orientation toward the importance of the nation are close at hand in the work of Jerry Falwell. In Falwell's role as an apostle of born-again activism in the 1980s he delivered and published versions of a standard "stump sermon" across the United States. In these sermons—delivered on television as well as live before thousands of congregants—Falwell made his case for the active participation of born-again Christians, and Christian values, into every aspect of American social and professional life. He warned of God's judgment on a nation without such intercession: "There is hardly a press conference in which someone doesn't ask me, 'Do you believe AIDS is God's judgment against homosexuals?' I always say, 'No, I don't believe that. I believe it is

God's judgment against America, for endorsing immorality, even embracing it.' I believe it is God's judgment against the whole society."³⁷ Messages such as these, widely available during the AIDS epidemic of the 1980s and early 1990s, were ignored or greeted with scorn by those whom Falwell and Robertson would identify as liberal "cultural elites." However, such arguments serve the purpose of constituting a particular conception of Bible-based history for conservative Christian followers.

To go further, such arguments help to constitute particular kinds of believers who anticipate and fashion their own understandings of reality in accord with the Word being preached to them. Anthropologist Susan Friend Harding, who quotes Falwell's AIDS stump speech, gets this aspect of conservative Christian theology dead on. She conceptualizes Falwell's authority as "produced by a community of believers through its interpretive practices"; and she conceptualizes the eternal verities of conservative Christian faith as "flexible absolutism," the generation of absolutes through the knitting together of "narrative gaps and excesses."³⁸ The "always already" of biblical truth is very much in need of always being created anew.

In fact, Robertson did not first make the connection between same-sex sexuality and terrorism in the chaotic days after September 11. In June, 1998, Robertson offered comments on a *700 Club* broadcast that foreshadow those he would later repeat and disavow. Addressing himself to the Orlando, Florida, gay pride parade and the controversy of "gay days" at Disneyland, Robertson said:

> We better respond according to what the Bible says. The Apostle Paul made it abundantly clear in the Book of Romans that the acceptance of homosexuality is the last step in the decline of Gentile civilization. But if a condition like this will bring about the destruction of your nation, if it will bring about terrorist bombs, if it will bring about earthquakes, tornadoes and possibly a meteor, it isn't necessarily something we ought to open our arms to. And I would warn Orlando that you're right in the way of some serious hurricanes, and I don't think I'd be waving those flags in God's face if I were you.³⁹

After Robertson's comments were circulated to media outlets by critics, he defended himself in another *700 Club* monologue, noting that his original comments were taken out of context and then affirming that "if we continue to engage in various types of sexual conduct which is [sic] displeasing to God, then this country will not have the defenses we've enjoyed for such a long time."⁴⁰

Adhering to his pattern in such circumstances, Robertson both obfuscates the details of the original statement and reaffirms the belief that God punishes the sin of homosexuality by striking the nation that tolerates it. In this belief, Robertson is on firm Christian right ground; for these believers, not only is same-sex sexuality "unbiblical and unnatural," but it is taken by Christian right leaders to be "emblematic of a civilization's decline."[41] In the context of such a belief, tolerance—of value disagreements in general and of same-sex sexuality in particular—is not a positive civic value that undergirds democratic regimes. It is an invitation to God to vent his wrath on the tolerant.

Christian right leaders often gesture toward "extremists" to legitimate their political beliefs, defending their public rhetoric and policy positions by denying that they represent a political extreme. These leaders frequently deny hateful motivations and bias and tacitly position themselves between purveyors of hate on the left and those on the right. Queer activists frequently stand in as leftist extremists and reinforce the reasonable and righteous nature of conservative Christianity. One example occurred when members of the AIDS Coalition to Unleash Power (better known as ACT UP) picketed Robertson's Harlem, New York, announcement of his 1988 presidential candidacy.[42] Such an equation between queers and stigmatized left political beliefs confirms for conservative Christians linkages of lesbians and gay men with communism, with the degradation of moral values, and with Satan's work in the world.

The general agreement on the Christian right that God permits nations to be punished for the sins of their people leaves open the question of how the deity apportions blame at particular historical moments. Falwell himself raised this question in an exculpatory fashion in his interview with the *Washington Post*. There, he noted that he was humbled by the many criticisms of his *700 Club* comments to reflect upon the many forms of tolerance of evil—citing, for example, a "sleeping church"—for which he and members of the born-again Christian community have been responsible. This statement appears apologetic—*it's not you who are at fault but we, the church*—but for one hermeneutic detail: when Falwell referred to the "sleeping church" he meant the body of Christians who have not arisen to seize control of the nation and purge its sinfulness. In his interview with the *Washington Post*, Falwell was not apologizing for his comments. He was actually apologizing for a "church"—a body of believers—that has not yet managed to put an end to the forms of sinfulness he cited in his original chat with Robertson on September 13.

During the uproar over the Falwell-Robertson comments, many Christian commentators pointed out that it was presumptuous for anyone to believe that they could discern the specific purposes of God, even though they agreed that the terrorist acts probably constituted some form of punishment on the United States as a nation. An anthropologist doing fieldwork with conservative Protestants in east Tennessee at the time of the attacks lends support to this formulation of the issue of terrorist strikes on American soil. Omri Elisha notes that although the evangelicals he worked with embrace a theology of blame, many were still critical of Falwell, believing not only that human beings cannot discern divine purposes but that "moral accusations must be tempered."[43] Despite his own emphasis on the diversity of viewpoints among conservative Protestants, however, even Elisha concedes that "millions" of conservative Christians "firmly support" Falwell and Robertson's attribution of desert for the attacks.

There is no doubt that same-sex sexuality evokes outrage in the majority of Christian right followers.[44] Descriptions of queers as committed to nothing more than intense sexual pleasure do have the ironic effect of heightening the attractiveness of homosexuality for anxious Christian right audiences. But they also stabilize distinctions between saved believers and the lubricious, demonic homosexuals who must be opposed. Even as Christian right leaders rhetorically and politically reinforce this distinction, a Christian right politics of desert often is not aimed directly at lesbians and gay men. Rather, it is aimed at Americans who do not use the levers of law and social policy to punish and proscribe homosexuality. In the final analysis, these Americans—tolerant, indifferent, or merely misled— are the "we" who bring down God's wrath on America.

The Politics of Desert

Jerry Falwell and Pat Robertson agreed with one another that Americans got "probably what we deserve" in the attacks on the Pentagon and World Trade Center. Whatever observers believe about the views the two Christian right leaders shared that day, it is clear that both were chagrined that their comments were broadcast to the nation and that both attempted to reverse the damage to their mainstream reputations. Falwell apologized in his fashion (disingenuously); Robertson both embraced the remarks and dissociated himself from them in his fashion (aggressively).

If Falwell and Robertson's comments assigning blame for the terrorist attack were no more than the appearance of isolated personal views in public discourse, there would be little more to say on the subject. Mill's elegant delineation of the "morality of public discussion" notwithstanding, it is utopian to expect that "malignity, bigotry, or intolerance of feeling" will ever be expunged from the political realm.[45] However, the sentiments these Christian right leaders expressed are neither isolated nor merely personal. Rather, they are theologically and politically complex rhetorics formulated by one group about others. Such rhetorics provoke and ratify the production and dissemination of ideology and the mobilization of financial, intellectual, and institutional resources.

However angry, eloquent, or sympathetic they were, the vast majority of rejoinders to Falwell and Robertson's comments individualized their sentiments without contextualizing them either theologically *or* politically. Political cartoons tell this individualizing story. Of dozens of cartoons I saw that lampooned Falwell and Robertson, only one depicted them as leaders of a movement with a coherent ideology. This was Tom Toles's cartoon, published in many American newspapers on September 19, 2001. In the cartoon, a woman and man watch a television on which, we presume from their comments, they have just viewed Jerry Falwell blaming immoral Americans for the September 11 attacks. Enraged, the man leans forward and shouts, "BOMB HIM!," while his wife reprimands, "We can't bomb Jerry Falwell." But the tiny figure lurking in the lower margin of the cartoon utters the key phrase: "It's Americans who are harboring him." Other cartoonists routinely figured the two as loony fringe figures or merely as comrades of that other religious extremist, Osama bin Laden.

Critics of Falwell and Robertson's comments also failed to inquire about the impact that the comments have on Christian right followers and on those named in the cultural indictment. Hence, these commentators missed opportunities—to explicate Christian right theology with regard to end-times, sexual sin, and national transgression and to explicate the rhetorical, ideological, and institutional components of the Christian right's politics of desert, a politics deeply related to its "national campaign against gay rights" from the 1980s to the present.[46]

The occasional eruptions of Christian right discourse into mainstream attention can yield considerable information about the cultural politics of the current "family values" movement, but to make sense of them we must be attentive to the multiple forms of address favored by Christian right leaders. These leaders practice small duplicities—such as apologies—in order to be misunderstood by the "major population." It is important to recognize that nonbelievers—for born-again believers, those (including Jews) who have not yet found Christ—have a crucial role to play in the theology and eschatology of the Christian right. In the little tribulation of present-day America, nonbelievers fulfill unaware the end-time narrative of descent into sin and secularism and are the objects of Christian missionary action. They fix and occupy the boundary of God's church, for "the disbelief of outsiders is a precondition of miraculous action."[47]

As for the other side of the political continuum, students of right-wing discourse point out that extreme right-wing ideas on race, gender, sexuality, and nationalism function to center and legitimize ostensibly more benign expressions. This is so even when there is little or no distinction between the content of the ideas themselves.[48] It turns out that there are a number of actors on the political right whose message reproduces the message that the reverends Falwell and Robertson delivered on September 13, 2001. Most of these spokespersons are less prominent and so less likely to attract the kind of attention that briefly flowed to the *700 Club* broadcast. Examining a variety of these documents helps to situate—indeed, to normalize—the comments that attracted so much attention to two outspoken Christian right leaders. These messages appear in a variety of media. Moderation of tone and language notwithstanding, what is striking is how similar are the sentiments and ideas expressed in these manifestos.

Soon after the fracas over Falwell and Robertson, D. James Kennedy, the late founder of Coral Ridge Ministries and the Center for Reclaiming America, produced a booklet, entitled "Why Was America Attacked? Answers for a Nation at War." The booklet is divided into three sections—"When the Towers Fall," "Answers from Dr. Kennedy," and "Two Questions for You"—and it evinces the two prime conservative Christian motives of our time: first, encouraging individual salvation, and second, punishing the guilty and redeeming America from the sins of its denizens, the *700 Club* politics of desert. Referring to the attacks on the World Trade Center, the Pentagon, and United Airlines Flight 93, Kennedy begins by noting that the nation "will need much prayer—and repentance—before the crisis has passed."[49]

Kennedy's diagnosis of the precipitating factors of the attack is the same as Falwell and Robertson's without the pointed identifications of sinful groups who, after all, need not be named for this audience: "when such things happen we should consider our own sins and the sins of our own nation." Here is a more complete version:

And so we should all consider ourselves and ask God for forgiveness for our individual sins and, as representatives of this nation, for our national sins. There is no doubt that in America we have been engaged in all kinds of immorality—every conceivable kind. We seem to be bent on plunging ourselves ever deeper and deeper into the mire of perversion and immorality. We need to repent as a nation or we can experience worse chastening from God.

Dear friends, we have enough sin in this country to keep terrorists busy for the next hundred years, and we need to confess those. We need, as citizens of this nation, to confess our national sins and ask God to cleanse us and forgive us that we might be spared that which God says He has intended to do to His people.[50]

Without the specific signifier, "perversion," this might be a Christian version of a left-wing political complaint against American foreign policy. Such a complaint would seek the reasons why foreign nationals might hijack commercial jets and use them as missiles against American targets and civilians. And it would locate the reasons for those actions in American acts of state. Both the left- and right-wing perspectives on culpability for September 11 can be indicted for paying too little attention to the ideologies of those who initiate terrorist attacks against civilians; these are empirical as well as theoretical questions.[51] Yet in spite of superficial similarities, the search for culprits on the political left and the Christian right could not diverge more.

The most important area of difference lies in Kennedy's notion of "national sins." Kennedy does not explain the difference between individual and national sins—that difference is already understood by his audience—but by "national sins" he does not refer to acts committed by representatives of the United States government. Rather sins become national when they are widely practiced violations of God's will and, in addition, when they are widely tolerated, or even not sufficiently contested. William Bennett's title phrase from the days of President Bill Clinton's impeachment, "the death of outrage," suggests the depth of the problem. The book of Genesis leads us to the concept of national sins through a story that is much invoked by conservative Christians for the purpose. Genesis chapter 18 records a conversation between God and Abraham about the sins of the cities of Sodom and Gomorrah and about God's plans to destroy the cities because of their iniquity. Abraham begs for the cities to be spared and barters with God, asking him to relent if a specifiable number of righteous people can be found in the cities. The two conclude their conversation with a deal: if ten righteous people can be found in the cities, God will not destroy them. As we know, the ten righteous people are not found. God rescues his servant, Lot, and some members of Lot's family, and then destroys the cities with fire. The only sin Christian conservatives explicitly associate with the destruction of Sodom and Gomorrah is the sin of homosexuality. It's unlikely that all, or most, of the citizens of these cities were practicing homosexuality, so it seems likely that widespread depravity in the cities was a matter of indifference to that vile sin or negotiation with it. Indeed, Lott even seems to share the latter response when he attempts to trade his virgin daughters to the crowd in return for the safety of his male visitors.

In Kennedy's account, it is not that there is no distinction to be made between Sodom and September 11. Unlike in Sodom, those killed in the conflagrations of September 11 are not more guilty than those who were spared. Their innocence—or, perhaps, the guilt they share with other Americans—can function as a confirmation that, as in Sodom, our national wickedness is pervasive and only can be cleansed by God's wrath.

Because of the greater length of his booklet compared to the brief *700 Club* comments, Kennedy delivers much more detail to his conservative Christian audience than Falwell and Robertson were able to do. To lay the foundation for a politics of desert, Kennedy repeats what his audience already knows about Osama bin Laden because he is a Muslim: "*of course,* he is descended from Ishmael, who, we are told in Scripture, 'will be a wild man, his hand will be against every man, and every man's hand against him.'"[52] Of course. More generally, those who identify with "militant Islam" are "but captives of our enemy, Satan." Kennedy exculpates himself, and by extension his readers ("I don't know about you, but"), from having ever "personally done anything . . . against a Muslim." In fact, Kennedy's care for Muslims extends to "shar[ing] the Good News of the Gospel with them."[53] He also exculpates

Christians throughout history, noting that when "Christians in past times . . . have killed people" they have done so not with the blessing of their faith but "in violation and opposition to the teachings of Jesus." This conviction begs the question of the possible ways in which God has used, or may yet use, Christians to fulfill his will, either to punish the sinfulness of peoples or to initiate their individual salvation. Or, more to the point, this teaching assumes that, like the ancient Hebrews, Christians may be used in this way. If God uses Christians to work his will, it is only their wayward individual actions that can be the objects of legitimate criticism.

God will "bring in the foreigner" to chastise his people, and when he does so their chastening is correct and a sign that they are "legitimate children of God." By the same token, Christians may be called of God to defend their nation from attack, and when they do so they must set aside the "Christian *personal* ethics" of the Sermon on the Mount and participate in their government's efforts to effectuate the "principle of justice." Kennedy is persuaded that all terrorist attacks and the efforts to bring justice from them must conclude with God bringing good "even out of the most horrid circumstances." This good will be dual, a national repentance from sins of perversion and immorality and a turning of many millions of individuals to Jesus; Kennedy hopes that "five million people or more will come to receive life everlasting" as a result of the events the terrorists initiated.[54] What commands our attention about these arguments is how very ordinary they are in the context of conservative Christian doctrine. The only unusual dimension of Kennedy's booklet is the context, a large-scale violent assault on American territory and American citizens. This assault gives urgency to the message, but it does not alter its content by a jot or a tittle.

A somewhat harsher version of the politics of desert is expressed by ACTS International. ACTS International is a "Christian teaching service" and a "dynamic resource for inspirational living." It provides Christians with an online bookstore, inspirational stories, devotionals and prayer tips, and information about important social and political issues from a conservative Christian perspective. Here is Dick Innes, author and founder of the organization, on September 11:

> In the wake of the September 11 barbaric terrorist attacks in New York and Washington and many other acts of terrorism in recent days, not only in America but around the world—one cannot help but wonder about the correlation of these events with the ever-increasing tearing down of the Christian beliefs upon which the U.S.A. was founded, and the Judaeo-Christian ethic upon which much of our Western society has been built. . . . Let us not forget other recent societies who also ignored God—including those of Hitler and Stalin![55]

As a political argument, this message may seem ideologically confused unless we fill in the connection between Hitler and Stalin. Innes certainly denounces the two leaders for their murderous acts and their totalitarian regimes. However, it is more productive to attend to the plain language of the text and conclude that what National Socialism and Soviet communism have in common is their satanic origins. This they share with the homosexual threat.

The ACTS International formulation, although somewhat more moderately phrased, is nonetheless difficult to differentiate from the version put forth by the Creator's Rights Party. Creator's Rights is a militant group whose rhetoric edges just into the territory of encouraging violence against God's foes. Its founder carefully renounces violence and advocates education and, as a last resort, secession as a solution to the failure of the United States to be governed by God's law. The group focuses its primary attention on abortion rights issues and abortion providers. It furnishes visitors to its website with photos of purported reproductive rights clinics and aborted fetuses. With its *Reader's Digest* style, and its many offerings of light-hearted lifestyle reading materials, ACTS International is like the soft suburban megachurch to God's own Creator's Rights guerillas. Nonetheless, in an essay entitled "Our Nation Under Attack: Will the USA be Nuked for Defending a False Freedom?" party founder Neal Horsely offers a by-now familiar reading of the events of September 11. Horsley considers President Bush's claim that the terrorists hate America because of our freedoms and offers both his agreement and a provocative demurral. He forcefully seconds Islamic fundamentalist charges that American freedoms and mores represent sinfulness and evil:

> We must not only hear the forces of Islamic fundamentalism say those things: we must agree that they are correct and that such sin should never be tolerated by any nation on earth. That is how repentance must begin. But that is only the start of repentance. We the people of the United States of America must demonstrate that our repentance is a true repentance by returning sin to its rightful place and outlawing those things that are an abomination before the God of Abraham.

He continues:

> The vast majority of American citizens have proven themselves willing to tolerate the most grievous sin rather than risk offending any significant group in this nation, like the abortion advocates or the homosexuals or other sexual outlaws. . . . But mark these words well[:] when nuclear or biological terror settles over this nation in the months and years ahead, that bold mocking of the God of Abraham will change.[56]

One virtue of this concise statement is that it explicitly makes the connections that often are implicit between the punishment meted out to "ordinary" Americans, tolerance, sexual sin (abortion and same-sex sexuality), and terror.

These linkages are also apparent in another recent work, and one that is more recognizable as a theological treatise. The book, *Defending a Higher Law: Why We Must Resist Same-Sex "Marriage" and the Homosexual Movement*, is produced by the American Society for the Defense of Tradition, Family and Property (TFP). Judged by obscurity alone, TFP may be an even less predictable messenger of Christian right doctrine than are some marginal figures who communicate with their followers through websites. TFP was founded in 1973 to resist liberalism, socialism, and communism and affirm tradition, family, and property.[57] Also unusual is the fact that *Defending a Higher Law* is a Catholic work with deliberate crossover appeal for conservative Protestants. The dedication reads: "This book is dedicated to the Holy Family, the sublime model for all families, and our sure guide in the reaction to the sexual revolution and homosexual offensive. May the Blessed Mother intercede with Her Divine Son for all Americans committed to defend the sacred institutions of marriage and the family."

The book as a whole traces the origins and development of the LGBT movement, rehearses the church's teachings on same-sex sexuality, and offers arguments for use against the rights claims and social appeals of homosexuals. However, it is the appendix to the book, a section often ignored even by studious readers, that is most interesting. Entitled "Are We Still 'One Nation Under God'?" the text of this section appeared as a full page ad in the *Washington Times* on July 9, 2003. Thus, the ad appeared two weeks after the Supreme Court announced its decision in *Lawrence v. Texas*. For TFP, *Lawrence* is America's "moral 9/11," a decision that "replicates in the moral realm the devastating physical attack perpetrated against the nation on September 11, 2001."[58] The decision "affirms that there is no morality"; the court, in defining liberty broadly enough to include the right to engage in same-sex sexual acts in private "profoundly undermine[s] public morality."[59] In many respects, the ad/appendix complements Justice Scalia's many jeremiads against court decisions that violate his understanding of natural law. It differs from these only in its explicit deference to scripture and to Catholic doctrine on the subject of same-sex sexuality.

The passages that are most relevant to the politics of desert are offered under the subhead "We Should Fear That God Will Withdraw His Blessings from America." In this section, the authors reject the cynicism of Europeans who deride the presidential custom of closing speeches with the prayerful "God bless America." They note that "God has blessed America abundantly" and pose the question that preoccupies many conservative Christians after September 11: "Will America continue to receive God's blessings in the wake of *Lawrence*? We certainly hope and pray that it will. This will certainly happen, if Americans resolve to reject the homosexual agenda despite the pressure brought to bear by a liberal media, the world of Hollywood, and more unwanted changes to our laws by the Supreme Court."[60] Here is the clarification of what it is about the court's decision in *Lawrence* that makes that decision the moral equivalent of the 9/11 paramilitary attack. Both events trigger visible and devastating effects of perilous national choices. In both, the indifference, ignorance, tolerance, or malice of many parties—for the TFP, the conservative bête noire, activist judges—is necessary to precipitate these consequences. TFP urges Americans to embrace two ideas: that God has blessed America and that our collective behavior is too egregious for him to continue to do so.

Finally, on the far right, there is Fred Phelps. In the months after the terrorist attacks, Phelps added specific commentaries to his Westboro Baptist Church websites that clarify the causal link between same-sex sexual conduct ("sodomy") and collective terrorist victimization.[61] Explaining that the September 11 attacks are the direct result of widespread social tolerance of the sin of sodomy, Phelps offers a timely set of lyrics to be sung to the tune of "America the Beautiful" and, for those with appropriate computer software, a choir singing those lyrics:

> O wicked land of sodomites
> Your World Trade Center's gone
> With crashing planes and burning flames
> To hell your souls have flown
> America
> America
> God showed his wrath to thee!
> He cursed this land
> With his own hand
> And showed His sovereignty.[62]

In addition to sermonizing on the causes of terrorism, Phelps helpfully denounces the more tepid Christianity of Billy Graham, Jerry Falwell, Pat Robertson, and George W. Bush. Such denunciations, whether offered by Phelps or by other marginal Christian figures such as the Reverend Tony Alamo, no doubt reinforce the claims of Graham, et al., to political moderation.

Phelps himself is not an important figure in Christian right politics, and his views do not resonate with large numbers of Americans. Quite the contrary: the majority of his followers are members of his own family, and his views seem to be anathema to most Americans who have heard of him. Even if these citizens do not need to understand themselves as "tolerant" in the sense of liberal pluralism, they probably find his gleeful sadism repugnant, especially since Phelps and his flock have begun picketing the funerals of soldiers killed in the Iraq War. Phelps's importance lies in the fact that his extremism, and that of other far right-wing actors, works to center the views of Christian right leaders like Falwell, Robertson, James Dobson, Gary Bauer, and others. Although the contents of the *700 Club*, ACTS International, Creator's Rights Party, TFP, and Westboro Church messages are strikingly similar, trusted mainstream messengers of antigay political beliefs benefit from the extravagant, even pornographic, hatred expressed by figures such as Phelps.

Mainstream Christian right leaders wish to deflect their followers from tolerance toward a degenerate society. But this mandate is perpetually in tension with a belief in America's special role in God's destiny for humanity. As a result, one theme that expresses and establishes the "moderation" of the Christian right is the hope for national atonement. Christian right leaders always temper anger and contempt for cultural sinfulness with the potential for salvation and national atonement. It is for this reason that leaders like Falwell, Robertson, Kennedy, Bauer, Dobson, and others are political actors and not simply prophets of divine retribution. Fred Phelps and his disciples do not expect either political or cultural change. And their contempt remains undimmed by hopefulness or by attempts to recruit others to their ranks. In this way, they violate the jeremiad tradition, which requires the hope of change and redemption.[63]

While some far right religious actors such as Phelps and his "church" eschew conventional means of effecting political change, Christian conservatives operate within the mainstream of contemporary political discourse and activism. They engage in political dialogue on consequential issues, both within the group of believers and with broader publics. One such issue is the separation of church and state, a rubric under which concerns about the extent to which sectarian religious beliefs and practices should influence law and public policy reside. Prominent Christian right leaders take slightly different positions on the separation of church and state. But many, such as Robertson and Dobson, deny that church-state separation is anything more than a fiction promulgated by irreligious liberals for the benefit of their own designs.

Of course, the conversation about what "separation" means, why it is important, and how to secure it continues in the United States, both at the level of legal scholarship and decisions and in political discourse. No single intervention can settle the question for disputing parties. But interventions are essential to interpret the terms of conflict for disputing sides. In conflicts of beliefs, we may misinterpret the story that the other side is telling and, in this way, fail to know precisely what kind of argument we are having. In this sense, separation of church and state does not only point to a set of legal, political, institutional questions. It is also a terrain of popular discursive struggle.

Where's the Harm?

Conservative Christian doctrine demands that conservative born-again Christians transform law and political institutions and punish dissenters in order to avert God's wrath from a sinful nation and prepare for the Second Coming of Christ. In light of these requirements, the principle of separation of church and state arouses little support and is frequently rejected altogether even by those who do not understand themselves as Christian reconstructionists. There is wide agreement among Christian conservatives that what is at hand is a struggle over ideas and values, the hearts and minds of any major ideological conflict. However, those outside the purview of the Christian right should bear in mind that it is also a struggle over political goals and the nature of the state. From *700 Club* broadcasts to Dobson's radio programming, from the Presidential Prayer Team's daily emails to the preaching at Rod Parsley's World Harvest Church, Christian conservatives receive constant reinforcement for the idea that it is time for born-again believers to take back their nation and its political institutions for God.

In responding to Christian right attempts to breach or nullify church-state separation, many secular students of politics are likely to recur to classic arguments in favor of separation and consider the debate well joined. A problem with this response, as David Gutterman suggests, is that the "relationship between religion and politics" in the United States is too complex for such a resolution. Forcing all questions of religion and politics through this particular sieve distorts political discourse about the role of religion in American political culture. We are dealing with issues that are not simply a matter of the allocation of resources or the proper application of the First Amendment. We are dealing with issues of culture, ethics, and identity. That is, the complex relationship between religion and politics in the United States challenges us to think about communication, argumentation, and what counts to whom as viable and legitimate evidence.[64]

What counts as viable and legitimate evidence for the various arguments that address the relationship between religion and politics? Secular and left religious advocates of church-state separation use arguments from a variety of sources to address religious tolerance and oppose theocratic politics. To the extent that its arguments have become background to this debate, John Locke's *Letter Concerning Toleration* is a first line of intellectual defense for many, including students of religion and politics.[65] Locke, a devout Puritan as well as political philosopher, delivers a litany of the bad outcomes associated with collapsing boundaries between church and state. Although he does not specify particular institutional boundaries between the two, his is an elegant argument for those who defend the necessity of boundaries between civil and religious authority. From our contemporary perspective, Locke's failure to protect a right of individuals to reject religious belief altogether is a significant omission. But he provides support to those who defend the right of individuals to be free of even well-intentioned religious pressure from those who wield state power.

One of Locke's central arguments in the *Letter* is that faith cannot be coerced. Hence, it is useless for believers or for their representatives to try to pressure unbelievers into belief or conversion. Conversion certainly has been one goal of organized religious activity in the political sphere. In her recent book, *Identity in Democracy*, Amy Gutmann accurately notes the propensity of believers to behave in "intolerant and aggressive" ways "in the name of saving lost souls."[66] The problem with extending this reading to account for the Christian right lies less with Locke than it does with the particulars of contemporary Christian right theology and politics. Locke understands the propensity of religious believers to save lost souls or, at least, to add those souls to their own doctrinal ledger. But Locke and many other representatives of church-state separation are silent on the goal of theologically driven cultural and political change and why those with such a goal should settle for the pale reward of religious minimalism. Although converting individual sinners to Christianity remains a ministerial imperative and a goal of many individuals and churches, it is not the principal goal of conservative Christian activists. Rather, the first goal of the Christian right is effecting political change, or effecting cultural change that results in political change. In fact, the goal of social, cultural, and political refashioning is not unique to the Christian right. In a recent study of "the prophetic pulpit," researchers found that ministers who constitute the leadership of the smaller and less politically influential American Christian left share this project with those on the Christian right.[67]

The primacy of this goal on the Christian right calls into question the relevance of appeals against the use of legal and political mechanisms to force conversion. It moots the implicit deal between believers and state authority that Gutmann outlines when she describes the impracticable ideal of "strict separation" of church and state: the state protects freedom of conscience and in exchange believers commit themselves to protect the state from the zeal of their fellows.[68] Gutmann's objection to strict separation is that democracies should do more than this principle allows to respect the conscientious objections of their citizens. But it is also accurate that believers have no need to strike such a deal if they can hope to control the direction of state action with regard to both religious expression and key moral issues.

As the internal discourse of the conservative Christian movement makes clear, the movement has two immediate, and closely related, political goals: first, to place the moral force and disciplinary resources of the state behind proscribing behavior deemed immoral and ungodly; second, to suppress freedom of expression and bad behavior on the part of disbelievers who, left to their own devices, might engage in the proscribed behaviors. The ultimate goal—one that more often than not is not disclosed openly in political discourse—is placing believers in charge of the state and enabling them to consolidate a politics that will deflect God's wrath away from the righteous and prepare the world for the Second Coming of Christ.

If Locke's *Letter* is less useful than many might imagine in confronting the political concerns and agendas of the Christian right, we would do well to turn to John Stuart Mill. In *On Liberty*, Mill makes an argument that has come to be known as the "harm principle." The principle confronts directly the criteria for coercing behavior that are consistent with the liberty interest of individuals in liberal democratic societies. Mill responds to the problem of religious believers who attempt to force behavior on the part of dissenters and nonconformists. He concludes that individuals can't be forced to give up even behavior that is repugnant to observers when there is no demonstrated harm to others. Mill acknowledges vices and personal failures over which individuals might rightly suffer the disapproval of their fellow citizens. However, he concludes that

> Whenever . . . there is a definite damage, or a definite risk of damage, either to an individual or to the public, the case is taken out of the province of liberty, and placed in that of morality or law. But with regard to the merely contingent, or, as it may be called, constructive injury which a person causes to society, by conduct which neither violates any specific duty to the public, nor occasions perceptible hurt to any assignable individual except himself; the inconvenience is one which society can afford to bear, for the sake of the greater good of human freedom.[69]

As is evident from his text and countless commentaries on it, Mill recognizes that religious antipathies to nonconforming behavior are likely to comprise a large subset of charges of "harm." This group of claims he rejects as merely an outrage to the feelings of those offended by the behavior of less pious others.

Many conservative Christians make one version or another of this basic claim: that immoral actors and those who tolerate them cause a "harm," the consequences of which are as bad as consequences can be. At times, this argument is straightforward and does not require additional understanding of conservative Christian theology. For example, in his book *The Tempting of America: The Political Seduction of the Law*, Robert Bork argues that "moral outrage is a sufficient ground for prohibitory legislation. . . . Knowledge that an activity is taking place is a harm to those who find it profoundly immoral."[70] However, at other times, the same argument gestures toward harmful consequences in a way that is more consistent with Mill's intention.

Most students of the harm principle would conclude that there are two fatal problems with the claim that particular categories of sinners must be constrained by law and public policy in order to protect the "major population" from God's purifying wrath. The first response of critics is the agnostic reply that such a claim manifests outraged feelings and that outraged feelings do not constitute a legitimate basis for harm under the harm principle. The second response is that God's punishment on an errant nation is insufficiently causally linked with social tolerance of putative immorality to be taken seriously under the harm principle. Case closed. However, those who wish to understand Christian right political activism would do well to reconsider the nuances of these arguments. Most secular and many religious citizens would probably agree that Christian right claims of harm at terrorist hands fail to meet the criteria for interference with individual liberty. Nonetheless, critics can learn something about these Christian right concerns and goals by examining the parallel tenets of the harm principle and arguments of Christian right leaders.

One link between the Christian right stance toward gays and same-sex sexuality is obvious and ubiquitous: the claim that homosexuals constitute a threat to children. The most direct version of this claim is that LGB people pose a sexual threat, but this claim is usually accompanied but the idea that same-sex sexuality irreparably spoils the environment required for children's moral and spiritual hygiene.[71] To these arguments, which are deployed in both in-group and public venues, we can add the in-group link between queers and harm to the nation. Communiqués within the movement resonate with the conviction that unrepented same-sex sexuality stimulates divine punishment. With regard to outrage, it may be that Mill himself countenanced much more of the kind of social disapprobation expressed through "distaste, contempt and shaming" than is usually identified with him, particularly when those shamed pursue "lower pleasures" and exhibit a "miserable individuality."[72] If anything, Christian right descriptions of same-sex sexuality are lurid accounts of the miserable individuality of gays.[73] Even in the compassionate quarters of Christian antigay politics, same-sex attracted people who refuse to abstain from sexual activity and romantic relationships are described as leading unhappy lives dedicated to low pleasures. As in the days of Noah, such sinfulness is bound to provoke a terrible judgment.

But in any case, Christian right politics of desert are not only aimed at LGB people themselves, those who are objects of distaste and presumed to be miserable individuals. Rather, they are aimed at wayward Americans who do not use the levers of law and social policy to punish and proscribe homosexuality. A more compelling and productive line of argument emerges with reference to these tolerant Americans. As a doctrinal matter, Christian right leaders teach that God exacts judgment and punishment not only on evildoers but also on the peoples/nations that tolerate them. "National sins jeopardize a people's covenant with God."[74] Further, leaders commonly invoke particular groups of evildoers and charge Christians with exhibiting intolerance toward them, not only because such intolerance is what God's inexorable justice commands, but also because it benefits Americans collectively. In this, Christian right leaders such as Falwell, Robertson, James Dobson, D. James Kennedy, and others employ something akin to a concept of "indirect" or "remote harms" to justify acts that range from social disapprobation to legal proscription.

Remote harms extend the harm principle, addressing circumstances in which bad conduct is not followed by an immediate and indisputably injurious consequence. In fact, even in the most ostensibly straightforward cases of individual conduct, the very notion of what constitutes a harm is elusive.[75] In cases of remote harms, these complexities proliferate. With remote harms, a number of issues, including the "gravity of the eventual harm" and the more difficult issue of fair imputation of fault to actors must be resolved before it is possible to find that a harm has occurred.[76] For the Christian right, these issues are already resolved: the gravity of the harm is nothing less than the destruction of America, and fair imputation proceeds from close adherence to scriptural prohibitions on sin and toleration of sin. Here, recall the Christian conservative reading of God's judgment on Sodom and Gomorrah, delivered by messengers as diverse as James Dobson and Jack Chick.

Critics of such notions as gravity and imputation of harm often attempt to dislodge conservative certainty about specific biblical prohibitions. These critics may unearth arcane rules and disingenuously question their contemporary standing. They might, for example, refer to such prohibitions as the one in Deuteronomy that forbids a married woman to help her spouse win a fight by grabbing his foe's genitals.[77] However, these tactics are more satisfying for the critics who wield them than they are useful in inciting conservative Christians to reconsider their case for harm. This is because basic conservative Christian pedagogy distinguishes "between moral law and ancient custom," between universally applicable principles (such as that same-sex sexuality is an abomination) and cultural rules that were meant to apply only to Jews of that era.[78]

The category of remote harms that best applies to the case of pernicious tolerance is "accumulative harms." In this category, "conduct does the feared injury only when combined with similar acts of others."[79] Thus, God does not "lift the curtain" of protection surrounding the United States because of the acts of a few isolated individuals. But there is presumed to be a tipping point for the removal of God's protection. In the teachings of prominent Christian right leaders, widespread tolerance of homosexuality and homosexuals, among other perversions, has already precipitated a withdrawal of God's protection. Only a return to Christian principles and prohibitions can reverse this withdrawal. As Stormie Omartian, author of *The Power of a Praying Nation*, puts it in her book about September 11,

How many of us have humbled ourselves in repentance for our sins and the sins of our nation? How many of us are brokenhearted about the things we tolerate in our nation that break the heart of God?[80]

For years we've been told by pastors and Godly spiritual leaders that, unless we repent, turn from our own ways, and return to God's ways, there will be serious consequences. We must heed their warnings.[81]

Perhaps the best irony of conservative Christians employing a harm argument to respond to the danger of national sins and the tolerance of them is the theoretical context in which the harm principle is nested. For Mill, the harm principle protects the normative end of diversity by constraining state action against nonconformity and difference. Mill is famously concerned with securing the social and political conditions that nurture and protect individuality, even if true individuality rarely makes an appearance. He is pitiless in his rejection of the precept that religion provides the best or only foundation of ethics. And he learned much from Alexis de Tocqueville's famous indictment of the tyranny of the majority in modern democracies. For Mill, the convictions of ordinary people, no matter how widely or deeply held, do not constitute a natural law for human conduct. Christian conservatives thus turn Mill on his head in constructing their own contemporary version of the harm principle that links queers and terrorists.

By reading the Christian right's rhetoric in light of the harm principle, I do not mean to suggest that the Christian right framing of the politics of desert is unassailable, either logically or politically. On the contrary, the extent to which same-sex sexuality constitutes a persuasive case of remote harm is ultimately a matter of how we interpret such disparate "evidence" as Christian scripture, contemporary prophetic preaching, and constitutional law. However, Christian right leaders do benefit from constructing a Millian framing of the politics of desert while their political adversaries are off trying to make a more persuasive Lockean case for separation of church and state.

This is so for many reasons. First, by hewing to a harm principle argument, the Christian right avoids the identification of its cultural politics with mere outraged feelings. This is so because the framing of preventing harm to the nation does not immediately evoke the punitive motivations sometimes associated with the Christian right. A second, related, point is that the Christian right benefits from affirmatively identifying with concern for the nation as a whole and not with concern for its own minority membership. Finally, because the harm principle only justifies coercive intervention to prevent harm to innocent bystanders, many Americans might well identify it as a principle that supports basic respect for individual rights, if not value pluralism. Many theorists have recently documented consequential ways in which the political right coopts and transforms the values, rhetorics, ideals, and tools of the political left, and here is yet another.[82] In the case of sins such as homosexuality, abortion, and the dismissal of God from public life, the Christian right casts the tolerant value pluralism of the left as nihilism and the rhetorical and policy interventions of born-again believers as prudential morality and patriotism.

For secular students of politics, acknowledging the ways in which a Christian right politics of desert bears a family resemblance to a Millian harm principle accomplishes two important ends: first, "reparative therapies" and the "ex-gay movement" notwithstanding, it confirms that Christian right antipathy toward homosexuals and other disfavored groups does not necessarily have individual conversion as a primary goal. Second, it helps to explain the attractiveness of conservative Christian politics to many Americans who probably would not identify themselves with the Christian right. In the days after September 11, several email messages that identified the cause of the disaster as Americans' loss of values zipped around the nation. I received a couple of variations on that theme from unlikely sources, people who did not understand themselves as bearers of a particular religious doctrine but who found the causal argument, and the national fix it recommended, intuitively persuasive and comforting.

If many Americans who might not otherwise identify with Christian right politics intuitively come to understand a politics of desert to be consistent with the harm principle, Christian right politics will be facially consistent with a liberal democratic political tradition. And to paraphrase one of our post-September 11 clichés, the Christian right will have won.

Bringing Us All Together

Besides those we've seen already, there is yet another way that queers and terrorists/terrorism may well be related to one another in the minds of many Americans, one that is implicit in much of the post-September 11 conservative Christian literature. Or perhaps this connection is just another perspective on the notion of national harm. It is that the scourge of terrorism provides a tableau that motivates, inspires, and provides the opportunity for national unity through moral cleansing. National unity and inspiration, in turn, can provide the impetus for ridding our land of other scourges, including that of sexual sin. Since the beginning of our national war on terror, mainstream conservatives such as Francis Fukuyama and David Brooks have declaimed on the bracing effect of national unity for dealing with the problem of "self-indulgence."[83] Christian conservatives agree with this assessment, they are just more specific in detailing self-indulgence and in retailing different versions of their message to their audiences.

Examining many forms of conservative Christian pedagogy, it is clear that a principal thrust of conservative Christian concern is promoting and maintaining American unity in the face of behavioral and ideological differences. One example of this pedagogy uses moral-theological instruction to direct political belief and action: the Presidential Prayer Team (PPT). Founded on September 18, 2001, the sole purpose of PPT is given as "mobilizing and encouraging Americans to pray daily for the President, his Cabinet and other leaders of our nation."[84] PPT is a nonpartisan, nonprofit 501 (c)3 membership organization headed by a president/CEO and a board of directors. Its activities are diversified and include a listserv that communicates with members, a volunteer ("Ambassadors") program, an "Adopt Our Troops" program, a radio show, PPT publications, unscientific member polls, and a children's program (Presidential Prayer Team for Kids).[85] The PPT website clarifies that George W. Bush is not officially connected to the organization, but the iconic image associated with PPT is President Bush, brow furrowed, head bowed in prayer.

The Presidential Prayer Team directs its rhetoric toward in-group members of the conservative Christian right, which makes it a useful mechanism for surveying the relation between unity, patriotism, moral good, and the production of out-groups who are responsible for threatening unity and the well-being of America. The religio-political rhetoric of PPT performs a number of functions. These include soliciting prayer for national leaders but also a number of other functions that are performed rather than named: consolidating the reconstructionist argument that past American leaders shared a political theology with contemporary conservative Christians, informing PPT members about the functions and institutions of government, providing information about the president's schedule and movements, introducing current domestic and foreign leaders (including political appointees in executive branch agencies), and detailing current policies and administration initiatives. In short, PPT has packaged the goals, projects, and key actors of the Bush administration and served them to members as neutral reportage in the service of informed prayer, suggesting that those who know what the president is doing and with whom will be more effective at praying for him. PPT executes its Christian right pedagogical function by collapsing the task of holding the born-again president up in prayer and the task of consolidating support for the president's agenda and policies.

How do these fused objectives play out in the Presidential Prayer Team's regular internet outreach to its members? One example is that, like, Robertson, Kennedy, Rod Parsley, Joyce Meyer, and countless other leaders of the Christian right, PPT urges members to "pray for a resurgence of godly character in America" and "a return to biblical values" (Presidential Prayer Requests for October 16, 2003). Such general exhortations are packed with end-times meaning for conservative Christians as they summon up the forms of national sin that provoke God's wrath. Even more consistent with conservative Christian politics are messages that remind members of a link between terrorism and American domestic sinfulness: "just as there is a physical threat to America from terrorists abroad, there is a spiritual threat to America from enemies within, who want to extinguish prayer and our trust in Almighty God from the very foundation of our country" (PPT, February 27, 2006).

And what does support for Bush have to do with the twin threats of terrorism and national sin? "No matter how the critics try to tear down the Office of the Presidency, no matter how hard the terrorists try to defeat America, we know that President Bush still needs our genuine prayers and support" (PPT, May 31, 2006). Support for America—that is, an America that dedicates itself to following God's will—requires support for Bush (the Christian president identical with the presidential office). Christian citizens devoted to the president and to a godly America will recognize that terrorists and fellow citizens who refuse devotion to Bush and godliness constitute equivalent threats to the nation. Through a persistent set of putatively neutral and apolitical messages, PPT evokes the associations that other Christian right leaders spell out in pedagogical detail: fractious forms of immorality (such as same-sex sexuality) constitute a spiritual threat to the nation against which godly leaders like Bush struggle to save us. Christian citizens have a role in saving the nation because it is they who hold up the president to God in prayer and specify the terms of their concern for him and the nation. Commenting on Bush's slide in public opinion polls, PPT advises: "Being popular is beyond one's control. Doing the right thing steadily, before God, as best one can, is within one's grasp. Let's keep praying that President Bush seek God everyday for guidance and wisdom to keep America on track as One Nation Under God. We must not fail to pray for our President. We must continue to pray for America" (May 31, 2006).

As the 2006 midterm election campaign drew to a close, Christian right leaders were emphasizing the conservative Christian interest in supporting the Republican Party. At The Washington Briefing: Values Voter Summit in Washington, DC, James Dobson urged the assembled activists to support the Republican Party because "the alternative is terrible." Gary Bauer was even more pointed about the need for conservative Christians to vote for godly candidates, including those who oppose the "radical gay rights movement." To make his point, Bauer noted that voting is not as difficult as wrestling with box cutter–wielding terrorists. As it was for the Republican Party, the electoral strategy of the Christian right in the campaign season was to tie the ungodly—principal among them queer people and those who campaign for LGBT rights—to the threat of terrorism. This equation was unavoidable at the Values Voter Summit and was documented by reports from PRA ("Running Against Sodom and Osama") and NGLTF ("Internal Enemy: Gays as the Domestic al-Qaeda")."[86]

Political discourse is agonistic. Partisans play rough, and successful political strategists accomplish the best fit between the characterizations of their adversaries and the anxieties of the electorate. This being so, it seems naïve to bemoan the uses of terrorism to advance partisan political agendas; such is the rough-and-tumble of democratic politics. Those who disagree with particular metaphors and metonyms are free to create and disseminate their own. With regard to the link between queers and terrorism, however, more remains to be said. LGBT people are already abjected members of the community, objects of disgust, contempt, and second-class citizenship. The multiple enemy constructions of homosexuals have had many ramifications for those who bear this stigmatized identity. This should be enough of a reason to justify the scrutiny of the ends, aspirations, and strategies of the Christian right movement. If it is not, there is an additional consideration: democracy is not reducible to its most agonistic elements. Because there is more to democracy than that, it is possible to mobilize knowledge and counter-discourses against the enemy rhetoric of the Christian right.

Another Gay Agenda

A soft answer turneth away wrath: but grievous words stir up anger. The tongue of the wise useth knowledge aright: but the mouth of fools poureth out foolishness.

—Proverbs 15:1–2

Listen Up!

Americans have a long history of fidelity to a Puritan tradition that enjoins the godly to endow the nation with spiritual significance and to steer it toward righteousness. Politically, of course, all social movements have national aspirations, so the mere existence of such ends and aspirations doesn't distinguish the Christian right from other groups, including the LGBT movement. However, one difference between groups is consequential to democratic knowledge and deliberation: groups and movements differ in how they formulate different sets of polemics, analyses, rationales, and aspirations for in-group and out-group audiences.

Besides considerable differences between the LGBT and Christian right movements in terms of ends and values, there is another difference that is relevant to this book. Semi-coordinated as it is, the LGBT movement is transparent about its goals. For example, many queers disapprove, but the movement has embraced the goal of same-sex marriage. The internal movement conversation about same-sex marriage, civil partnerships, employment protection, and integration into the military forces continues even as civil rights organizations enunciate and defend positions on these issues.[1] On other issues related to sexuality, family life, politics, economics, and movement ethics there is a multiplicity of perspectives and voices: religious and nonreligious, monogamous and polyamorous, traditionalist and libertarian, closeted and assertively public. The LGBT movement, constructed as monolithic by its adversaries, is a very big tent indeed.

Leaders in the Christian right teach that there is a sinister agenda behind the goal of same-sex marriage, and that is the goal to destroy the institution of marriage altogether. However, this claim rests on the quite different conceptions of marriage that those on different sides of the debate hold rather than on a secret queer agenda to wreck the sacred institution. People on the LGBT side of this divide frequently wonder why conservative Christians believe that same-sex marriage will destroy marriage itself, but this confusion is a matter of theo-political ignorance that as easily characterizes many heterosexuals outside the Christian right as it does many queers. Such confusion can be resolved by learning what marriage, gender nonnormativity, and same-sex sexuality mean to conservative Christians. The knowledge is unlikely to foster comity between adversaries, but it would inform the kinds of conversations citizens have with one another and the way those who disagree with the Christian right practice politics.

For the record, this book is an exercise in documenting and analyzing dimensions of conservative Christian ideology, because it is important for all citizens to understand the political ideology of the movement. However, I am not suggesting that conservative Christians be pressured to recant their perspectives on the satanic foundations of same-sex sexuality, the misery of same-sex relations, and the linkages between homosexuality and terrorism. Tolerance *is* only valuable in cases in which expression is undesirable; these ideas are undesirable to me, and I still believe that a good society is one that tolerates them. As students of elementary civics learn, the answer to such ideas is more expression. What we don't always absorb in civics class is the problem that even ordinarily attentive citizens may not be aware of the convictions that undergird ostensibly benign or rational political rhetorics. Particularly misleading to some and satisfying to others are those rhetorics that furnish citizens with an identity that is centrist, rational, patriotic, virtuous, or godly.

I can testify with a clear conscience that homosexuals do not gather away from prying conservative ears and discuss or acknowledge a plot to destroy the institution of marriage by participating in it. Further, the conflict between these two social and political movements is often characterized by false parity. I can say with complete honesty that I know of no move afoot in the LGBT rights movement to deprive nonhomosexuals of civil rights, convert heterosexuals to homosexuality, or prohibit the free exercise of religion. Of course, unlike many of my peers, I understand that these assurances are all beside the point. Homosexuals and transgender people are dangerous not because we intend or aspire to do anything *to* anyone but because we are more emboldened than ever to live openly and without apology, to call into question the settled beliefs of our fellow citizens, and to alter historical patterns of the distribution of rights and status. Make no mistake: these are radical acts, and it is understandable that those challenged by them are dismayed, disgusted, anxious, angry, and determined. Of my fellow citizens who are conservative Christians I can only say: we disagree. More, we disagree about issues that both sides believe are inescapable dimensions of citizenship and the possibility of a good (if not eternal) life.

Out in the Public

The conservative Christian movement commands impressive support from Americans. Scholars disagree about measurement issues and offer a variety of methods to establish who constitutes this movement, but most agree that the movement represents an impressive 20 to 30 percent of the electorate.[2] This is important information for those who care about the public philosophies upon which the operation of American democracy rests. Yet, offering an answer to the question, how large is the Christian right? doesn't settle questions of political appeal and influence. However broad support for the movement and its political goals, a movement with broad cultural and political aspirations still needs to influence and persuade as many citizens as possible to either identify with it or, at the least, to fail actively to disidentify. When Christian right ideologists and opinion leaders pursue the goal of enlarging the numbers of citizens who identify with the political aspirations of the movement, they do not require those citizens to become attentive subscribers to religious foundations. Indeed, many adherents are drawn to a theological politics because it is the mode of their childhood socialization or because it promises family values, a generalized respect for God, the confirmation of American traditions, and stable identity in a culturally chaotic world. Political competition for votes on issues of great concern, including those on the basic civil rights of queer citizens, does not require theological rigor.

Scholars and citizens on the American left often point out that a majority of Americans do not share the beliefs and political goals of the Christian right. This reality is clearly comforting to many, especially when democracy is in dark times.[3] Nevertheless, in a political realm of institutionally supported and strategic political leaders reinforced by committed activists, it simply doesn't matter whether a majority of Americans know or share all the theological foundations of the Christian right. In addition, crucial coalitions may be more functional when leaders elide the most potentially troublesome facts about the theological foundations of their political beliefs and aspirations. These are desirable effects for the conservative Christian movement: the intuitive support of anxious citizens with low levels of political knowledge, the willingness of political elites to execute its agenda—even if for their own selfish purposes—and the ability to curry favor and create coalitions with those who might well disapprove of the movement's narrow theology. Needless to say, these conditions exact a cost on democratic processes that, at their best, rely upon transparency for their functioning.

Why is transparency—and the debate it enables—important for democracy? One theorist who took up these questions is the political philosopher

Hannah Arendt, and her responses fruitfully can be applied to present circumstances in the politics of sexuality. Arendt wrote two essays that address these questions: "Truth and Politics" and "Lying in Politics." "Lying" is Arendt's passionate response to the Pentagon Papers and the lies of American political elites during the Vietnam War era. In it, she returns briefly to an argument she explored at much greater length in the earlier essay, which she wrote in response to the controversy over her book *Eichmann in Jerusalem*.[4] There is an important difference between the two essays; while "Lying" addresses the democratic problem of official deception, "Truth" defines the democratic problem more expansively. In "Lying," Arendt puts the problem this way:

> The lie did not creep into politics by some accident or human sinfulness. Moral outrage, for this reason alone, is not likely to make it disappear. The deliberate falsehood deals with *contingent* facts; that is, with matters that carry no inherent truth within themselves, no necessity to be as they are. The historian knows how vulnerable is the whole texture of facts in which we spend our daily life; it is always in danger of being perforated by single lies or torn to shreds by the organized lying of groups, nations, or classes or denied and distorted, often carefully covered up by reams of falsehoods or simply allowed to fall into oblivion.[5]

In her earlier consideration of "Truth and Politics," Arendt lays out the grounds of this argument. There, she confronts the intuition that truths cannot be suppressed with a distinction between different kinds of truths: rational and factual. In the category of rational truths that are less vulnerable to extinction are such objects as mathematical and scientific propositions, while factual truths are historical and political; they involve the events of common life. This latter category of truths are more fragile; indeed, they are "always in danger of being maneuvered out of the world, not only for a time but, potentially, forever."[6] Arendt notes that the earliest concerns with truth in political discourse were articulated in the ancient world with regard to rational truths, but that our contemporary concerns ought to be with factual truths, those that are "politically most relevant."

Using Arendt's categories, it is fruitful to allow that many Christian right projects in the arena of knowledge are likely to fail including, for example, challenges to evolution. That is to say, such challenges, even if successful in local domains, will not erase the scientific evidence for evolution or the continuing advancement of the life sciences. Of course, while the different parties argue about the legitimacy of evolutionary science and use the tools of state and local politics to carve out domains of pedagogical control, many American children will miss the opportunity to understand science. This reality alone makes the fight against creation science or Intelligent Design worth waging even if disputes against evolution use theology to target rational truths.

By the same logic, other knowledge, say about historical information such as the religious commitments of the American Founders, the unchanging nature of "the family," and the miserable individuality of LGBT people is more fragile and requires vigilance and public discussion to illuminate its complexities. Even when these discussions occur, there is no guarantee that factual truths will prevail. For example, those who are not part of the in-group may dispute the knowledge of the Christian right to little discernable effect. When I teach my department's Introduction to Women's Studies in the Social Sciences course I briefly instruct students about the origins and existence of federal antidiscrimination law and the categories of identity covered by such laws. This is factual stuff, uninflected by the kinds of haranguing and intimidation that many who disagree with me politically might assume would be part of the lesson plan. In recent years, and in response to students' questions about this material, I've discovered that large numbers of students at my Big Ten university do not believe me when I state that sexual orientation is not a protected category in federal antidiscrimination law. They simply do not believe that I am telling them the truth, and they express their skepticism to me and to each other through words, gestures, and meaningful looks. How could they accept the accuracy of the lesson plan when they have heard for most of their lives about the special rights afforded to homosexuals? Not that some of them care, of course; many are quite laissez faire about LGBT identities and same-sex sexuality. Still, I'm sure I fail to persuade many of these students about the status of sexual orientation in the law because they have already learned this lesson elsewhere.[7]

Although we would disagree about the particulars, skepticism about Truth is common across the political spectrum. Much academic political theory consists of critiques of foundations, putative truths upon which political regimes and ideologies might be erected and maintained. Most contemporary political theorists are antifoundationalists of one sort or another, but such antifoundationalism does not entail a disregard for all truths. Certainly, those who believe in democracy and wish to strengthen its practice must have a respect for evidence and for empirical forms of knowledge. Either sexual orientation is a protected category in federal antidiscrimination law or it is not. Either queers are rich (and therefore not in need of the protection of the laws) and unhappy (and therefore in need only of salvation) or the reality—to say nothing of democracy itself—is much more complicated.

We inhabit a public realm in which citizens have access to a wide range of facts; who among us is incapable of discovering the truth about federal antidiscrimination law? Yet it is incontrovertible that many of us accept what we are told by trusted elites or what seems to us consistent with our ideological impulses. This is a problem with which democratic theorists must grapple. The complicated interrelationship of facts and values, contingent truths and passionate beliefs, also suggests a broader "gay agenda" than the one we're used to hearing of from the Christian right.

Another Gay Agenda

It's important for gay people to know the reasons that shape and sustain antigay attitudes and politics as antigay individuals and groups understand them. This is not to suggest that antigay individuals—any more than others—have privileged access to their own minds. Antigay beliefs may be unconscious and multidetermined; they may reveal socialization by authorities as well as expressions of broad fears of contamination. Some research suggests that they may even expose the disclaimed desires of the prejudiced.[8] These psychological questions are significant and scholars should continue to investigate the broad subject matter of the hidden and disclaimed dimensions of antigay bias.[9]

But antigay politics cannot be reduced to psychologies of prejudice. Even if political ideologies were merely elaborate facades of rationalization for psychic tics and quirks it would still be useful for those of us who embody some kind of widely loathed or mistrusted identity to listen carefully to the baroque and tenacious beliefs that ground public policies that touch our lives and livelihoods. Many of the putative truths that motivate political ideologies—of the left and of the right—are not matters of fact but, rather, matters of values, core commitments, deeply held beliefs about the world, and affective investments. For the most part, it does no good to argue over the truth of these. On the other hand, the fact that genealogies of theological belief and commitment provide foundations for political beliefs and policy positions is a political fact—a factual truth, in Arendt's language—that is capable of being revealed, documented, disclaimed, and debated. Asking public questions and demanding public answers about the foundations, strategies, and aspirations of political actors is itself a task for democratic citizens.

The mandates to translate private languages and beliefs into public ones and to engage in common forms of democratic discourse are laudable. Indeed, it is difficult to see how the goal of mutual respect can be achieved without democratic talk that is broadly comprehensible. At the same time, most democratic theorists underestimate the side effects—intended or unintended—that may follow from this process of translation. What of, for example, the beliefs that cannot be translated into common discourse without doing violence to their sacredness or exposing their adherents to ridicule? When Pastor Ted Haggard wrote the members of his congregation about the upcoming visit of journalists to New Life Church and urged the members of his flock not to "be weird" in front of the guests, he was engaging in a time-honored ritual of cleaning up for company. It is respectful of company to put one's best foot forward, to clean up one's speech and not employ the mannerisms accepted among one's bosom companions. Among conservative Christians, as well as members of many faiths, it may also smack of impiety to expose precious aspects of belief to a secular mass audience. Why would one want to share the "things of the spirit" with those who not only will fail to appreciate them but who will almost certainly see them as "foolishness"?

Christian conservatives have long maintained that American society is hostile to their religious beliefs, for example, interpreting awkward rhetorical attempts to accommodate non-Christian sensibilities as a "War on Christmas." And criticisms of policy perspectives are easily read as malevolent assaults on sacred beliefs or on religion itself. My purpose in this study is expository and analytical rather than directly political. But this does not mean that no strategic political implications may be gleaned from the examination of Christian right antigay "cases" such as Chick tracts, the ex-gay movement, and the rhetorical equation of homosexuals and terrorists.

Critics of the antigay politics of the Christian right can and should explicitly address the range of messages on LGBT people and same-sex sexuality that the movement conveys to its in-group and to the broader public. We should be able to demonstrate that we understand the multiple ways in which believers of many varieties translate core matters of faith with regard to gender, sexuality, and family formation into social and policy positions. We should be prepared to discuss the ways in which the different messages produced and consumed within the Christian right movement expose gaps and contradictions that are, at least at times, inconvenient for those who represent the movement's interface with the broad public and with at least some political decision-makers. We should know not only the old and still viable rhetoric of sin and abomination, but be able to map the movements back and forth across the terrain of sin and rights, damnation and choice. Some ideological gaps that are papered over in the course of conservative Christian movement politics represent old fault lines between religious traditions and denominations. Even if strategies such as cobelligerency prevail in constituting political coalitions among a vague class of religious traditionalists, we should understand how such coalitions are always ideologically unstable and vulnerable.

The diversity of beliefs within the Christian right movement is great, and the movement succeeds best when it elides doctrinal differences to focus on broad agendas and specific goals: for example, turning back the LGBT rights movement and promulgating laws and constitutional amendments that prohibit same-sex marriage. Hence, the movement's critics must highlight the underlying beliefs, motivations, and sometimes enmities that lie beneath these popular goals.

At the same time that the Christian right is its own big tent, the tent of Christianity is larger still, and denominations, traditions, Christian organizations, and individual churches now openly debate issues about sexuality, welcoming or excluding LGBT individuals and reshaping the boundaries of faith and fellowship. One of the greatest rhetorical triumphs of the Christian right movement may be its success in constructing and defending the belief that queer people, by definition, are not Christian believers. This belief is a powerful wedge for separating LGBT people from their communities and families, if not from faith itself. Even so, American Christians of all sexual identities who share some skepticism about the social and policy agenda of the Christian right are potential allies in opposing the inegalitarian aspirations of the antigay Christian right.

Over the last twenty years, there has been considerable debate about the "gay agenda," whether such a singular object of opposition exists and, if so, of what it consists. Although they have changed over time, a recognizable set of aspirations has been endorsed by the LGBT movement: the repeal of discriminatory legislation, equal treatment in public institutions such as schools and the military, inclusion in human rights policies, protection of LGBT youth, equality in family policies and public entitlements, and more diffuse goals of social recognition and equal respect. Even though these goals are not universally endorsed by all queer people, they surely constitute a kind of gay agenda. Opposition to this gay agenda, including the position that stigma and discrimination are positive social goods, has a variety of sources, but it is undeniable that traditionalist religious belief motivates most antigay bias and activism.[10] Thus, whether we like it or not, the conservative Christian movement defines LGBT people, our issues, and our aspirations for millions of Americans and for countless people around the world.

The Christian right is constantly changing and includes within its boundaries a rich variety of theological commitments, discourses, projects, and goals. Its leaders speak in both therapeutic and political registers and, within these different contexts, to each other and also to the rest of us. So listening in and making sense of what we hear is no small challenge. It's likely that no amount of conversation about sexuality is going to enable us all just to get along. Instead, this afterword suggests another gay agenda, one we can share with all citizens who oppose the social and policy aspirations of the conservative Christian movement. This other gay agenda involves learning the theo-political language of the Christian right and taking its sexuality discourse seriously as an ideology that informs the political goals, projects, and yearnings of a large percentage of our fellow citizens. We can't—and won't—share the same language, but we can become better translators and, in the process, more able democratic citizens.

Notes

Introduction: We Are Family

1. Kenneth L. Woodward, "Do You Recognize This Jesus?" (*New York Times*, 2004), http://www.nytimes.com/2004/02/25/opinion/25WOOD.html ?ei=5007&en=397eb9139d213af3&ex=1393045200&partner=USER LAND&pagewanted=print&position (accessed April 3, 2004).

2. The Christian cartoon tracts of Jack Chick are the subject of chapter 2. Robert Fowler, the most careful collector of Chick's publications, notes that "Jack's favorite part of Jesus' life is the gory crucifixion." Indeed, Fowler divides Chick's depictions of the Passion of Christ into three categories, two of which are "gory pre-crucifixion appetizers" and "gory pictures of Him on the cross, suitable for E.C. comics," Robert B. Fowler, *The World of Jack T. Chick (The History of the World According to Jack T. Chick)* (San Francisco: Last Gasp, 2001), pp. 3–10 to 3–11. For one example see "The Sissy?" in which a drawing of a flayed and bleeding Christ is accompanied by the text "you see, Duke, he was beaten to a pulp for you! That's how much he loved you!"

3. Garry Wills, *Under God: Religion and American Politics* (New York: Simon and Schuster, 1990), p. 15.

4. For another perspective on God and sexuality in Texas, see Angelia R. Wilson, *Below the Belt: Sexuality, Religion and the American South* (London: Cassell, 2000).

5. James W. Lamare, Jerry L. Polinard, and Robert D. Wrinkle, "Texas: Religion and Politics in God's Country," in *The Christian Right in American Politics: Marching to the Millennium*, ed. John Green, Mark Rozell, and William Clyde Wilcox, pp. 60–61 (Washington, DC: Georgetown University Press, 2003).

6. Jessica Stern, *Terror in the Name of God: Why Religious Militants Kill* (New York: Harper Perennial, 2004).

7. Actually, a more recent version substitutes "vehicle" for "car," no doubt a confirmation of the great popularity of SUVs and the misnamed "light" trucks.

8. Peter Applebome, *Dixie Rising: How the South Is Shaping American Values, Politics, and Culture* (San Diego: Harcourt Brace and Company, 1996), p. 5.

9. Paul Boyer, *When Time Shall Be No More: Prophesy Belief in Modern American Culture* (Cambridge, MA: Harvard University Press, 1992), p. 13.

10. Wilson, *Below the Belt*, p. 165.

11. Dana Milbank, "Religious Right Finds Its Center in Oval Office: Bush Emerges as Movement's Leader after Robertson Leaves Christian Coalition," *Washington Post* (December 24, 2001): A2.

12. Lou Cannon, *President Reagan: The Role of a Lifetime* (New York: Simon and Schuster, 1991), p. 288.

13. The email was reproduced in many sources. See Cara DeGette, "New Life Church: 'Don't Be Spooky or Weird'" (*Colorado Confidential*, 2006), http://www.coloradoconfidential.com/showDiary.do?diaryId=947 (accessed December 1, 2006). Reverend Haggard stepped down from his leadership position in November 2006, over a sex and drug scandal involving a male prostitute. He announced that he had been cured of homosexuality in February 2007, three weeks after beginning treatment.

14. Pew Forum on Religion and Public Life, "Religion and Politics: Contention and Consensus," (Pew Forum, 2003), http://pewforum.org/docs/index.php?DocID=26 (accessed September 7, 2003).

15. Steve Stone, "Robertson Defends Statement That God Says Bush Will Be Reelected," (*Hampton Roads*, 2004), http://home.hamptonroads.com/stories/story.cfm?story= 655 20&ran=236535 (accessed August 4, 2005).

16. In my notes from the event, no speaker actually used the word "torture," but all who spoke on the subject supported the President's (pro-torture) position and/or spoke disdainfully of liberal discomfort with, or opposition to, the use of practices prohibited under the Geneva Conventions. The most virulent comments on the issue were offered by Gary Bauer, Sean Hannity, William Bennett, and Ann Coulter.

17. On Bush's reputed incompetence, see George Lakoff, Sam Ferguson, and Marc Ettlinger, "Bush Is Not Incompetent," (Rockridge Institute, 2006), http://www.rockridgeinstitute.org/research/lakoff/incompetent (accessed January 22, 2007).

18. Steve Chapman, "George W.'s Heart Attack," (*Slate*, 2001), http://www.slate.com/id/1 00424/ (accessed July 13, 2001).

19. David S. Gutterman, "Presidential Testimony: Listening to the Heart of George W. Bush," (*Project Muse*, 2001), http://muse.jhu.edu/journals/theory_and_event/v005/ 5.2gutterman.html (accessed October 2, 2002).

20. Jim VandeHei, "GOP Looks to Move Its Social Agenda," (*Washington Post*, 2002), http://www.washingtonpost.com/wp-dyn/articles/A34450–2002Nov24.html (accessed December 1, 2002). See Anna Marie Smith, "The Politicization of Marriage in Contemporary American Public Policy: The Defense of Marriage Act and the Personal Responsibility Act," *Citizenship Studies* 5, 3 (2001): 303–320.

21. One example is President Bush's speech in support for a constitutional amendment forbidding same-sex marriage. Christian right groups began pressing for the president's public support for such an amendment shortly after the June 2003 Supreme Court decision in *Lawrence v. Texas*.

22. See, e.g., Doris Buss and Didi Herman, *Globalizing Family Values: The Christian Right in International Politics* (Minneapolis: University of Minnesota Press, 2003); Stephen Zunes, "The Influence of the Christian Right on U.S. Middle East Policy," *Foreign Policy in Focus* (Silver City, NM: Interhemispheric Resource Center, 2004).

23. Duane M. Oldfield is one author who makes this case in the course of a sophisticated analysis of the political setting for the contemporary Christian right: Oldfield, *The Right and the Righteous: The Christian Right Confronts the Republican Party* (Lanham, MD: Rowman and Littlefield, 1996), pp. 30–34.

24. A similar formulation is "multiple modes of outreach" in Julia Lesage, "Christian Media," in *Media, Culture, and the Religious Right*, ed. Linda Kintz and Julia Lesage, p. 28 (Minneapolis: University of Minnesota Press, 1998). While Lesage uses this term to describe institutional and organizational outlets for Christian right ideology, I use a variation on this formulation to point toward the rhetoric itself rather than the outlets through which it is disseminated.

25. Tony Horwitz, *Confederates in the Attic: Dispatches from the Unfinished Civil War* (New York: Random House, 1999).

26. Howard Winant, "Racial Dualism at Century's End," in *The House That Race Built*, ed. Wahneema Lubiano, pp. 87–115 (New York: Vintage, 1998).

27. Bill Keller, "God and George W. Bush," *New York Times* (May 17, 2003): A27.

28. Al Franken, *Lies and the Lying Liars Who Tell Them: A Fair and Balanced Look at the Right* (New York: Dutton, 2003), pp. 222–224.

29. The germinal investigation of this concept is found in C. Wright Mills, *The Power Elite* (New York: Oxford University Press, 2000).

30. See Amy Gutmann and Dennis Thompson, *Democracy and Disagreement* (Cambridge: Harvard University Press, 1996); Stephen Macedo, *Deliberative Politics: Essays on Democracy and Disagreement* (Oxford: Oxford University Press, 1999).

31. Actually, Lindblom spoke of "businessmen" in his 1977 book and, at the risk of failing to acknowledge the slow process of women's mobility in the upper strata of the business world, I bring his language up to date.

32. Charles E. Lindblom, *Politics and Markets: The World's Political Economic Systems* (New York: Basic Books, 1977), p. 171.

33. Jacob Weisberg, "Dobson's Choice: Religious Right Leader James Dobson's 'My Way or the Highway' Tactics Spell Trouble for the GOP," (*Slate*, 1998), http://slate.msn.com/id/2314/ (accessed September 14, 2004); see also Phil Brennan, "Christian Right Talks of Bolting GOP in 2004," (*NewsMax*, 2003), http://www.news max.com/archives/articles/2003/5/6/110046.shtml (accessed February 10, 2004).

34. Alan Cooperman, "Churchgoers Get Direction from Bush Campaign," (*Washington Post*, 2004), http://www.washingtonpost.com/wp-dyn/articles/A19082–2004Jun30.html (accessed September 15, 2004).

35. Alan Cooperman, "Pastors Issue Directive in Response to Reelection Tactic," (*Washington Post*, 2004), http://www.washingtonpost.com/wp-dyn/articles/A9533–2004Aug17.html (accessed August 19, 2004); Jamie Shor, "Evangelical/Moderate Religious Leaders Criticize Bush Campaign for Misuse of Churches; Call on President to Repudiate Violations," (*US News Wire*, 2004), http://releases.usnewswire.com/Get Release.asp?id=34700 (accessed September 15, 2004).

36. A. James Reichley, Paul Weyrich, Terry Eastland, Ralph Reed, Robert Dugan, Richard D. Land, and Donald Wildmon, "Comments," in *No Longer Exiles: The Religious New Right in American Politics*, ed. Michael Cromartie, pp. 82–83 (Washington, DC: Ethics and Public Policy Center, 1993).

37. Lindblom, *Politics and Markets*, p. 175.

38. Another consideration is Lindblom's claim that sometimes interest groups besides business in polyarchies occupy a "limited privileged position." See Lindblom, *Politics and Markets*, pp. 176–177.

39. Although his applied psychodynamic analysis of George W. Bush is not dispositive, Justin A. Frank provides support for the half of this conclusion that bears on the president's character. See Frank, *Bush on the Couch: Inside the Mind of the President* (New York: ReganBooks, 2004), pp. 53–76.

40. PBS Video, *Frontline: The Jesus Factor*, 60 minutes, 2004.

41. Boyer, *When Time Shall Be No More*, pp. 142–146.

42. John J. Dilulio Jr., "Attacking 'Sinful Inequalities'," *Perspectives on Politics* 2, 4 (2004): 669.

43. See Francis Schaeffer, *Plan for Action: An Action Alternative Handbook for* Whatever Happened to the Human Race? (New York: Flemming H. Revell, 1980).

44. Charles B. Strozier, *Apocalypse: On the Psychology of Fundamentalism in America* (New York: Beacon Press, 1995).

Chapter 1. Speaking Right

1. The actual text takes the form of a proverb: "Marriage is honourable in all, and the bed undefiled: but whoremongers and adulterers God will judge."

2. Hannah Arendt, "'What Remains? The Language Remains': A Conversation with Günter Gaus," in *Essays in Understanding 1930–1954: Uncollected and Unpublished Works by Hannah Arendt*, ed. Jerome Kohn, p. 12 (New York: Harcourt Brace and Company, 1994). The original quote reads: "If one is attacked as a Jew, one must defend oneself as a Jew. Not as a German. . . ."

3. See Chris Bull and John Gallagher, *Perfect Enemies: The Religious Right, the Gay Movement, and the Politics of the 1990s* (New York: Crown Publishers, 1996); M. V. Lee Badgett, *Money, Myths, and Change: The Economic Lives of Lesbians and Gay Men* (Chicago: University of Chicago Press, 2001).

4. Didi Herman, *The Antigay Agenda: Orthodox Vision and the Christian Right* (Chicago: University of Chicago Press, 1997), pp.127, 125.

5. Paul Cameron, "Gay Domestic Violence Finally Measured," (Family Research Institute, 2001), http://www.familyresearchinst.org/FRR_01_12.html (accessed May 21, 2005).

6. Herman, *Antigay Agenda*, p. 102.

7. Paul Cameron, *The Gay 90s: What the Empirical Evidence Reveals about Homosexuality* (New York: New York University Press, 1994).

8. Michael J. Sandel, *Democracy's Discontent: America in Search of a Public Philosophy* (Cambridge, MA: Harvard University Press, 1996); Arlene Stein, *The Stranger Next Door: The Story of a Small Community's Battle over Sex, Faith, and Civil Rights* (Boston: Beacon Press, 2001), p. 216.

9. Pat Robertson, "Pat Robertson Quotes," (*Brainy Quotes*, 2006), http://www.brainyquote.com/quotes/authors/p/pat_robertson.html (accessed December 1, 2006).

10. Nicole Hollander, *Female Problems: An Unhelpful Guide* (Chicago: PreviewPort Editions, 2001), p. 136. In her cartoon, Hollander attributes the statement to "spokesmen from the right wing of the Republican Party" rather than to Pat Robertson.

11. Jean Hardisty, *Mobilizing Resentment: Conservative Resurgence from the John Birch Society to the Promise Keepers* (Boston: Beacon, 1999), p. 114; R. Claire Snyder, "Neopatriarchy and the Antihomosexual Agenda," in *Fundamental Differences: Feminists Talk Back to Social Conservatives,* ed. Cynthia Burack and Jyl J. Josephson (Lanham, MD: Rowman and Littlefield, 2003), pp. 166–167.

12. Jeffrey K. Hadden and Anson Shupe, "Televangelism: The Story the Media Missed," (*Boston Review,* 1988), http://bostonreview.mit.edu/BR13.2/hadden.html (accessed February 1, 2002).

13. "News of the Year: Far Right," *The Advocate* (January 22, 2002): 25.

14. Ann Burlein, *Lift High the Cross: Where White Supremacy and the Christian Right Converge* (Durham, NC: Duke University Press, 2002), pp.147–148.

15. Burlein, *Lift High the Cross,* p. 26.

16. John D. Woodbridge, "Culture War Casualties: How Warfare Rhetoric Is Hurting the Work of the Church," *Christianity Today* 39, 3 (1995): 26.

17. Quoted in James Carney, "The Rise and Fall of Ralph Reed," (*Time,* 2006), http://www.time.com/time/magazine/article/0,9171,1218060,00.html (accessed October 10, 2006).

18. In his critique of Christian fundamentalism and its social and political effects, Bruce Bawer links the effectiveness of the Christian right to the low religious literacy of many Americans. See Bruce Bawer, *Stealing Jesus: How Fundamentalism Betrays Christianity* (New York: Random House, 1997).

19. Paul Boyer, *When Time Shall Be No More: Prophesy Belief in Modern American Culture* (Cambridge, MA: Harvard University Press, 1992), pp. 248–249.

20. Martin E. Marty, *A Nation of Behavers* (Chicago: University of Chicago Press, 1976), p. 23.

21. Lisa McGirr, *Suburban Warriors: The Origins of the New American Right* (Princeton, NJ: Princeton University Press, 2001).

22. The Barna Group, "Americans Speak: Enron, WorldCom and Others Are Result of Inadequate Moral Training By Families," (Barna, 2002), http://www.barna.org/FlexPage .aspx? Page=BarnaUpdate&BarnaUpdateID= 117 (accessed November 8, 2005).

23. Even if conservative Christians understand themselves as biblical literalists, scriptural interpretation is always a work in progress. See Susan Friend Harding on "fundamentalism's flexible absolutism": *The Book of Jerry Falwell: Fundamentalist Language and Politics* (Princeton, NJ: Princeton University Press, 2001), pp. 166–168.

24. Nancy L. Rosenblum, *Membership and Morals: The Personal Uses of Pluralism in America* (Princeton, NJ: Princeton University Press, 1998), pp. 3–46. For a similar argument and debate see Will Kymlicka, "Liberal Complacencies," in *Is Multiculturalism Bad for Women?*, ed. Susan Moller Okin, Joshua Cohen, Matthew Howard, and Martha C. Nussbaum, pp. 31–34 (Princeton, NJ: Princeton University Press, 1999).

25. Kathleen M. Sullivan, "Defining Democracy Down," (*Prospect*, 1998), http://www. prospect.org/print/V9/41/sullivan-k.html (accessed February 2, 2002).

26. Rosenblum, *Membership and Morals*, p. 269.

27. Pew Forum on Religion and Public Life, "Religious Beliefs Underpin Opposition to Homosexuality," (Pew Forum, 2003), http://pewforum.org/docs/index.php?DocID=37 (accessed July 22, 2005).

28. Snyder, "Neopatriarchy and the Antihomosexual Agenda," pp. 157–171.

29. Anna Marie Smith, "Why Did Armey Apologize?" in *Unraveling the Right: The New Conservatism in American Thought and Politics*, ed. Amy E. Ansell, p. 167 (New York: Westview Press, 1998).

30. Bishop Wellington Boone, The Washington Briefing: Values Voter Summit, September 22, 2006.

31. Anna Marie Smith, *New Right Discourse on Race and Sexuality: Britain, 1968–1990* (Cambridge: Cambridge University Press, 1994), p. 68.

32. Anna Marie Smith, "The Centering of Right-Wing Extremism through the Construction of an 'Inclusionary' Homophobia and Racism," in *Playing with Fire: Queer Politics, Queer Theories*, ed. Shane Phelan, p. 114 (New York: Routledge, 1997).

33. Smith, "Why Did Armey Apologize?" p. 163. Many others note these same tactics. See, e.g., Bull and Gallagher, *Perfect Enemies*, p. 90.

34. John C. Green, "Antigay: Varieties of Opposition to Gay Rights," in *The Politics of Gay Rights*, ed. Craig A. Rimmerman, Kenneth D. Wald, and Clyde Wilcox, pp. 129–130 (Chicago: University of Chicago Press, 2000).

35. Rogers M. Smith, "Beyond Tocqueville, Myrdal, and Hartz: The Multiple Traditions in America," *American Political Science Review* 87, 3 (1993):

549–565; Linda Kintz, *Between Jesus and the Market: The Emotions That Matter in Right-Wing America* (Durham, NC: Duke University Press, 1997).

36. Paul M. Weyrich, "Paul Weyrich Letter," (Religious Freedom Coalition, 2000), http://www.rfcnet.org/archives/weyrich.htm (accessed November 11, 2001).

37. James L. Conn, "Rift on the Right: Right-Wing Strategist Paul Weyrich Says the Culture War Is Lost, but Dobson, Robertson and Other Religious Right Leaders Insist They've Just Begun to Fight" (*Church and State*, 1999) http://www.au. org/churchstate/cs4991.htm (accessed November 16, 2001).

38. Josh McDowell and Bob Hostetler, *The New Tolerance: How a Cultural Movement Threatens to Destroy You, Your Faith, and Your Children* (Wheaton, IL: Tyndale House, 1998).

39. Peter Carlson, "Jerry Falwell's Awkward Apology: What Did He Mean and When Did He Mean It? Huh?" *Washington Post* (November 18, 2002): F5. Emphasis in the original.

40. Smith, "Centering of Right-Wing Extremism," p. 121.

41. Tim LaHaye and Bob Phillips, *Babylon Rising: The Secret on Ararat* (New York: Random House, 2004), p. 80.

42. Michael Walzer, *On Toleration* (New Haven: Yale University Press, 1997), pp. 2, 10–11, 55, 81–82.

43. Amy Gutmann, *Identity in Democracy* (Princeton, NJ: Princeton University Press, 2003), pp. 33–34, 154.

44. John L. Sullivan, James Piereson, and George E. Marcus, *Political Tolerance and American Democracy* (Chicago: University of Chicago Press, 1982), p. 10.

45. Daniel Taylor, *Is God Intolerant? Christian Thinking about the Call for Tolerance* (Wheaton, IL: Tyndale House, 2003), p. 1.

46. Taylor, *Is God Intolerant?* pp. 105–106.

47. Ryan Dobson and Jefferson Scott, *Be Intolerant: Because Some Things Are Just Stupid* (Sisters, OR: Multnomah, 2003), p. 120.

48. Robertson made these comments on the January 14, 1991, broadcast of the *700 Club*. Robertson, quoted in David Cantor, *The Religious Right: The Assault on Tolerance and Pluralism in America* (New York: Anti-Defamation League, 1994), p. 26.

49. The "Roman Road" (sometimes "Romans Road") is one term for a series of Bible verses found in the book of Romans that are read collectively to outline the path to salvation.

50. These references can be found on fifteen pages, although only two are listed in the index.

51. For quite different sorts of arguments about how political toleration contributes to human flourishing see, e.g., John Stuart Mill, *On Liberty and Other Writings* (Cambridge and New York: Cambridge University Press, 1994); Martha C. Nussbaum, *Women and Human Development: The Capabilities Approach* (New York: Cambridge University Press, 2000).

52. Taylor, *Is God Intolerant?* pp. 13–16.

53. Michael Lienesch, *Redeeming America: Piety and Politics in the New Christian Right* (Chapel Hill and London: University of North Carolina Press, 1993), pp. 169–171.

54. McDowell and Hostetler, *The New Tolerance*, pp. 70–71.

55. Gaines M. Foster, *Moral Reconstruction: Christian Lobbyists and the Federal Legislation of Morality, 1865–1920* (Chapel Hill: University of North Carolina Press, 2002).

56. Ruth Murray Brown, *For a "Christian America": A History of the Religious Right* (New York: Prometheus Books, 2002), pp. 81–84.

57. This is the most common intellectual history of premillennial dispensationalism. A challenge to this genealogy can be found in Dave MacPherson, *The Rapture Plot* (Simpsonville, SC: Millennium III, 1994).

58. For a popular rendering of these theological arguments, see the *Left Behind* series of novels by Tim LaHaye and Jerry B. Jenkins. The books have been staples on the *New York Times* Best Sellers list since they debuted in 1995.

59. For the brief discussion of Christian right eschatology in this section, I rely primarily on the following resources: Timothy P. Weber, *Living in the Shadow of the Second Coming: American Premillennialism, 1875–1982* (Chicago: University of Chicago Press, 1987); Stephen J. Stein, ed., *The Encyclopedia of Apocalypticism. Volume 3: Apocalypticism in the Modern Period and the Contemporary Age* (New York: Continuum, 1998); Boyer, *When Time Shall Be No More*; Brenda E. Brasher, ed., *The Encyclopedia of Fundamentalism* (New York: Routledge, 2001). For a more entertaining take on conservative Christian apocalyptic beliefs, see Jason Boyett, *Pocket Guide to the Apocalypse: The Official Field Manual for the End of the World* (Orlando, FL: Relevant Books, 2005).

60. Cathleen Falsani. "Bishops Warn Catholics about 'Left Behind' Books," (*Sun Times*, 2003), http://www.suntimes.com/output/religion/cst-nws-left06.html (accessed May 20, 2005).

61. Boyer, *When Time Shall Be No More*, p. 234.

62. Tim LaHaye and Jerry B. Jenkins, *The Rising: Antichrist Is Born* (Wheaton, IL: Tyndale House, 2005). For those who listen to the *Left Behind* series, the audio version of several installments of the series helps establish the evil character of the Antichrist by conferring effeminate accents on both Nicolae and Pontifex Maximus Peter Matthews. The reader who voiced these characters is Frank Muller, who was replaced after he died in an accident in 2001.

63. Boyer, *When Time Shall Be No More*, p. 80.

64. Herman, *The Antigay Agenda*, p. 192.

65. Herman, *The Antigay Agenda*, p. 189.

66. Tim LaHaye, *The Battle for the Mind* (Old Tappan, NJ: Fleming H. Revell, 1980).

67. Harding, *The Book of Jerry Falwell*, p. 241.

68. See Sara Diamond, *Roads to Dominion: Right-Wing Movements and Political Power in the United States* (New York: Guilford Press, 1995); Chip Berlet, "The Christian Right, Dominionism, and Theocracy," (Political Research Associates), http://www.publiceye.org/christian_right/dominionism.htm (accessed September 30, 2006).

69. Boyer, *When Time Shall Be No More*, pp. 302–304, 137–138.

70. *Christianity Today.* "Worship as Higher Politics," (*Christianity Today,* 2005), http://www.christianitytoday.com/ct/2005/007/16.22.html (accessed June 24, 2005).

71. Stephen Prothero, *American Jesus: How the Son of God Became a National Icon* (New York: Farrar, Straus and Giroux, 2003), p. 66.

72. Burlein, *Lift High the Cross*.

73. Mark Noll, quoted in Derek H. Davis, "God and the Pursuit of America's Self-Understanding: Toward a Synthesis of American Historiography," (*Journal of Church and State,* 2004), http://www3.baylor.edu/Church_State/journ2004Summer.htm (accessed June 27, 2005).

74. Boyer, *When Time Shall Be No More*, pp. 148, 174–176, 241, 209–217.

75. Hal Lindsey, *The Late Great Planet Earth* (Grand Rapids, MI: Zondervan, 1970), p. 68.

76. Public schools are often a site of anxiety for Christian conservatives for reasons other than the quality of education they provide. In October 2005, the Reverend Willie Wilson banned a gay African American speaker from the podium of the Millions More March in Washington, DC. Wilson had previously cited concerns with rampant lesbianism in public schools to LGBT movement representatives.

77. Even as other Christian right leaders have come to represent conservative Christian prophesy, Lindsey seems to have renounced his early ambivalence about the survival of the United States as the sole world superpower. In a recent book, Lindsey sadly concludes that America's decline before the Rapture is irreversible. See Hal Lindsey, *The Everlasting Hatred: The Roots of Jihad* (Murrieta, CA: Oracle House, 2002), p. 242.

78. Pat Robertson, *The New World Order* (Nashville, TN: W, 1991), p. 256.

79. See Tim LaHaye and Thomas Ice, *Charting the End Times: A Visual Guide to Bible Prophesy and Its Fulfillment* (Eugene, OR: Harvest House, 2001).

80. Martin E. Marty, "The Future of No Future: Frameworks of Interpretation," in *The Encyclopedia of Apocalypticism. Volume 3: Apocalypticism in the Modern Period and the Contemporary Age*, ed. Stephen J. Stein, p. 480 (New York: Continuum 1998).

81. Julia Lesage, "Christian Media," in *Media, Culture, and the Religious Right*, ed. Linda Kintz and Julia Lesage, pp. 23–44 (Minneapolis: University of Minnesota Press, 1998).

82. Michael Barkun, *A Culture of Conspiracy: Apocalyptic Visions in Contemporary America* (Berkeley: University of California Press, 2003), p. 23.

83. John A. Moran, a cochair of the Republican Leadership Council, was quoted as saying that the Republican Party needed to "soften the image of the party" and "avoid ideological purity." James L. Conn, "Rift on the Right: Right-Wing Strategist Paul Weyrich Says the Culture War Is Lost, but Dobson, Robertson and Other Religious Right Leaders Insist They've Just Begun to Fight," (*Americans United*, 1999), http://www.au.org/churchstate/cs4991.htm (accessed November 16, 2001).

84. Pat Buchanan, "Address by Patrick J. Buchanan," in *Official Report of the Proceedings of the Thirty-Fifth Republican National Convention Held in Houston, Texas* (Washington, DC: Republican National Committee, 1992), pp. 371–376.

85. For an account of antigay rhetoric in the 1992 Republican Convention see Bull and Gallagher, *Perfect Enemies*, pp. 63–96.

86. Herman, *The Antigay Agenda*, pp. 60–91.

87. Such mainstream appearances include, for example, Pat Robertson's appearances as a talking head on CNN during the 2000 presidential campaign and the subsequent electoral debacle.

88. Bull and Gallagher, *Perfect Enemies*, pp. 113–114.

89. Lesage, "Christian Media," p. 44.

90. See, e.g., Harding, *The Book of Jerry Falwell*; Arlene Stein, *The Stranger Next Door*; Dawne Moon, *God, Sex, and Politics: Homosexuality and*

Everyday Theologies (Chicago: University of Chicago Press, 2004). Moon defines "everyday theologies" as "how individuals, as parts of communities and societies, come to make sense of their world and its sacred aspects," p. 62.

91. Bryan Anderton, "'Ex-Gay' Ads Reappear in Metro Stations: Free Ads Slammed as 'Harmful' Were also Posted Last Year" (*Washington Blade*, 2003), http://www.washblade.com/2003/10–24/news/localnews/exgayad.cfm (accessed July 6, 2005).

92. David Domke, *God Willing: Political Fundamentalism in the White House, the "War on Terror," and the Echoing Press* (London: Pluto Press, 2004).

Chapter 2. The Nightmare of Homosexuality

1. All emphases in quotes from Chick tracts are in the original. With their italics, underlining, exclamation points, and other symbols, the tract texts are highly dramatic.

2. Heidi Ewing and Rachel Gracy, Directors, *Jesus Camp*, 2006.

3. Chick Publications Catalog, 2003.

4. I have found many Chick tracts since. As I began to write this chapter in early 2004 I found a Chick tract in the dining room of the student union at Ohio State University. When I showed it to the manager of one of the franchise food operations where I regularly eat lunch she took it to pass along to her young nephew. I didn't intend to proselytize, so this may be an example of God working in a mysterious way. A few months later, at the Festival Latino in Columbus, Ohio, I came across a church group distributing Spanish-language tracts—"Rumbo Al Hogar" ("Going Home," 1991), "El Sueño Espantoso de un Demonio" ("A Demon's Nightmare," 1972)—as well as the ever-popular "This Was Your Life!" (in English). As I completed a draft of the chapter in the summer of 2005, I found a tract at Kaladi's, my favorite Sioux Falls, South Dakota, coffeehouse. That same week, Freshman U.S. Senator John Thune (R-SD) was spotted in the coffeehouse, but I do not believe there is any connection between his visit and the appearance of the tract. Between the autumn of 2005 and the summer of 2006, I found tracts in the Washington, DC, Metrorail system, in DC's Union Station, and in the women's restroom of Penn Alps Restaurant in Grantsville, Maryland. The last find was "Somebody Loves Me" (1969), the story of a child beaten to death, which some Chicklets believe is the most vicious of all Chick tracts. It's hard to argue with them.

5. Arguably, analysts of the Christian right have given inadequate attention to an important dimension of the movement: the production, distribution, and reception of conservative Christian cultural products. See Heather Hendershot, *Shaking the World for Jesus: Media and Conservative Evangelical Culture* (Chicago: University of Chicago Press, 2004).

6. Alleee and Franc, "Jack T. Chick, Cartoonist for the Lord," (Insolitology, 2002), http://www.insolitology.com/topten/jackchick.htm (accessed October 2, 2003). Other sources give Chick's birth year as 1924.

7. Robert Ito, "Fear Factor," (Find Articles, 2003), http://www.findarti cles.com/p/articles /mi_m1346/is_5_48/ai_101173128 (accessed April 28, 2004).

8. Lisa McGirr, *Suburban Warriors: The Origins of the New American Right* (Princeton, NJ: Princeton University Press, 2001). McGirr does not mention Chick in her impressive analysis of the conservative movement of Orange County and vicinity, but she provides a context for Chick's work that is not available in other studies of New right formation.

9. Kurt Kuersteiner, *The Unofficial Guide to the Art of Jack T. Chick: Chick Tracts, Crusader Comics, and Battle Cry Newspapers* (Atglen, PA: Schiffer, 2004), p. 136. Much of the material for his book is drawn from Kuersteiner's "Jack T. Chick Museum of Fine Art" on his Monsterwax website at http://members. aol/monsterwax/Contents.htm.

10. One of these authors is James R. Lewis, *Satanism Today: An Encyclopedia of Religion, Folklore, and Popular Culture* (Santa Barbara, CA: ABC-CLIO, 2001), p. 46.

11. Donald H. Gilmore, *Sex in Comics: A History of the Eight Pagers. Volumes 1–4* (San Diego: Greenleaf Classics, 1971), pp. 11–12.

12. Gilmore, *Sex in Comics*, pp. 110–119.

13. Tom McIver, *Anti-Evolution: A Reader's Guide to Writings before and after Darwin* (Baltimore: The Johns Hopkins University Press, 1992), p. 38.

14. Many commentators dismiss rumors of a "third artist," but Kurt Kuersteiner tracks down the storied third artist, who drew for Chick between 1988 and 1992. Much of the work of this artist was subsequently redrawn by Fred Carter.

15. Daniel K. Raeburn, *The Holy Book of Chick with the Apocrypha and Dictionary-Concordance. King Imp Edition* (Chicago, IL: Imp Publications, 1998), p. 20.

16. Raeburn, *The Holy Book of Chick*, pp. 7–8. Emphasis in the original.

17. Stephen Prothero, *American Jesus: How the Son of God Became a National Icon* (New York: Farrar, Straus and Giroux, 2003), pp. 65–66.

18. Mark J. Estren, *A History of Underground Comics, Fourth Edition* (Berkeley: Ronin, 1993).

19. For a recent example in this genre see the 1990s graphic novel series *Preacher*, by Garth Ennis and Steve Dillon, which has been collected in ten volumes. Unlike in Chick or the eight pagers, in *Preacher*, the money shot is what one blogger calls a "grievous head-wound." The website, no longer available, featured a "grievous head-wound count" (172 in the entire *Preacher* series).

20. In a brief entry, Shame.org notes that Chick tracts use "comics to teach children to hate": "Chick Publications," (Shame, 2003), http://www.shame.org/detail. html?61 (accessed October 2, 2003).

21. "The Comics Code Authority," (Comicartville Library), http://www.comicartville.com/comicscode.htm (accessed December 14, 2006). See also Hans Sidén, *Sadomasochism in Comics: A History of Sex and Violence in Comic Books* (San Diego: Greenleaf Classics, 1972).

22. Richard von Busack, "Comic-Book Theology: Unearthing Famed Christian Artist Jack T. Chick," (*MetroActive*, 1998), http://www.metroactive.com/papers/metro/04.02.98/ comics-9813.html (accessed April 28, 2004).

23. The second colleague tells the story of her encounter with a Chick tract in a brief memoir: Bonnie Morris, "Playing with Fire," in *Word of Mouth Volume 2: Short-Short Stories by 100 Women Writers*, ed. Irene Zahava, pp. 80–81 (Berkeley: Crossing Press, 1991). On those born-again after reading a tract, Dave Burchett bemoans salvation as a "get-out-of-hell card in the game of life." See Burchett, *When Bad Christians Happen to Good People: Where We Have Failed Each Other and How to Reverse the Damage* (Colorado Springs, CO: Waterbrook Press, 2002), pp. 52–53.

24. Psycho Dave is the nom de plume of David W. Irish.

25. Psycho Dave, "The Holy and the Homo," (Weirdcrap, 2000), http://www.weirdcrap.com/chick/archive.html (accessed September 30, 2004).

26. Psycho Dave, "The Trucker and the Mind-Fucker," (Weirdcrap, 2000), http://www.weirdcrap.com/chick/archive.html (accessed September 30, 2004).

27. David W. Irish, personal email, (December 20–26, 2004).

28. Psycho Dave, "The Jack T. Chick Parody Archives," (Weirdcrap, 2000), http://www. weirdcrap.com/chick/index.html (accessed October 2, 2003).

29. Robert B. Fowler, *The World of Jack T. Chick (The History of the World According to Jack T. Chick)* (San Francisco: Last Gasp, 2001), pp. 6–38.

30. Jim Huger, "Jhuger—'Effing the Ineffable Since 1996'," (Jhuger, 2004), http://www.jhuger.com/index.mv (October 1, 2004).

31. Adult! Christianity. "Jack T. Chick's Fairy Tales," (Post Fun, 1998), http://www.postfun.com/pfp/features/98/feb/jtchick.html (accessed April 20, 2004).

32. Adult! Christianity, "Jack T. Chick's Fairy Tales."

33. Thanks to Dennis Brumm for including some of these photos on his *An Early History of Gay Liberation in Ames, Iowa* website and for responding to my questions.

34. Ralph Graves, "Homosexuals in Revolt: The Year that One Liberation Movement Turned Militant," *Life: The Year in Pictures 1971*, 26 (1971): 66.

35. On this view, see Spatula/Nick Johnson, "The Gay Blade," (The Gay Blade, 2004), *http://web.morons.org/chick/gayblade.jsp* (accessed January 13, 2004). Spatula/Nick Johnson reproduces the "Gay Blade" illustration inspired by the *Life* photo and adds this comment: "Let me make sure I state this loud and clear, because I don't want anyone to miss it: NO SELF-RESPECTING GAY MAN WOULD DRESS LIKE THIS OR DO THIS TO HIS HAIR." It goes without saying that the emphasis is in the original.

36. The quote is taken from the "The Gay Blade": "Out of Satan's shadowy world of homosexuality, in a display of defiance against society, they come forth— those who suffer the agony of rejection, the despair of unsatisfied longing— desiring—endless lusting and remorse crying that gay is good—their tragic lives prove that there isn't anything gay about being 'gay'." I can't demonstrate the provenance of this final phrase, but it continues to show up frequently in Christian right discourse. Most recently, I heard it delivered by Rick Scarborough at the Values Voter Summit, sponsored by FRC in Washington, DC, in September 2006.

37. The case is *Baker v. Nelson*.

38. Dennis Brumm, "Gays Protest Pamphlet," (Brumm, 2004), http://www.brumm.com/ gaylib/gaybladeprotest1974_1.html (accessed January 13, 2004).

39. I explore the importance of compassion in the developmental model of the origins of same-sex sexuality in chapter 3. For another version of this material see Cynthia Burack and Jyl J. Josephson, "A Report From Love Won Out: Addressing, Understanding, and Preventing Homosexuality," (The Task Force, 2005), http://www.thetaskforce.org/downloads/lovewonout.pdf (May 5, 2005).

40. I borrow the term "central gay content" from Timothy E. Cook and Bevin Hartnett, "Splitting Images: The Nightly Network News and the Politics of the Lesbian and Gay Movement, 1969–1978," in *Sexual Identities, Queer Politics*, ed. Mark Blasius, p. 290 (Princeton, NJ: Princeton University Press, 2001).

41. On the Chick Publications website, Chick accompanied "Birds and the Bees" with "A Personal Message from Jack Chick." (The letter can be found at http://www.chick.com/birdsandbeesletter.asp.) In the message, Chick defends his decision to set an antigay tract in a school by citing the aggressiveness of the gay agenda. The letter ends this way: "So please, let the kids read 'The Birds and the Bees.' It could save them from a homosexual nightmare in the future."

42. I am not arguing that the linkage between witchcraft and lesbianism is peculiar to conservative Christians. It has a long history and shows up in English literature as well as in mainstream popular culture.

43. George Johnson, *Architects of Fear: Conspiracy Theories and Paranoia in American Politics* (Los Angeles: J. P. Tarcher; Boston: distributed by Houghton Mifflin, 1983), pp. 87–88.

44. Andrew Clark, "The Twisted World of Christian Comix," (*Eye Weekly*, 2003), http://www.eye.net/eye/issue/issue_02.04.93/NEWS/nv0204.htm (accessed October 2, 2003).

45. Rebecca Brown, *He Came to Set the Captives Free* (New Kensington, PA: Whitaker House, 1986); *Prepare for War* (New Kensington, PA: Whitaker House, 1987). Chick Publications originally published Brown's books and provided gag cartoon-style illustrations for them.

46. G. Richard Fisher, Paul R. Blizard, and M. Kurt Goedelman, *Drugs, Demons and Delusions: A Christian Investigation of the Testimony and Claims of Rebecca Brown, M.D.* (St. Louis, MO: Personal Freedom Outreach, 1991). On the subject of the sources of false witness the authors expose, the book's cover material contains the following warning: "Christians face tremendous peril with each trip to their local Christian bookstore."

47. See, for example, Gary Metz, "Jack Chick's Anti-Catholic *Alberto* Comic Book Is Exposed as a Fraud," *Christianity Today* 25, 5 (1981): 50–52; Johnson, *Architects of Fear*, pp. 87–88; Daniel Pipes, *Conspiracy: How the Paranoid Style Flourishes and Where It Comes From* (New York: The Free Press, 1997), p. 148; von Busack, "Comic-Book Theology"; James R. Lewis, *Satanism Today*, pp. 45–47.

48. Raeburn, *Holy Book of Chick*, p. 1.

49. A note on the bookstores: It is increasingly common for suburban megachurches to run their own internal bookstores. The stores I visited were freestanding retail outlets.

50. Richard McMunn, quoted in Metz, "Jack Chick's Anti-Catholic *Alberto* Comic Book is Exposed as a Fraud," p. 52. McMunn, editor of the Catholic publication *Our Catholic Visitor*, was quoted on the Chick tract phenomenon in 1981.

51. See Armageddon Books at http://www.armageddonbooks.com/

52. For a personal account of this movement and the work of Catholic Answers, see Jimmy Akin, "Meet Jack Chick," (*Defensor Fidei: Jimmy Akin's Blog*, 2004), http://members.cox.net/jimmyakin/x-meet-jack-chick.htm (December 6, 2004).

53. See Susan Friend Harding, *The Book of Jerry Falwell: Fundamentalist Language and Politics* (Princeton, NJ: Princeton University Press, 2000).

54. TFP Committee of American Issues (The American Society for the Defense of Tradition, Family and Property), *Defending a Higher Law: Why We*

Must Resist Same-Sex "Marriage" and the Homosexual Movement (Spring Grove, PA: TFP, 2004), pp. 191–192.

55. Pat Robertson, "Operation Supreme Court Freedom," (The Official Site of Pat Robertson, 2005), http://www.patrobertson.com/PressReleases/supremecourt.asp (January 16, 2006).

56. McIver, *Anti-Evolution*, p. 38.

57. F. Clark Howell, *Early Man* (Englewood Cliffs, NJ: Silver Burdett Press, 1987).

58. Raeburn, *Holy Book of Chick*, p. 12.

59. For the development of the synergy between rejection of state provisioning and social conservatism in the politics of the 1960s, see McGirr, *Suburban Warriors*.

60. Steven P. Brown, *Trumping Religion: The New Christian Right, the Free Speech Clause and the Courts* (Tuscaloosa: University of Alabama Press, 2003).

61. See David H. Bennett, *The Party of Fear: The American Far Right from Nativism to the Militia Movement* (New York: Vintage, 1995).

62. Yonder Moynihan Gillihan, "Rapture," in *The Encyclopedia of Fundamentalism*, ed. Brenda E. Brasher, p. 407 (New York: Routledge, 2001). See also Matthew Goff, "Apocalyptic Literature," in *The Encyclopedia of Fundamentalism*, ed. Brenda E. Brasher, p. 33 (New York: Routledge, 2001).

63. There are many sources for Catholic amillennialism. Some of these are oriented toward ordinary readers in forms that are easy to consult. One example of an accessible source that is an obvious response to the popularity of the *Left Behind* series is Fr. Sean Wales, *What You Should Know About the "End Times"* (Liguori, MO: Liguori Publications, 2004).

64. Barbara R. Rossing, *The Rapture Exposed: The Message of Hope in the Book of Revelation* (New York: Basic Books, 2004), pp. 19–46.

65. Ruth Murray Brown, *For a "Christian America": A History of the Religious Right* (New York: Prometheus Books, 2002), pp. 81–84.

66. Dawne Moon, *God, Sex, and Politics: Homosexuality and Everyday Theologies* (Chicago: University of Chicago Press, 2004), pp. 206–227.

67. An example in this category includes "Love the Jewish People" (1976).

68. Laurie Schulze and Frances Guilfoyle, "'Facts Don't Hate: They Just Are,'" in *Media, Culture, and the Religious Right*, ed. Linda Kintz and Julia Lesage, p. 333 (Minneapolis: Minnesota University Press, 1998). See also Burack and Josephson, "Introduction," *Fundamental Differences: Feminists Talk Back to Social Conservatives*, pp. 1–8 (Lanham, MD: Rowman and Littlefield, 2003).

69. Granted, no doubt the more important motivator is the need to evade a series of court decisions barring the teaching of creationism in public schools.

70. Paul Cameron, *Exposing the AIDS Scandal* (Lafayette, LA: Huntingon House, 1988).

71. Paul Boyer, *When Time Shall Be No More: Prophesy Belief in Modern American Culture* (Cambridge, MA: Harvard University Press, 1992), p. 310.

72. The phrase is found in Ezekiel 22:30: "And I have sought for a man among them, that should make up the hedge, and stand in the gap before me for the land, that I should not destroy it: but I found none." "Stand in the gap" has been used by the conservative Christian organization Promise Keepers as a charge to Christian men, but it was in wide usage before the inauguration of this group. I've also encountered the noun "gap-stander" in some conservative Christian literature.

Chapter 3. Origin Stories

1. Jean Hardisty, *Mobilizing Resentment: Conservative Resurgence from the John Birch Society to the Promise Keepers* (Boston: Beacon, 1999), p. 116.

2. American Psychiatric Association, *Diagnostic and Statistical Manual of Mental Disorders* (Arlington, VA: American Psychiatric Publishing, 2000). See also, Hannah Lerman, *Pigeonholing Women's Misery: A History and Critical Analysis of the Psychodiagnosis of Women in the Twentieth Century* (New York: Basic Books, 1996).

3. Some current antigay psychological literature refers to same-sex attracted people by the abbreviation SSA, hence, "SSA men" and "SSA women."

4. For many stories of those who left ex-gay ministries, see Human Rights Campaign, "Finally Free. Personal Stories: How Love and Self-Acceptance Saved Us from 'Ex-Gay' Ministries," (2000), http://www.hrc.org/Content/Content Groups/Publications1/FinallyFREE.pdf (accessed September 14, 2006).

5. *The Onion,* "Church Group Offers Homosexual New Life in Closet," (*The Onion,* 1999), http://www.theonion.com/content/node/28799 (accessed January 20, 1999).

6. American Psychiatric Association, "Position Statement on Therapies Focused on Attempts to Change Sexual Orientation (Reparative or Conversion Therapies)," (American Psychiatric Association, 2000), http://www.psych.org/pract_of_psych/ copptherapyaddendum83100.cfm (accessed November 28, 2001). It is useful to note that there are differences between the responses of mental health organizations to reparative therapies. In 1997, the American Psychological Association passed a resolution that stopped short of labeling the therapies

unethical and merely imposed some safeguards on their applications. Organizations such as NARTH strongly opposed the resolution. In May 2005, the American Psychological Association approved a statement urging legal recognition of same-sex marriage.

7. Cynthia Burack and Jyl J. Josephson. "A Report From 'Love Won Out: Addressing, Understanding, and Preventing Homosexuality,'" (National Gay and Lesbian Task Force Policy Institute, 2005), http://www.thetaskforce.org/downloads/reports/reports/LoveWonOut.pdf (accessed May 5, 2005).

8. For an excellent analysis of this integration and its discontents, see Tanya Erzen, *Straight to Jesus: Sexual and Christian Conversions in the Ex-Gay Movement* (Berkeley: University of California Press, 2006).

9. For a discussion of these currents within the Lutheran denomination, see Jyl J. Josephson and Cynthia Burack, "Inside, Out, and In-Between: Sexual Minorities, the Christian Right and the Evangelical Lutheran Church in America," in *Religion, Politics, and American Identity: New Directions, New Controversies*, ed. David S. Gutterman and Andrew R. Murphy, pp. 247–265 (Lanham, MD: Lexington Books, 2006).

10. James Dobson, *Bringing Up Boys: Practical Advice and Encouragement for Those Shaping the Next Generation of Men* (Wheaton, IL: Tyndale House, 2001), p. 117.

11. Our experience with security and the suppression of dissent is consistent with other observations of LWO conferences, which have been circulated to members of PFLAG on the organization's listserv.

12. Focus on the Family, "Toward an Open Debate on Homosexual Behavior," (Focus on the Family, 1998), http://www.family.org/cforum/research/ papers/ a0002800.html (accessed November 28, 2001).

13. Religious Tolerance, "'Ex-Gay' Advertisements: In Newspapers and on TV," (Religious Tolerance, 2001), http://www.religioustolerance. org/hom_ads.htm (accessed November 6, 2001).

14. Focus on the Family, "Toward a New National Discussion of Homosexuality," (Focus on the Family, 1998), http://www.family.org/cforum/research/ papers/a0002799.html (accessed November 28, 2001).

15. Hardisty, *Mobilizing Resentment*, p. 118. See also a critique of the ex-gay movement as "calculated compassion": Surina Khan, "Calculated Compassion: How the Ex-Gay Movement Serves the Right's Attack on Democracy," (Public Eye, 1998), http://www.publiceye.org/equality/x-gay/X-Gay.htm (accessed November 6, 2001).

16. For connections between the usual arenas of Christian social conservatism and those of the economic right see Linda Kintz, *Between Jesus and the*

Market: The Emotions That Matter in Right-Wing America (Durham, NC: Duke University Press, 1997).

17. Unpacking LGBT identity in different Christian right contexts is complicated. At LWO, we heard no mention of bisexuals, an elision characteristic of much of the ex-gay movement. Transgender identity is not a sexual orientation, and although some ex-gay literature does include discussion of transgender issues (as the Christian right understands them) there was no mention of these issues at the event we attended.

18. Russell Shorto, "What's Their Real Problem with Gay Marriage? (It's the Gay Part)," (*New York Times*, 2005), http://www.nytimes.com/2005/06/19/magazine/19ANTI GAY.html (accessed June 22, 2005).

19. See, e.g., Cathy J. Cohen, *The Boundaries of Blackness: AIDS and the Breakdown of Black Politics* (Chicago: University of Chicago Press, 1999); Angela D. Dillard, *Guess Who's Coming to Dinner Now? Multicultural Conservatism in America* (New York: New York University Press, 2001).

20. There is some variation in the ways that scholars treat this question of origins. For example, Mary Wood ignores the narrative of development in favor of an analysis of the Christian right's emphasis on narratives of choice and biology. Rather than concentrating exclusively on the Christian right rejection of arguments for biological immutability, she elucidates the points of similarity between Christian antigay discourse and scientific discourses related to evolutionary biology and nineteenth-century sexology. See Mary E. Wood, "How We Got This Way: The Sciences of Homosexuality and the Christian Right," *Journal of Homosexuality* 38, 3 (2000): 19–39.

21. Laurie Schulze and Frances Guilfoyle, "'Facts Don't Hate: They Just Are'," in *Media, Culture, and the Religious Right*, ed. Linda Kintz and Julia Lesage, p. 336 (Minneapolis: Minnesota University Press, 1998).

22. Hardisty, *Mobilizing Resentment*, p. 118.

23. Peter B. Wood and John P. Bartkowski, "Attribution Style and Public Policy Attitudes Toward Gay Rights," *Social Science Quarterly* 85, 1 (2004): 58–74.

24. The extent to which immutability is embraced varies widely, from its replacement in some quarters by human rights arguments to its continued viability for many individuals. Some LGBT people who rely upon immutability arguments are not active in the LGBT civil rights movement.

25. Didi Herman, *The Antigay Agenda: Orthodox Vision and the Christian Right* (Chicago: University of Chicago Press, 1997), p. 73.

26. Herman, *The Antigay Agenda*, p. 71.

27. The speaker was Alan Chambers.

28. Herman, *The Antigay Agenda*, pp. 121–122.

29. John J. Smid, "Exploring the Homosexual Myth," (Love in Action, 2001), http://www. loveinaction.org/default2.aspx?pid=62 (accessed September 28, 2005).

30. Mark A. Yarhouse, Erica S. N. Tan, and Lisa M. Pawlowski, "Sexual Identity Development and Synthesis Among LGB-Identified and LGB Dis-Identified Persons," *Journal of Psychology and Theology* 33, 1 (2005): 3–16.

31. Tim LaHaye, *The Unhappy Gays: What Everyone Should Know about Homosexuality* (Wheaton, IL: Tyndale House, 1978), p. 64.

32. LaHaye, *The Unhappy Gays*, pp. 66–77.

33. LaHaye, *The Unhappy Gays*, p. 85.

34. Frank M. du Mas, *Gay Is Not Good* (Nashville: Thomas Nelson, 1979), p. 203.

35. du Mas, *Gay Is Not Good*, pp. 294–299. Emphasis in the original.

36. Michael R. Saia, *Counseling the Homosexual: A Compassionate and Biblical Guide for Pastors and Counselors as well as Non-Professionals and Families* (Minneapolis: Bethany House, 1988), p. 49.

37. Saia, *Counseling the Homosexual*, pp. 51–52.

38. Saia, *Counseling the Homosexual*, pp. 57–58.

39. Marlin Maddoux and Christopher Corbett, *Answers to the Gay Deception* (Dallas, TX: International Christian Media, 1994), p. 34. Emphasis in the original.

40. Maddoux and Corbett, *Answers to the Gay Deception*, p. 35.

41. Jeffrey Satinover, M.D., *Homosexuality and the Politics of Truth* (Grand Rapids, MI: Baker Book House, 1996), pp. 221–225.

42. Dobson, *Bringing Up Boys*, p. 115.

43. For one perspective on the Paulk affair and the ex-gay movement as a whole, see Wayne Besen, *Anything but Straight: Unmasking the Scandals and Lies Behind the Ex-Gay Myth* (New York: Harrington Park Press, 2003). For a critique of Dr. Spitzer's research, see Besen, pp. 229–241; B. A. Robinson, "Analysis of Dr. Spitzer's Study of Reparative Therapy," (Religious Tolerance, 2002), http://www.religioustolerance.org/hom_spit.htm (accessed August 4, 2004); Jack Drescher and Kenneth J. Zucker, eds., *Ex-Gay Research: Analyzing the Spitzer Study and Its Relation to Science, Religion, Politics, and Culture* (New York: Harrington Park Press, 2006).

44. Dobson, *Bringing Up Boys*, p. 123.

45. Joseph Nicolosi and Linda Ames Nicolosi, *A Parent's Guide to Preventing Homosexuality* (Downer's Grove, IL: InterVarsity Press, 2002), p. 76.

46. Nicolosi and Nicolosi, *A Parent's Guide to Preventing Homosexuality*, p. 30.

47. Jack Drescher, "I'm Your Handyman: A History of Reparative Therapies," in *Sexual Conversion Therapy: Ethical, Clinical and Research Perspectives*, ed. Ariel Shidlo, Michael Schroeder, and Jack Drescher, p. 22 (New York: Haworth Medical Press, 2001). See also Thomas Domenici and Ronnie Lesser, eds., *Disorienting Sexuality: Psychoanalytic Reappraisals of Sexual Identities* (New York: Routledge, 1995).

48. On the psychology of binary exclusion of gender and sexual orientation, it is interesting to compare the following theoretical works with Nicolosi: Nancy J. Chodorow, *Femininities, Masculinities, Sexualities: Freud and Beyond* (Lexington: University of Kentucky Press, 1994); and Judith Butler, *The Psychic Life of Power: Theories in Subjection* (Palo Alto, CA: Stanford University Press, 1997).

49. Anne Paulk, *Restoring Sexual Identity: Hope for Women Who Struggle with Same-Sex Attraction* (Eugene, OR: Harvest House, 2003), pp. 36–47.

50. Although her husband John's gay credentials are beyond dispute (John Paulk was at one time a cross-dressing male prostitute), critics of the ex-gay movement have called Anne Paulk's claim to lesbian identity into question and challenged her to provide information that would confirm that she ever lived a lesbian "lifestyle." She has declined to provide such substantiating information. For one example of skepticism about Paulk's pre-salvation sexual orientation, see Besen, *Anything but Straight,* pp. 33–34.

51. Jeffry G. Ford, "Healing Homosexuals: A Psychologist's Journey Through the Ex-Gay Movement and the Pseudo-Science of Reparative Therapy," in *Sexual Conversion Therapy: Ethical, Clinical and Research Perspectives,* ed. Ariel Shidlo, Michael Schroeder, and Jack Drescher, pp. 69–85 (New York: Haworth Medical Press, 2001).

52. See A. Lee Beckstead, "Cures versus Choices: Agendas in Sexual Reorientation Therapy," in *Sexual Conversion Therapy: Ethical, Clinical and Research Perspectives,* ed. Ariel Shidlo, Michael Schroeder, and Jack Drescher, pp. 87-115 (New York: Haworth Medical Press, 2001).

53. Thomas E. Schmidt, *Straight and Narrow? Compassion and Clarity in the Homosexuality Debate* (Downer's Grove, IL: InterVarsity Press, 1995), p. 169.

54. Surina Khan, "Calculated Compasion: How the Ex-Gay Movement Serves the Right's Attack on Democracy," (Political Research Associates, Policy Institute of the National Gay and Lesbian Task Force, and Equal Partners in Faith, 1998), http://www.publiceye.org/equality/x-gay/X-Gay.htm (accessed November 6, 2001), p. 2.

55. The original name of the ministry, founded by Frank Worthen in 1973, was Love in Action. In 1994, Love in Action relocated to Memphis, Tennessee under different leadership and Worthen renamed his California ministry New Hope. See Erzen, *Straight to Jesus*, pp. 27–42.

56. The terms "strugglers" and "ex-gays" are both used within the ex-gay movement. At LWO, one volunteer referred to herself as an "ex" in a brief conversation with us. According to Erzen, "ex-gay identity . . . is constantly in flux and incorporates the idea of sexual falls and subsequent redemption." Tanya Erzen, "We Shall Overcome? Changing Politics and Changing Sexuality in the Ex-Gay Movement," in *Local Actions: Cultural Activism, Power, and Public Life in America*, ed. Melissa Checker and Maggie Fishman, p. 132 (New York: Columbia University Press, 2004).

57. Erzen, "We Shall Overcome?" pp. 127–131.

58. See Khan, "Calculated Compassion," p. 17, unnumbered first page of Executive Summary, and p. 7, respectively.

59. Kirk Cameron, "No, Dr. Dobson, Homosexuality Is a Choice," (Family Research Institute, 2002), http://www.familyresearchinst.org/FRR_02_07.html (accessed October 2, 2003).

60. Fred Phelps, "Love Crusades," (God Hates Fags, 2004), http://www.godhatesfags. com/fliers/pickets.html (accessed August 23, 2004).

61. For this process, see Anna Marie Smith, *New Right Discourse on Race and Sexuality: Britain, 1968–1990* (Cambridge: Cambridge University Press, 1994); Anna Marie Smith, "The Centering of Right-Wing Extremism Through the Construction of an 'Inclusionary' Homophobia and Racism," in *Playing with Fire: Queer Politics, Queer Theories*, ed. Shane Phelan, pp. 113–138 (New York and London: Routledge, 1997); Cynthia Burack, "Getting What 'We' Deserve: Terrorism, Tolerance, Sexuality, and the Christian Right," *New Political Science* 25, 3 (2003): 329–349.

62. Dillard, *Guess Who's Coming to Dinner Now?*; Herman, *The Antigay Agenda*.

63. See Amy Ansell, ed. *Unraveling the Right: The New Conservatism in American Thought and Politics* (Boulder, CO: Westview, 2001).

64. Nancy D. Campbell, "Reading the Rhetoric of 'Compassionate Conservatism'," in *Fundamental Differences: Feminists Talk Back to Social Conservatives*, ed. Cynthia Burack and Jyl J. Josephson, pp. 113–126 (Lanham, MD: Rowman and Littlefield, 2003).

65. Ideological compassion and the policies associated with it are not coextensive with personal charity, but on charity, see Arthur C. Brooks, *Who Really Cares: The Surprising Truth about Compassionate Conservatism* (New York: Basic Books, 2006).

66. Valerie Lehr, *Queer Family Values: Debunking the Myth of the Nuclear Family* (Philadelphia: Temple University Press, 1999), pp. 135–136.

67. Angelia R. Wilson, *Below the Belt: Sexuality, Religion and the American South* (London: Cassell, 2000), p. 125.

68. PFLAG. "Our Daughters and Sons," (Parents, Families, and Friends of Lesbians and Gays, 1995), http://www.pflag.org/PFLAG_Publications.297.0.html (April 21, 2004).

69. PFLAG, "Our Daughters and Sons."

70. Emphasis added.

71. Emphasis in the original.

72. Regina Griggs, "Sample Letters You Can Follow," (Parents and Friends of Ex-Gays and Gays, 2004), http://www.pfox.org/asp/newsman/templates/newstemplate.asp?articleid=238&zoneid=4 (accessed July 15, 2004).

73. Jamie Babbit, *But I'm a Cheerleader!* (USA: Lions Gate Films, 1999).

74. PFLAG, "Our Trans Children" (Parents, Families, and Friends of Lesbians and Gays, 1999), http://www.youth-guard.org/pflag-tnet/booklet.html (accessed June 4, 2004).

75. Focus on the Family, "Helping Boys Become Men, and Girls Become Women," (Focus on your Child, 2004), http://www.focusonyourchild.com/develop/art1/A0000687.html (accessed August 9, 2004).

76. See Jyl J. Josephson, "The Missing Children: Safe Schools for Some," in *Fundamental Differences: Feminists Talk Back to Social Conservatives*, ed. Cynthia Burack and Jyl J. Josephson, pp. 173–187 (Lanham, MD: Rowman and Littlefield, 2003).

77. One example is California, which changed its school code in 2002 to include protection from discrimination based on sexual orientation. There, Christian conservatives have worked to ensure that parents who are opposed to the inclusion of sexual orientation in school policies can withdraw their children from any instruction that includes mention of sexual orientation. See Pacific Justice Institute, "California: Where the Worst Is Happening," (Pacific Justice, 2000), http://www.pacificjustice.org/articles_9.html (accessed November 6, 2001).

78. Debra Chasnoff and H. S. Cohen, *It's Elementary: Talking about Gay Issues in School* (Women's Educational Media, 1996); American Family Association, *It's Not Gay* (American Family Association, 2000).

79. This anxiety about the same-sex seduction of children by adults is usually aimed at gay men. However, it is interesting to note that some of the same concern circulates around the seduction of girls by other girls and by older women. In her recent book, Anne Paulk writes that 17 percent of her sample of ex-lesbians reported being molested by a female, a category that includes

babysitters, mothers, sisters, family friends, and church leaders. Paulk's definition of sexual molestation is as follows: "any kind of sexual interchange between a child and anyone bigger, stronger, or older, from inappropriate touching to kissing, contact with another's genitals, also [sic] includes exposure to another's genitals, exposure to pornographic materials, or use of child to make pornographic materials (may or may not include vaginal, oral, or anal intercourse)." Paulk, *Restoring Sexual Identity*, pp. 246–247.

80. John Stuart Mill, *On Liberty and Other Writings* (Cambridge: Cambridge University Press, 1994), pp. 9, 83–85.

81. Dawne Moon, *God, Sex, and Politics: Homosexuality and Everyday Theologies* (Chicago: University of Chicago Press, 2004), p. 183.

82. I heard this formulation, and close variations, in several presentations at the Washington Briefing: Values Voter Summit, Washington, DC, September 22–24, 2006. The summit was sponsored by Family Research Council Action, Focus on the Family Action, Americans United to Preserve Marriage, and American Family Association Action.

Chapter 4. Getting What "We" Deserve

1. Chip Berlet, "Following the Threads," in *Unraveling the Right: The New Conservatism in American Thought and Politics*, ed. Amy Ansell, pp. 27–28 (Boulder, CO: Westview, 2001).

2. Janet R. Jakobsen, "Can Homosexuals End Western Civilization As We Know It? Family Values in a Global Economy," in *Queer Globalizations: Citizenship and the Afterlife of Colonialism*, ed. Arnaldo Cruz-Malavé and Martin F. Manalansan IV, pp. 49–70 (New York: New York University Press, 2002).

3. Florence Tamagne, *A History of Homosexuality in Europe: Berlin, London, Paris 1919–1939. Volume I* (New York: Algora, 2004), pp. 383–384.

4. Scott Lively and Kevin Abrams, "The Pink Swastika: Homosexuality in the Nazi Party," (The Pink Swastika, 1998), http://www.mega.nu:8080/ampp/pinkswastika.hold/index.html (accessed April 27, 2005). Perhaps "The Pink Swastika" is a rejoinder to Richard Plant, *The Pink Triangle: The Nazi War Against Homosexuals* (New York: Owl Books, 1988).

5. Pat Robertson, *The 700 Club*, January 21, 1993.

6. Interview with Molly Ivins, *Fort Worth Star Telegram*, September 14, 1993.

7. Incidentally, the theme of American Christian martyrdom is neither occasional nor the work of fringe figures on the right. For one recent book in the genre, see David Limbaugh, *Persecution: How Liberals Are Waging War Against Christianity* (Washington, DC: Regnery, 2003).

8. James Dobson, *Marriage Under Fire: Why We Must Win This Battle* (Sisters, OR: Multnomah, 2004), pp. 29, 41. See also Didi Herman's discussion of the link between gays and Nazis in her interview with Lon Mabon: Didi Herman, *The Antigay Agenda: Orthodox Vision and the Christian Right* (Chicago: University of Chicago Press, 1997), pp. 90–91.

9. See Corrie ten Boom, *The Hiding Place* (New York: Bantam, 1984).

10. See David K. Johnson, *The Lavender Scare: The Cold War Persecution of Gays and Lesbians in the Federal Government* (Chicago: University of Chicago Press, 2004).

11. Mary K. Bloodsworth-Lugo and Carmen R. Lugo-Lugo, "'The War on Terror' and Same-Sex Marriage: Narratives of Containment and the Shaping of U.S. Public Opinion," *Peace and Change* 30, 4 (2005): 469–488.

12. For a domestic example of such denial and its effects in the African American community, see Cathy J. Cohen, *The Boundaries of Blackness: AIDS and the Breakdown of Black Politics* (Chicago: University of Chicago Press, 1999).

13. James Kimball, "'Gay' Activists Not Allowed to Enter U.S. as Married Couple," (Ex-Gay Watch, 2003). The original article is available at many locations on the Web, including in "Antigay Group Censors Itself," (Ex-Gay Watch, September 29, 2003), http://www.exgaywatch.com/xgw/2003/09/antigay_group_c.html (accessed January 16, 2005).

14. Dobson, *Marriage Under Fire*, p. 85.

15. See Jamiel Terry, "A Rising Son," (Out.com, 2004), http://www.out.com/feature. asp?ID=4811 (accessed September 30, 2005); Michael Powell, "Family Values: Randall Terry Fights Gay Unions. His Son No Longer Will," (*Washington Post*, 2004), http://www.washingtonpost.com/ac2/wp-dyn/A32934–2004Apr21?language=printer (accessed October 1, 2005).

16. After White came out as gay in 1993, he repudiated the Christian right and cofounded the LGBT organization Soulforce.

17. John D. Woodbridge, "Culture War Casualties: How Warfare Rhetoric Is Hurting the Work of the Church," *Christianity Today* 39, 3 (1995): 22, 25; James Dobson, "Why I Use 'Fighting Words': A Response to John Woodbridge's 'Culture War Casualties,'" *Christianity Today* 39, 7 (1995): 28–30.

18. John D. Woodbridge, "Why Words Matter: A Response to James Dobson" *Christianity Today* 39, 7 (1995): 32.

19. Human Rights Watch, "'We Are Not the Enemy': Hate Crimes Against Arabs, Muslims, and Those Perceived to Be Arab or Muslim After September 11," (Human Rights Watch, 2002), http://www.hrw.org/reports/2002/usahate/ (accessed January 16, 2005).

20. Bruce Lincoln, *Holy Terrors: Thinking about Religion after September 11* (Chicago: University of Chicago Press, 2003), p. 30. For this analysis, see chapter 2, "Symmetric Dualisms: Bush and bin Laden on October 7."

21. Bruce Lincoln analyzes and contextualizes Jerry Falwell and Pat Robertson's September 13 remarks in chapter 3 ("Jihads, Jeremiads, and the Enemy Within") of *Holy Terrors*. My discussion here does not rely on Lincoln, but his analysis of the *700 Club* broadcast highlights some of the same themes as well as offering some different perspectives. See Cynthia Burack, "Getting What 'We' Deserve: Terrorism, Tolerance, Sexuality, and the Christian Right," *New Political Science* 25, 3 (2003): 329–349.

22. John F. Harris, "God Gave U.S. 'What We Deserve,' Falwell Says," *The Washington Post* (September 14, 2001): C3.

23. Elizabeth Birch, "Speech by Elizabeth Birch at HRC's Fifth Annual National Dinner," (Human Rights Campaign, 2001), http://www.hrc.org/news releases/2001/011008eb speech.asp (accessed October 10, 2001).

24. Jerry Falwell, "Jerry Falwell Apologizes," (Banner, 2002), http://www.banner.org.uk/wtc/patrob.html (accessed May 20, 2002).

25. The satirical magazine *The Onion* featured the following ersatz "head-line" in response to the controversy: "Jerry Falwell: Is That Guy a Dick or What?"

26. Many conservatives, including William F. Buckley Jr. and Rush Limbaugh, joined this chorus of disapprobation. See William F. Buckley Jr., "Invoking God's Thunder on the Reverend Jerry Falwell," (*National Review*, 2001), http://www.nationalreview.com/ buckley/buckley091801.shtml (accessed March 4, 2002); People for the American Way, "Media Reactions to Jerry Falwell-Pat Robertson Comments on the September 11 Tragedies," (People for the American Way, 2001), http://www.pfaw.org/911/media reacts.shtml (accessed October 18, 2001).

27. Pat Robertson, "Pat Robertson Addresses Comments Made by Jerry Falwell," (PatRobertson.com, 2001), *http://www.patrobertson.com/Press Releases/falwell.asp* (accessed October 9, 2001).

28. Pat Robertson, "Robertson's Statement Regarding Terrorist Attack on America," (PatRobertson.com, 2001), *http://www.patrobertson.com/pressreleases/ TerroristAttack.asp* (accessed October 10, 2001).

29. Pat Robertson, "Pat Robertson's Letter to U.S. Newspaper Editors," (*Cross + Word*, 2001), http://www.banner.org.uk/wtc/patrob.html (accessed May 18, 2002).

30. Americans United for Separation of Church and State, "Jerry Falwell Tries to Cash in on Controversy: TV Preacher's Ministry Sends out Fund-Raising

Appeal Exploiting His Controversial Tirade over Terrorist Attacks," (Americans United, 2001), http://www. au.org/press/pr102201.htm (accessed October 25, 2001); Lloyd Grove, "The Reliable Source," *Washington Post* (October 24, 2001): C3.

31. Peter Carlson, "Jerry Falwell's Awkward Apology: What Did He Mean and When Did He Mean It? Huh?" *Washington Post* (November 18, 2001): F5.

32. Jerry Falwell, "Jerry Falwell Apologizes," (Banner, 2002), http://www.banner.org.uk/ wtc/patrob.html (accessed May 18, 2002).

33. See Jeffrey K. Hadden and Anson Shupe, *Power and Politics on God's Frontier* (Reading, MA: Addison-Wesley, 1988).

34. One author who excels at this kind of conceptual translation is Jeff Sharlet. See, e.g., Jeff Sharlet, "Soldiers of Christ: Inside America's Most Powerful Megachurch" (Harper's.org, May 26, 2005) http://www.harpers.org/SoldiersOfChrist.html (June 24, 2005).

35. Omri Elisha, "A Theology of Blame," (American Anthropological Association, 2002), http://www.aaanet.org/press/an/0203ElishaBlame.htm (accessed March 2, 2002).

36. Harding, *The Book of Jerry Falwell*, pp. 125–152.

37. Jerry Falwell, quoted in Susan Friend Harding, *The Book of Jerry Falwell*, p. 160.

38. Harding, *The Book of Jerry Falwell*, pp. 88, 275.

39. PFAW. "Right Wing Watch Online," (People for the American Way, 1998), http://www.pfaw.org/pfaw/general/default.aspx?oid=3939 (accessed November 11, 2001).

40. Jeffery Jay Lowder, "The God of Terrorism," (Infidels, 1998), http://www.infidels.org/secular_web/feature/1998/robertson.html (accessed November 20, 2001).

41. Michael Lienesch, *Redeeming America: Piety and Politics in the New Christian Right* (Chapel Hill: University of North Carolina Press, 1993), p. 59.

42. Chris Bull and John Gallagher, *Perfect Enemies: The Religious Right, the Gay Movement, and the Politics of the 1990s* (New York: Crown, 1996), p. 32.

43. Elisha, "A Theology of Blame." Some Christians challenge those who attend principally to saving America to minister instead to the "brokenness" of individuals who are "postmodernists," feminists, homosexuals, and liberals. See Rich Nathan, *Who Is My Enemy? Welcoming People the Church Rejects* (Grand Rapids, MI: Zondervan, 2002).

44. See reporting of Barna Group research on Christians' views of homosexuality (2001). The Barna Group is a Christian marketing research company that provides information and analysis on attitudes and cultural trends. Barna Research Online, "Born Again Adults Remain Firm in Opposition to Abortion and Gay Marriage," (Barna, 2001), http://www.barna.org/cgibin/PagePressRelease. asp?PressReleaseID=94& Reference=B (accessed March 10, 2002).

45. John Stuart Mill, *On Liberty and Other Writings* (Cambridge: Cambridge University Press, 1994), p. 55.

46. Bull and Gallagher, *Perfect Enemies*, p. 161.

47. Harding, *The Book of Jerry Falwell*, p. 86.

48. Anna Marie Smith, *New Right Discourse on Race and Sexuality: Britain, 1968–1990* (Cambridge: Cambridge University Press, 1994); Jessie Daniels, *White Lies: Race, Class, Gender, and Sexuality in White Supremacist Discourse* (New York: Routledge, 1997); Ann Burlein, *Lift High the Cross: Where White Supremacy and the Christian Right Converge* (Durham: University of North Carolina Press, 2002).

49. D. James Kennedy, *Why Was America Attacked? Answers for a Nation at War* (Nashville, Tennessee: Broadman and Holman, 2001), p. 8.

50. Kennedy, *Why Was America Attacked?* pp. 39, 16.

51. See Paul Berman, *Terror and Liberalism* (New York: W. W. Norton, 2004).

52. Kennedy, *Why Was America Attacked?* p. 11. Emphasis is added. Kennedy's source text here is Genesis 16:12.

53. Kennedy, *Why Was America Attacked?* pp. 43, 17.

54. Kennedy, *Why Was America Attacked?* pp. 12, 34, 19–22, 31.

55. Dick Innes, "Why Terrorism?" (Gospelcom.net, 2001), http://www.gospelcom.net/act si/helps_terrorism1.htm (accessed January 20, 2002).

56. Neal Horsley, "Our Nation Under Attack: Will the USA be Nuked for Defending a False Freedom?" (Christian Gallery, 2001), http:// www.christiangallery.com/nukethreat.html (accessed March 3, 2002).

57. See the website of the American Society for the Defense of Tradition, Family and Property at http://www.tfp.org.

58. TFP Committee of American Issues (The American Society for the Defense of Tradition, Family and Property). *Defending a Higher Law: Why We Must Resist Same-Sex "Marriage" and the Homosexual Movement* (Spring Grove, PA: TFP, 2004), pp. 191–192.

59. TFP, *Defending a Higher Law,* p. 192.

60. TFP, *Defending a Higher Law,* pp. 200–201.

61. Lest anyone mistake the message of the site, it can be located on the Web at http://www.godhatesamerica.com with links to http://www.godhates fags.com.

62. Fred Phelps, "God Hates America Sermons from WBC Pastor Fred Phelps, Sr.," (God Hates America, 2002), http://www.godhatesamerica.com/html/songsnsermons.html (accessed April 6, 2002).

63. See Sacvan Bercovitch, *The American Jeremiad* (Madison, WI: University of Wisconsin Press, 1978).

64. David S. Gutterman, "Presidential Testimony: Listening to the Heart of George W. Bush," (*Muse,* 2001), http://muse.jhu.edu/journals/theory_and_event/v005/5.2gutterman.html (accessed October 2, 2002).

65. John Locke, *A Letter Concerning Toleration* (Indianapolis, IN: Hackett, 1689/1983).

66. Amy Gutmann, *Identity in Democracy* (Princeton, NJ: Princeton University Press, 2004), p. 162.

67. Paul A. Djupe and Christopher P. Gilbert, *The Prophetic Pulpit: Clergy, Churches, and Communities in American Politics* (Lanham, MD: Rowman and Littlefield, 2003).

68. Gutmann, *Identity in Democracy,* p. 178.

69. Mill, *On Liberty and Other Writings,* p. 82.

70. Robert H. Bork, *The Tempting of America: The Political Seduction of the Law* (New York: Free Press, 1990), p. 124.

71. For recent examples of texts that deploy general arguments for child well-being against gay rights, see: Alan Sears and Craig Osten, *The Homosexual Agenda: Exposing the Principal Threat to Religious Freedom Today* (Nashville, TN: Broadman and Holman, 2003); James Dobson, *Marriage Under Fire*; Erin W. Lutzer, *The Truth About Same-Sex Marriage: 6 Things You Need to Know About What's Really at Stake* (Chicago: Moody, 2004); Peter Sprigg, *Outrage: How Gay Activists and Liberal Judges Are Trashing Democracy to Redefine Marriage* (Washington, DC: Regnery, 2004).

72. Joseph Hamburger, *John Stuart Mill on Liberty and Control* (Princeton, NJ: Princeton University Press, 1999), p. 189. For a complete discussion of Mill on liberty and miserable individuality, see chapter 8: "How Much Liberty?"

73. Antigay "researcher" Paul Cameron has specialized in these characterizations, but he is only one of the more visible spokespersons. See, for exam-

ple, Robert Dreyfuss. "The Holy War on Gays," (Parents, Family, and Friends of Lesbians and Gays, 1999), http://www.pflagdetroit.org/Holy_War_OnGays. htm (accessed March 6, 2002).

74. Harding, *The Book of Jerry Falwell*, p. 162. This belief resonates with the frequent promises made by President Bush after September 11 to punish not only the terrorist evildoers but also the nations that harbor them. This parallel is one of many ways in which Bush effectively has spoken to conservative Christians as *their* leader and not just as *ours*. For other examples of these codes, see Bruce Lincoln, *Holy Terrors*.

75. Gerald F. Gaus, *Social Philosophy* (Armonk, NY: M. E. Sharpe, 1999), pp. 137–159.

76. Andrew von Hirsch, "Extending the Harm Principle: Remote Harms and Fair Imputation," in *Harm and Culpability*, ed. A. P. Simester and A. T. H. Smith, pp. 265–271 (Oxford: Oxford University Press, 1996).

77. The text of Deuteronomy 25:11–12 reads: "When men strive together one with another, and the wife of the one draweth near for to deliver her husband out of the hand of him that smiteth him, and putteth forth her hand, and taketh him by the secrets: then thou shalt cut off her hand, thine eye shall not pity [her]."

78. Thomas Caramagno, *Irreconcilable Differences: Intellectual Stalemate in the Gay Rights Debate* (Westport, CT: Praeger, 2002), p. 56. See also L. William Countryman, *Dirt, Greed, and Sex: Sexual Ethics in the New Testament and Their Implications for Today* (Philadelphia: Fortress Press, 1988).

79. von Hirsch, "Extending the Harm Principle," p. 265.

80. Stormie Omartian, *The Power of a Praying Nation* (Eugene, OR: Harvest House, 2002), p. 24.

81. Omartian, *The Power of a Praying Nation*, p. 72.

82. See Herman, *The Antigay Agenda*; Angela D. Dillard, *Guess Who's Coming to Dinner Now? Multicultural Conservatism in America* (New York: New York University Press, 2001).

83. Corey Robin, *Fear: The History of a Political Idea* (Oxford: Oxford University Press, 2004), pp. 156–157.

84. Presidential Prayer Team, "The Story of the Presidential Prayer Team," (September 2005), http://www.presidentialprayerteam.org/site/Page Server?pagename=ppt_History (accessed June 28, 2006).

85. The polls administered in email alerts have a clear pedagogical function, asking such questions as: "Is the Bible as relevant to the governing of our

nation today as it was during the time of our Founders?" PPT publications include a devotional and matching prayer journal. See Presidential Prayer Team, *The Presidential Prayer Team Devotional* (Nashville: Countryman, 2003).

86. Chip Berlet and Pam Chamberlain, "Running Against Sodom and Osama: The Christian Right, Values Voters, and the Culture Wars in 2006" (Political Research Associates, October 2006), http://www.publiceye.org/ pdfs/Running_Against_Sodom_And_Osama_Appendices.pdf (accessed November 1, 2006); Sean Cahill and Cynthia Burack, "Internal Enemy: Gays as the Domestic al-Qaeda: A Report from the Family Research Council's Values Voter Summit, September 22–24, 2006," (The National Gay and Lesbian Task Force, October 27, 2006), http://www.thetaskforce.org/downloads/Internal_ enemy_ValuesVoter.pdf (accessed November 1, 2006).

Afterword: Another Gay Agenda

1. For a substantial collection that suggests some of the shades of opinion on the subject see Greg Wharton and Ian Phillips, eds., *I Do/I Don't: Queers on Marriage* (San Francisco: Suspect Thoughts Press, 2004). Full disclosure: My partner, Laree Martin, and I contributed an essay for the volume that suggests our own somewhat different perspectives.

2. On this question of measurement and demographics of the conservative Christian movement, I offer some key works: Duane M. Oldfield, *The Right and the Righteous: The Christian Right Confronts the Republican Party* (Lanham, MD: Rowman and Littlefield, 1996); Grant Wacker, "The Christian Right," (*National Humanities Center*, Divining America: Religion and the National Culture, TeacherServe, 2000), http://www.nhc.rtp.nc.us:8080/tserve/ twenty/tkeyinfo/chr_rght.htm (accessed October 3, 2002); John C. Green, Mark J. Rozell, and Clyde Wilcox, eds., *The Christian Right in American Politics: Marching to the Millenium* (Washington, DC: Georgetown University Press, 2003). For a skeptical reading of the measurement literature, see Lee Sigelman and Stanley Presser, "Measuring Public Support for the New Christian Right: The Perils of Point Estimation," *Public Opinion Quarterly* 52 (1988): 325–337.

3. I draw the phrase and its underlying pessimism from Jeffrey C. Isaac, *Democracy in Dark Times* (Ithaca: Cornell University Press, 1998). Isaac, in turn, draws his inspiration from the work of Hannah Arendt and her book *Men in Dark Times* (New York: Harcourt, Brace, and World, 1968).

4. Hannah Arendt, *Eichmann in Jerusalem: A Report on the Banality of Evil* (New York: Penguin Books, 1965).

5. Hannah Arendt, "Lying in Politics," in *Crises of the Republic* (New York: Harcourt Brace Jovanovich, 1972), p. 6.

6. Hannah Arendt, "Truth and Politics," in *Between Past and Future: Eight Exercises in Political Thought* (New York: Penguin Books, 1968), p. 231.

7. I have observed a similar dynamic in effect with regard to race. White university students often use popular historical revisionisms to express counterfactual beliefs about the causes of the American Civil War, the symbolism of the Confederate battle flag, the egalitarian effects of the Civil Rights movement, and the vulnerability of African Americans to, for example, heightened scrutiny from police.

8. See Henry E. Adams, Lester W. Wright Jr., and Bethany A. Lohr, "Is Homophobia Associated with Homosexual Arousal?" *Journal of Abnormal Psychology* 105, 3 (1996): 440–445.

9. There is a considerable amount of literature on the psychologies of fundamentalism and right-wing ideology and their relationship to social and political issues. A principal construct in this literature is right-wing authoritarianism. See Aubyn S. Fulton, Richard L. Gorsuch, and Elizabeth A. Maynard, "Religious Orientation, Antihomosexual Sentiment, and Fundamentalism Among Christians," *Journal for the Scientific Study of Religion* 38, 1 (March 1999): 14–22; Bruce Hunsberger, "Religious Fundamentalism, Right-Wing Authoritarianism, and Hostility Toward Homosexuals in Non-Christian Religious Groups," *The International Journal for the Psychology of Religion* 6, 1 (1996): 39–49; Jonathan P. Schwartz and Lori D. Lindley, "Religious Fundamentalism and Attachment: Prediction of Homophobia," *International Journal for the Psychology of Religion* 15, 2 (2005): 145–157; Wayne W. Wilkinson, "Religiosity, Authoritarianism, and Homophobia: A Multidimensional Approach," *International Journal for the Psychology of Religion* 14, 1 (2004): 55–67; Bob Altemeyer and Bruce Hunsberger, "Changes in Attitudes toward Homosexuals," *Journal of Homosexuality* 42 (2001): 63–75; Bob Altemeyer and Bruce Hunsberger, "Why Do Religious Fundamentalists Tend to Be Prejudiced?" *The International Journal for the Psychology of Religion* 13, 1 (2003): 17–28. For a provocative psychodynamic account of the prejudices, including antigay prejudice, see Elisabeth Young-Bruehl, *The Anatomy of Prejudices* (Cambridge, MA: Harvard University Press, 1996).

10. The Pew Research Center for the People and the Press, "Religious Beliefs Underpin Opposition to Homosexuality," (The Pew Research Center, 2003), http://peoplepress.org/reports/display.php3?ReportID=197 (accessed December 29, 2005).

Index